All
in a
Day's
Work

Publisher's Note

All names, locations and other identifying features have been changed to protect the privacy of all the individuals that the author has worked with.

Many of the characters are not based on any one person but are composite characters drawn from the author's extensive career in Social Services.

Becky Hope is a pseudonym.

All in a Day's Work

No child should ever be forgotten

BECKY HOPE

HODDER &
STOUGHTON

First published in Great Britain in 2011 by Hodder & Stoughton
An Hachette UK company

1

A CIP catalogue record for this title is available from the British Library

ISBN 978 1 444 72363 2

Typeset in Monotype Sabon by Ellipsis Books Limited, Glasgow

Printed and bound by
CPI Mackays, Chatham ME5 8TD

Hodder & Stoughton policy is to use papers that are natural,
renewable and recyclable products and made from wood grown in
sustainable forests. The logging and manufacturing processes are expected
to conform to the environmental regulations of the country of origin.

Hodder & Stoughton Ltd
338 Euston Road
London NW1 3BH

www.hodder.co.uk

This book is dedicated to every child who has struggled with the circumstances of their family life.

It is also dedicated to all those social workers who, on a daily basis, work tirelessly to ensure the safety and well-being of the many vulnerable children in our society.

Finally it is dedicated to my family, and my mother.

Contents

Preface

From the moment a child enters this world as a tiny baby, everything that happens to that child, be it positive or negative, will affect his or her future. It used to be thought that children were pretty much unaffected by early experiences, the thinking 'too young to remember' would often be thrown about as an excuse, as if the marks on the canvas only began at some later critical date, maybe aged one, or maybe later.

Research is now beginning to show us something many parents instinctively always knew: that bonding, attachment and interactive responsive behaviour begins in earnest from the very start of life. Within months the effects of a lack of care can be seen in a child's responses.

Children whose basic needs for responsive loving care are not met, and who are left to flounder, have been found to suffer clear detrimental effects to their brain development long before they reach anywhere near their first birthday. It has also been found that children who have experienced severe neglect as tiny babies, but are placed in long term adoptive homes before the age of six months, are able to make far greater progress overall than a child placed after that age.

These research findings make uncomfortable reading for all of us working in the field of child protection, because at present this research is not infiltrating social work practice in a way that best supports the children who depend upon us. To allow these research findings to change our practice will require a change in the mind-set of all involved in the process of child protection, and it would require the understanding and support of our society.

Children do have rights, including the right to a caring environment in which they can grow physically, mentally and emotionally.

We owe our children the best that we can offer in terms of care and protection. They are the future of this world, and if we stand by and take no action when a family is struggling then we send out damaged children who will struggle in so many ways, and society will in turn stand to be damaged, badly at times.

So some families need support from an early point to help them to provide the care their children need; and where a family is in itself so damaged that it cannot, even with help, provide that care, then society has to protect the child as an absolute priority, and place that child in a home where such care will be his or her right. Furthermore, the child needs that action to be taken before the damage to him or her has become too great.

This work with both families and children is the role of the child protection social worker. Demanding and challenging, both intellectually and emotionally, but with the potential to be life changing.

Sadly we are desperately short of good calibre, well trained social workers. There is a country wide shortage, with an overall 12% vacancy rate. It is estimated that we are short by as many as 15,000 social workers.

I decided to write this book to open up a door into the world of social work. Why? . . . For several reasons.

Firstly, it is my hope to try to encourage more able people of all ages to consider entering the profession. I also hope to increase the understanding of some of the very serious dilemmas surrounding a social worker's task, by allowing the reader to step into that world and actually come face to face with the children, and their families.

Very few really understand a social worker's job and the tremendous stresses social workers are required to deal with; the difficult decisions, the physical risks of the work, the sheer quantity of cases, the emotional impact, all sometimes against a background of limited support both administratively and supervisory. Add to that the wide ranging misconceptions held about the work by most people, is it any wonder that too many young people have not considered social work as a career?

But this has always frustrated me. I know what those outside the profession could not know: that this is one of the most challenging and exciting jobs one could wish for, with a potential to actually change the lives of some of the most vulnerable children in society.

For competent people seeking a real challenge, rather than looking to the third world, or to the many other alternative options, perhaps they will see here something much tougher on their own doorstep.

I truly believe that social work provides a satisfaction that cannot be matched by very many other careers.

Further, for those who organise and manage social work teams, perhaps they may recognise so many of the short-comings that are touched on in my story – which very much add to the enormous stress of my work and the work of my colleagues – and consider how they, as individuals, might seek to bring about real change in their own areas.

For others, I hope that through a deeper understanding of the consequences of neglect, abuse and delay on children, society may look hard at itself, and at the most vulnerable children within it, and consider whether this society really does put its children first.

This is a question that should be addressed by all those in the 'system', be it legal, the social work profession, politicians or the man or woman in the street. All of us.

Children can't wait whilst we adults play at getting it right. If we insist on them waiting then the children will pay a very high price, and so, in time, will society.

I

One Tuesday

I leaned against the doorframe, savouring for one brief moment a relaxing pause, helped by the heat of the mug of coffee I was nursing between my hands. The sun was pouring through the rather grimy window, creating the illusion of warmth on what was actually a rather cold early autumn day. I took a very deep slow breath. In that moment of quiet I mentally stepped back from the office, with its back-cloth of hustle and bustle, only hearing the constant barrage of phones ringing as a background, and I felt my muscles slightly relax.

I had worked for Barton's child protection team for some considerable time now, having gone in on a short-term contract which had fairly quickly become permanent. I had, as they say, hit the ground running, and so far had not stopped, but life was certainly never dull. I loved the work and the sense that I could, at least on occasions, make a difference to some of the most vulnerable children in society. I'd been qualified for over six years now, and most days drove to work with a real sense of excitement, and purpose. The occasional sleepless nights, which walked hand in hand with the job, seemed a small price to pay.

As today's duty officer I took anything and everything that happened to come through the door – by phone, in writing or by carrier pigeon! So far this morning I had received a hectic couple of calls first thing, dealing with contact meetings between parents and their children in foster care. This was an area that often sparked problems. Any slight hitch would trigger disproportionate outbursts of rage from parents who were often already very stressed by events. Another call was about a child who had absconded from a children's home overnight, and whose social worker was out of the office. And, oh yes, there had been two referrals from the police relating to domestic violence, and one distraught mother who rang for advice about her sons. I had also spoken to two people in reception who had serious housing problems. Any spare moments between these calls had been filled with paperwork and follow-up from earlier issues.

It was still only ten o'clock.

Sandy, our team secretary, had helped me to run multiple checks on various people's background history; she also braved the cellars periodically to find old and often misplaced files for individuals on whom we did have past records. When she was busy we often had to do this hunt ourselves, though that left the desk unmanned.

The descent down from a hectic duty desk to the silence of the cellars was always a dramatic contrast. They were cool and dark, down what seemed endless stone stairs; I always found them slightly spooky. Rows and rows of shelving stood silently waiting, perhaps hoping for our enquiries. Unlocking the secrets from the clues on their pages was what it was all about and, when we failed, those files were the only repository left of the tragic events that had led to the crippling of yet another child's life.

The forgotten cruelties or neglects that had been the stuff of daily life for that child: there to be seen, yet not; there to be read, but not; there to be acted on, but, sadly, not.

Even though all these issues kept me fully occupied, I was constantly aware of the in-tray of papers from yesterday, the day before that and indeed the days before that: ever-mounting piles of referrals that previous duty workers had not got round to handling. They gave one the feeling that, however hard one worked to clear the backlog, it would never happen; indeed, I could swear that whenever my back was turned someone added more, from a pile that was breeding in a quiet cupboard somewhere. If that sounds like early paranoia, well, you may be right.

I thought back to a desperate call I had taken earlier that morning from a single mother who was clearly at the end of her tether, coping with two stroppy teenage boys who were walking all over her. Frankly, my heart really went out to her. I had dredged up all I could think of to point her to a better outcome, and gave her the names of some support agencies, parenting groups, etc. But what I really wanted to say was, look, let's meet up and tackle this, because I knew she needed some ongoing support more than anything and that, without it, sheer exhaustion would probably prevent her from changing anything.

Sadly, I knew that was the one thing I could not offer. The ever-swelling pile of referrals of actual abuse and neglect prohibited us from taking on any work that was not already in crisis. Basically we often stepped in when the harm was done, and did the best we could, but too often we fought fires.

My reveries were brought to an abrupt halt by Sandy's

voice penetrating my silence: 'Becky, Mr Duncan, the head of St Dominic's Primary School is on the phone. Could you take the call please?'

Snapping back into function mode, I grabbed my chair, shuffled through the paper on my desk, found my pad and pen, and picked up the phone.

'Becky Hope speaking. I'm today's duty worker, how can I help you?'

Mr Duncan, the head, sounded fraught and worried; normally a placid and calm man, his voice was now laced with emotion.

'OK,' he said, and I heard him taking a deep breath, as if to steady himself, 'I'll start at the beginning. We've this poor kid Sarah Peters in Mrs Thomas's class, you may know her, she's on the Child Protection Register. Her social worker is Wendy Watkins but she's on holiday. This kid is usually pretty grubby, and really struggles with any form of schoolwork. But she's cheerful – in fact she's a real joy to have around. We've often wondered how things are at home, and from the conferences I know there are worries. We thought that her mum just found it hard to cope, did her best, and honestly we felt the concerns about her were a bit over the top.'

There was a pause; it was as if he was wrestling with his thoughts, and in a weaker, almost agonised voice he added, 'The mother has always seemed genuinely fond of the child.'

Again he paused, and added, 'That's what we all believed. But . . .' his voice tailed off, and as if he made a mental effort to take charge again, he continued in a stronger voice. 'Anyhow, this morning, Mrs Thomas, her class teacher, took the children for games and noticed Sarah was reluctant to change into her top. When Mrs Thomas went to help her, she saw huge red, angry weals across the child's body, and the skin was actually broken.'

His voice faltered again. 'There was blood on her t-shirt.' Again he paused, and this time in an almost pleading voice added, 'She's only a little scrap of a thing, how could anyone . . .' It seemed as if the effort of recounting this was too much, and Mr Duncan went silent for a time, apparently reflecting again on the sheer horror of the child's situation.

He continued after a moment. 'Mrs Thomas took her aside to talk to her, and Sarah became very upset, and wouldn't say how the marks got there. So of course she called me in, and I spoke to Sarah myself.'

As Mr Duncan continued, I carefully jotted down exactly what Sarah had said to him. My mind was racing. This family was well known to us, and while I had been talking to Mr Duncan, Sandy, worth all her considerable weight in pure gold, had checked in the records and dug out a very large, dog-eared file, bursting with papers. The file also had a large hand-written warning across it: 'Matthew Jones, boyfriend, known to police as violent offender!'

I told Mr Duncan that I'd get back to him, and put the phone down. I needed to contact the mother as a priority, and rang my way through endless possible phone numbers to try to get hold of her. The first three numbers were no go – she had sold on those mobiles – so I kept on trying more numbers, reading the file notes as I ploughed on through the possibilities. I felt that old familiar rush of adrenaline that always seemed to allow me to think clearer and faster, and it helped me to work my way through the long list of tasks ahead. Eventually I located the mother, managed to explain what had happened, and held on while she exploded.

Liz, the other duty worker, gestured frantically at me, and stuck a note in front of me while I was on the phone. I read this as I was trying to calm the mother down. 'Back at 12.30, going to a court hearing; make sure you take James with you if you have to see the boyfriend!' James was our team's social work support worker, a fanatical member of the local gym, and just looking at him made you feel safer. I'd already got him on my list, but it was nice to feel Liz was thinking about me; or perhaps she was wondering how she'd man the duty desk later, if I got myself hospitalised by the boyfriend! No, I don't mean that. Liz is one of those really caring people with an endless capacity for thinking about others. She's the first to produce the tea when you put down the phone after 15 minutes with what one might call a 'rather challenging' client. To the non-social worker, this is the client who has no inhibitions about swearing, screaming and threatening violence and whose menacing voice can usually be heard all over the office. They are a well-known feature of the job; most social work caseloads have several! They are very wearing and seriously test one's self control!

I knew I had to get going, so I began to put together all the paperwork that might be needed for whatever eventuality might arise. As I was squeezing the last bundle of papers into my already bursting briefcase, ready to dash, Sandy waved a hand at me. She was on the phone, and I heard her saying, 'One moment please I'll see if a duty worker is available to speak with you,' before pressing the silence button.

Sandy's face was anxious as she continued: 'Becky, you're not going to be happy, but I've got Mrs Cliff, the assistant head of Grove Road School on the line. She is insisting that she speaks to someone about a child in her school, and now!'

'Look, Sandy, tell her I will get back to her as soon as I can.' Sandy grimaced, and began to assume the look of a trapped animal. 'Er, Becky, I really don't think I can. She says she has rung five times and refuses to be put off any more. She is rather worked up . . . actually, apoplectic might better sum up her mood.'

I thought for a moment, realising that this had to be tackled and that I couldn't expect Sandy to fend her off any longer. I went into deliberate slow tempo, took a deep breath, and reached out for the phone. 'OK then, I'll have a quick word.'

After fifteen minutes, my head was buzzing. Mrs Cliff began by launching a meaty and furious attack on Social Services' poor response rate. I could only apologise and say we were extremely short-staffed. The fact was, we always were. Her comments were totally justified, but what could I do? We were seriously over-stretched and half the time, well, often far more, we could only prioritise from a list of already high priorities.

Anyhow, her fury vented, she proceeded to relate her concerns about a very vulnerable young teenager in her school, only thirteen. She was alleging that her stepfather was abusing her, and had now revealed that she was about five months' pregnant, but had been afraid to tell for fear of the consequences. This had only come out when another girl had finally told someone. The girl was apparently hysterical, screaming that her stepfather would kill her for revealing all this, and her mum would think she was making more trouble for her. The school day ended at 4.30 p.m. for this girl, provoking an understandably angry question from Mrs Cliff: 'What,' she said to me, in a sharp voice rapidly rising in tone, 'am I supposed to do? Let the girl go home as if nothing has happened because Social Services are too busy?'

The criticism made me wince inside – not my fault I knew, but I was the front line and I understood where she was coming from. I promised to speak to a senior and get back to her as soon as I was able. Her tone reflected her utter disbelief in me, but finally she accepted my word.

I looked around the office as I put the phone down. There were now only three people in: one new trainee, one student, and James, the social work assistant . . . great! Or not . . .

My senior was out on a review in some remote part of the country, there was a managers' meeting at County Hall, and the duty senior was with Liz in court. There wasn't even another social worker in the office; they were either out on visits, in court, on leave or sick. I will admit here to a moment of panic, which I controlled in the certain knowledge that panic would get me nowhere, so it wasn't an option. I just had to keep going.

The phone rang again and, expecting it to be the school,

I unwisely picked it up. It was a problem with another supervised contact. The mother – who was only allowed contact with her child under supervision because of past abuse – was not about to be reasonable over the difficulties. I summoned my last reserves of calm, and dealt with this, replacing the receiver with exaggerated slow motion.

Sandy came over, the look on her face an interesting mixture of real concern and anxiety. 'Look, Becky, is there anything I can do?'

I looked up at her. When she was stressed, she went an interesting shade of blotchy pink, and her hair seemed to curl in sympathy. She had large pale blue eyes, which registered her emotions very openly. Somehow it helped me to have her at hand; I knew she was in this with me, and that felt good. I knew she was batting on my side.

'Sandy, I need you to talk to the duty senior when she returns from court, and explain what has been going on. In the meantime I need to get up to see the St Dominic's child and deal with that. I will have to get the child checked out at the hospital. I could be there until this afternoon, but I'll check my mobile regularly so you can leave a message for me. I've asked the assistant head at Grove Road to hold onto the girl until I'm back, unless another worker comes in. I am fairly certain that this will be a case of moving her first to a safe home if all is as recounted, depending on what the mother has to say. Would you check the records for other family members, a safe granny perhaps, and I will check that out if needed?'

While I was talking, Sandy was jotting down my list. I was confident that she would follow all my requests to the letter; she was such a brilliant person to have by you, especially in a crisis. She dashed off and I knew I could leave that with her. I knew also that what was ahead at St Dominic's was not likely to be good. From having skim-read the file, it was clear that this child was on the Child Protection Register for many reasons and had sustained a series of injuries that had raised concern, but we had been unable to prove what was happening. I knew this might lead to an emergency admission to care while we checked further. The child's file made grim reading, and the last conference found that nearly all the professionals had serious concerns.

As for Mrs Cliff at Grove Road, I simply knew I could not even begin to tackle her problem until I had dealt with Sarah.

Sandy reappeared with a pile of files and I said to her, 'You're going to have to take messages for all calls now; there is absolutely nothing else I can do. Also, would you mind telling James I'm going to need him.'

As I was speaking, the phone rang again, and I left Sandy to cope with it as I needed the other line to flag up with legal what was brewing. For once, the solicitor involved was not in court or elsewhere. At last, the wind was blowing with me. Putting the phone down, I redialled to the foster care team, and flagged up the possibility of needing a placement for the two girls. It was always wise to warn them in advance as foster carers are scarce resources. This way they could line up potential carers should they be needed.

I grabbed my bag to finally leave, but caught Sandy's eyes following me rather frantically. With real effort, I paused, asking, 'Are you OK, Sandy?' I think this was an example of extremely hopeful thinking, as it was as clear as the nose on your face that Sandy was far from OK! Her face was turning an even deeper shade of pink now and her eyes were looking like those of someone suffering from a terrible nightmare. She was clearly trying to hold back, but couldn't – as though she was afraid of what my reaction might be. I wasn't known for dramatic outbursts in response to stress, but perhaps she thought that this time I would crack, and be seen running in hysterics down the High Street, never to return. Anyhow, she finally blurted out: 'It's Forth Lodge, Becky. It's Steven Howell, the new manager. About Martin Jones. He sounds seriously angry. He is saying that he understands that the Lodge has been asking for Martin to be removed for three months now, and they refuse to keep him any longer. Martin attacked his key worker yesterday. Mr Howell insists on speaking to Martin's social worker. Apparently this is the third time Martin has exploded like this.' There was a short silence, and in a small voice Sandy added: 'Isn't Martin one of your cases, Becky?'

I leaned against the desk while I collected my disparate thoughts. Martin's angry face came into my mind. 'Oh no, Martin, what are you doing? Why today of all days?'

'OK, Sandy tell Forth Lodge that they must hang on until tomorrow and we will sort this out then.' I reached once more for my briefcase, and then added, 'Sandy, would you do me a huge favour please? Could you ring down to the fostering placement team and update them on Martin. They are fairly clued up as I have had several discussions with them about him in the last few weeks. Tell them it's critical and we will have to find a new placement tomorrow! If you could fill them in on today, that would be really helpful, and please send my apologies for not going down myself. If they need to talk they can get me on my mobile, so if you could make sure they have my number.'

I rather woodenly smiled my goodbyes, signed the red security book and purposefully strode, at speed, to the door, not stopping to look left or right lest some imaginary person should heap another social tragedy upon me and expect me to run with it. James was waiting for me in the reception area and we made our way out in silence.

In the car park I put my keys in the lock, opened my car and sank into the familiar comfort of my little, rather untidy sky blue car. I shovelled enough of the clutter to one side to allow James to squeeze in, took a deep breath and pointed the car in the direction of onward!

2

Sarah

The traffic was chaotic and made the journey frustratingly slow as James and I drove over to see Julie Peters, Sarah's mother. She lived in a fairly notorious road; in other words, it saw a great deal too much of social workers, for many reasons. I pulled up outside Julie's house, number 9, but long ago the screws at the top had fallen out, and it actually read number 6. The front garden was a small square of mud with tufts of grass, surrounded by a hedge, which many years ago someone had tried to trim. Projecting from the hedge was a rusty, broken scooter, which seemed to have ended its days unable to disentangle itself. It now seemed to be growing with the foliage, along with many items of rubbish that nature was now valiantly trying to hide in its greenery.

The paved area was littered with drinks cartons, plastic bags, odd broken toys and chocolate wrappers. At the side of the house was an impressive mountain of beer bottles. Those that were not broken were beginning to sprout green life. The door had several cracked panes, and a large dent at foot level where someone, it seemed, had grown tired of waiting for an answer or had been denied access and had tried to kick the door in. Torn and grey net curtains blurred the interior from curious eyes, but I suspected that our arrival was not unseen from the inside. I knocked on the door and waited, wondering during that time what would happen next.

I didn't have long to wait. Julie half opened the door, snarling at us, 'Are you from the Social?' and promptly began to shout at us. She was a pale thinly built young woman with straggles of blonde hair falling in locks out of a frayed band, which had been pushed carelessly onto her head in a vain attempt to tie it all back. She smelt strongly of alcohol and although she was a little unsteady, she could certainly still shout.

I'm not sure anyone ever becomes really accustomed to the aggressive shouting that you so often have to listen to in this job. As she shouted abusively at me, she kept up an angry stabbing gesture with her forefinger, directed at me. She screamed that she knew the school and Social Services had it in for her, she knew how corrupt we all were, hand in glove, and she was going to prove this in court.

At one point she made a sudden forward movement, and I wondered if she was going to lash out at me, but I think she had just lost her balance.

If I wasn't enjoying this, the neighbours certainly were. They were fast gathering in their front gardens, laughing among themselves, having a jolly good chin-wag, and passing frequent loud comments about Julie and social workers in general. Best thing since *Big Brother*, I assumed.

A brief thought crossed my mind as I stood there listening to Julie screaming very menacing abuse at me – a sign I had seen in the local post office yesterday: 'WE DO NOT TOLERATE ABUSE OF OUR STAFF'. I imagined that the nearest thing to abuse that the post office lady was likely to get was a moan about the price of stamps. I could cope with that.

Julie continued her rant, but would not let us into the house. The injuries, she claimed, were from school, which again she raged at for their neglect. At first she tried to say that Sarah must have had an accident at school, and then she said she had been out with her friend last night, and perhaps had been in a fight.

I needed to interview Matthew, but Julie claimed he was not at home and that she could not contact him. She was adamant that he had been out all morning and was not expected back that day, so we had no choice but to move on and have Sarah checked over.

It took a while to calm Julie down sufficiently to make her understand that she needed to come with us to pick up Sarah and take her to the hospital for a check-up. In time, she accepted – with great ill will – that she had little option. After a frantic search for her bag, her coat, then her phone, she followed us to the car, pausing only to swear colourfully at her neighbours, who were still lurking in the road enjoying a bit of free entertainment. I kept my face expressionless and James looked as though he had heard nothing, but to tell the truth I rather thought they had asked for it. Getting your kicks from other people's traumas was pretty low.

On the way to the school to pick up Sarah, it was clear that all was not well. Julie was making desperate mobile calls to someone I strongly suspected was the ostensibly missing boyfriend. I could hear an angry voice shouting at the other end of the line before the phone appeared to cut off suddenly. Julie became clearly more agitated and disconnected from what was happening.

Sarah was waiting with her teacher in the school office. She was a rather small child for her age, extremely thin, with greasy tangled strands of unkempt fair hair falling about her shoulders. Her eyes reminded me of a terrified rabbit, nervously looking under her brows at her mother.

The meeting with her mother was of concern in itself. There were no hugs and no concerned questions. Sarah was greeted with, 'What you been saying you lying little sod? You know you'll get Matthew and me into trouble. You don't want him to clear off again do you?' Sarah looked down at the floor, not moving an inch; I suspected she knew she could not win no matter what, so silence was a better response.

After a minute or two she mumbled, 'I didn't say nothing mum, honest.'

One could imagine what the child must have been feeling, but it was not a comfortable place to go. The aura of pervading misery around her was grim, her head hung down and arms wrapped tightly across her bony little chest as if to comfort and protect herself. I put an arm across the small child's shoulders to guide her along and offer her some comfort, and we made our way to my car.

Fortunately it was a very short drive to the hospital and before long we were wending our way through the rabbit warren of corridors to the paediatrics department. James had left us once we reached the hospital, as he had other appointments that could not wait. There was a bit of a wait before the check-up. To describe this time as 'somewhat tense', would be a huge understatement.

Maintaining a reasonable level of interaction between an incensed, angry and drunken mother, her terrified child and myself, while being aware of other hospital patients – and confidentiality – was not a task for the fainthearted.

At one point Julie became very agitated, once more beginning to work herself up into a state. As her voice rose, and she began issuing menacing threats to many institutions in general and me in particular, people began to look over. Nervous glances were exchanged between staff; clearly someone had summoned security to be on hand, which was not such a bad thing.

I knew Wendy, Julie's social worker, and had seen her bruised and stressed face on the day, some months ago, that Julie had taken a swing at her. Fortunately for me on this occasion, Julie calmed down when she received a text and was momentarily distracted. At that moment the doctor called us in.

Sarah was examined by a pleasant young doctor who was clearly nervous about the situation but did her best to cope with Julie's very abstracted replies to any questions. In spite of her evident anxiety over dealing with someone in such a fluctuating and unpredictable mental state, she managed to keep calm. At times, her questions were met with total silence. I suspect Julie's preoccupation was with the cut-off mobile call, which for her might have signified the end of yet another relationship.

I had to be sure that nothing was missed. X-rays and photos of Sarah's injuries were taken, and details of all Julie's explanations had to be noted carefully. There was a glum and rather concerned look on the doctor's face when she examined the X-rays. She turned to Julie and said, 'Sarah has several broken ribs – this must have been quite an injury. And there are also clear signs of previous damage here. It looks like Sarah has had a broken arm which was not set; can you remember when this might have happened?'

Julie looked blankly at the doctor, completely at a loss for words, then she muttered something about Sarah having fallen and that she had complained about her arm, adding that it hadn't seem worth taking her to the doctor as she was always making a fuss about nothing. I watched the child as she stood on the scales, her frail little arms and her ribs sticking out from her little body, which was only skin and bone. Her underclothing was filthy, some little more than rags hidden under her uniform and I couldn't help smelling the inevitable result of neglect, which was potent in that tiny room.

I found myself with time to reflect. How long had this child been left to suffer, how long had everyone talked their way through endless conferences, accepted the mother's excuses for her daughter's 'accidents' and still not seen how neglected this child was? I suggested to Julie that she needed time to sort things out at home and we needed to be sure that Sarah was safe while we discovered what had happened. I managed to persuade Julie to allow Sarah to spend a couple of nights with a foster carer whom she had stayed with earlier that year when her mother had gone missing for a week or so. This way I would not yet need to take emergency admission measures.

We could not place her in the family. The grandparents were well known dealers on the streets of Barton and

Sarah's only uncle was resting at her majesty's pleasure for a variety of offences. The other relations lived a long way away and had no intention of any involvement with Sarah and her family. Their only contribution to the situation was, 'I can't understand why you let the kid go home again last time!' Fair point! I did know, from talking to the fostering team earlier, that the foster carer who cared for Sarah previously had become very fond of her during her stay, and Sarah had been extremely happy with her.

In the meantime, I had to ensure that all Julie's ploys to get Sarah alone, and possibly whisper threats in her ear, were thwarted. So Julie's periodic offers to take Sarah for a drink, to the loo, etc had to be met with me accompanying them. My gut feeling was that this child would be under heavy threat, and when Julie made her first attempt to isolate Sarah, the swift anxious glance from the child towards me confirmed that she was well aware of this fact. At one point it began to strike me clearly that although still mute, Sarah was tending to walk closer to me than to her mother, yet any comments she received from Julie were met with placatory replies. This child was scared and horrendously vulnerable.

Julie seemed strangely unmoved once she had agreed to allow Sarah to go into temporary care. It was almost as if she had more pressing issues to deal with, issues which preoccupied her and made Sarah's situation almost irrelevant, just a huge irritation in her life. She had Matthew to deal with and his possible, indeed very likely, disappearance in the face of 'trouble'.

It was clear from the files that Julie, raised in a chaotic and abusive family by her own mother and her multiple partners, had never been wanted, loved or cared for herself. Indeed, the records noted that she had, along with her siblings, survived at times by eating from the kitchen bin. She had mattered to no one, except perhaps as a messenger for drug deals. Now, as an adult, she continued to crave that love she had never had and sadly this often meant she was the victim of more abuse, and was used and dumped on a regular basis. The result was that her need for 'love', in whatever form she could get it, was so great that her only priority in life was keeping her partners. Keeping them for whatever drops of warmth they might provide before they moved on to pastures new. This priority would possibly always come so high on her list that the needs of a mere child were totally irrelevant.

This is a frequent pattern of behaviour, one that we saw over and over and over, but it never ceased to leave me saddened. So often it was clear to me, and tragically to the child also, that their needs were very low on their parents' list of priorities. Also, that they, or their needs, would often be ignored in favour of anything, however trivial, that the latest partner might want.

Did I feel anger at these parents? This is a question often asked of social workers, and the truth of the matter is we are usually dealing with generations of neglected and abused children. Given the opportunity to take histories from the abusing parents, what one often meets behind the angry, menacing or cold adult who sits in front of you is another small, hurt and damaged child. And what do they tell you of their lives? So often, tales of more neglect and hurt, handed out to them by parents who themselves may have experienced the same. Generation through generation, so the trail of hurt persists.

Someone somewhere has to shout 'Stop! This is where it ends!' Intervention can take the form of support, classes on parenting, drug and alcohol rehabilitation and ongoing help in every area of a parent's life. The dilemma is that while this help is given, time passes and there is a child being damaged. The longer they are left, the greater the damage.

Sadly, some of these parents will never become 'good enough'; they have so many hurts and addictions themselves that the struggle is too great. The best that we as social workers can do is to place their children in a foster or adoptive home and try to give that child a chance, by breaking the endless cycle, and do this before the child has sustained too great a level of damage.

Too often I have sat with parents and wished with all my heart that someone in the past had given them the chance of a better life.

Sometimes this work makes you sad.

We waited while the doctors completed the necessary examinations and I endeavoured, by all means known to man, or at least to me, to keep the atmosphere as calm as possible. Eventually everything was finished, and as soon as Julie could escape from us she disappeared off. Her goodbyes to Sarah were again distracted and without any emotional content. As she left, Sarah gazed after her. I really couldn't read her expression, but it held some very strange and mixed emotions.

By this time, the heavens had opened and a constant

heavy rainfall added to the grey grimness of the day. It was still the afternoon, but seemed almost like night. Sarah and I made our way as quickly as possible out to the car park. I found myself burdened by an overwhelming weight of misery. They say that you often 'pick up' the mood of people you are working with, but this was a very potent example and I struggled to adjust my thinking into a more positive frame.

It wasn't until we had seated ourselves in my car that I was able to turn to Sarah and talk openly and I hoped reassuringly about her situation. But how could anyone really reassure a child whose world – all they had ever known, however awful, tough or rejecting – was being turned upside down? At times like this no amount of training could make one feel anything more than inadequate.

As we drove to the home of the foster carer, I tried to explain to Sarah what was going to happen and where she was going to stay. Initially she listened in silence, but seemed to be pleased that that she was going to Patty, with whom she had stayed before. As time passed, her reaction when I said she would be spending a night, possibly two, with Patty, was telling. She asked initially for frequent reassurances: that Patty would actually be there, that she would not have other children in 'her' bed, and that Patty wanted her. When I told Sarah that Patty's reaction to her visit had been one of real delight, and repeated some of the nice things she had said about her, Sarah listened so hard and attentively, that I felt her eyes almost boring into my face. She then retreated into a thoughtful silence, and said very quietly, 'Will Mum visit me?' On being reassured that this would be organised, Sarah then continued, 'Can Patty come with me on the visit; I don't want to be alone.'

I suddenly felt the burden of this child's fears. As if all this small child was feeling had really got to me, and the trust she was placing in me could be destroyed by a careless or thoughtless word or action. So much could go wrong, so many mistakes could be made in handling her fragile situation. The responsibility felt very heavy at that moment.

I gently asked Sarah whether she was a little worried about seeing her mum. Sarah retreated into silence and I feared that perhaps this had been too direct a question. After a long pause she replied that she thought her mum would be very angry and, if Matthew left, would blame her. She paused again and added that Matthew might also be angry, and as if to clarify this thought she continued, 'Very angry.' I asked whether Matthew frightened her when he was angry and she replied after a pause, 'He shouts, and . . .' again she paused, and then added 'he throws things.' By now we were pulling into the drive of Patty's home. Patty was always full of energy; her husband was often away, as he was in the army and on long tours, but she seemed to cope regardless. At the window Patty was watching for us and in seconds she was out the front door with Bumble, her 57 varieties bundle of canine affection.

Bumble waited on the step, wagging his tail with enthusiasm, though no doubt possibly wondering who was now coming to join their busy family. Sarah was greeted with a big hug and together we went straight to the kitchen where Sarah was treated to a drink and a slice of Patty's special, very highly rated chocolate cake. Case conferences at Patty's house were much the better for her chocolate cake; indeed, I had begun to suspect that her home was a popular venue for reviews and meetings for this very reason. It was certainly one of the comforting highlights in a social worker's day (unless on a diet, when sitting before said cake could truly be described as purgatory).

Sarah began noticeably to relax a little. Patty made a big fuss of her and, while we talked over the basic issues, she sat on the sofa with Patty and Bumble, stroking Bumble's long silky fur. It had been a difficult afternoon, but I still had another school to visit and, as soon as I was able, I left Patty and Sarah, now about to sort out some overnight things in her room.

I shot over to Grove Road Secondary, glad to have snatched that drink and a slice of cake at Patty's as it would be my lunch today; not perhaps the healthiest option, but that was the least of my concerns.

3

Martin

I glanced down at my watch. Nearly midnight. Bother. Another late night. I'd never get all my write-ups completed. I thought back over the day, and what a day.

It had taken most of it to deal with Sarah's situation. Once she was safely placed with Patty, I had torn up to Grove Road School, and reported to Mrs Cliff, who was by this time extremely tight-lipped. I decided that any attempt at an explanation would be met with incredulity and none of it would sound like anything but a poor excuse, so I made a brief comment on my day, ignored her expression and jumped right in to what turned out to be a very distressing situation.

Several hours passed before I could sort out some safe-keeping for Christie, the young girl that all the concerns were about. Finally I chose to place her temporarily in the care of the mother of a close friend of hers from school, and further steps were put on hold until the morning. Many people would, I knew, have a very difficult night! But I left Mrs Cliff in a very different frame of mind. The revelations disclosed over the course of the interviews with Christie clearly horrified her. These, coupled with her now understanding that I had come straight from placing another child in crisis, put the tardy response of the duty social worker into a completely different perspective, and she had become a staunch ally.

I was glad. I had great respect for Mrs Cliff. Our paths had crossed at a case conference when I first came to Barton and it was clear that this lady cared for a great deal more than the exam results of her children. She had been passionate in fighting the corner of the child who was the subject of that conference and I knew her present anger sprang from a deeply caring nature, frustrated by our inability to respond quickly. I shared her frustration but I had had to learn that there was truly only so much I could do in a day, however much I wanted to do more and however much I tried.

The mantle clock struck twelve, so I made another cup of coffee and carried on recording all that had happened and been said on that hectic day. I knew that leaving my report writing until the morning would mean that I would forget critical little things, which might later, perhaps in court, prove vital to the overall picture.

I often felt that understanding a family in trouble began like a jigsaw thrown onto the floor by a tantruming toddler, with scattered pieces, all unrelated and jumbled up, such that the overall scene was chaotic and meaningless. Slowly, over the months, through endless interviews with the many people involved in the child's life, through conversations with as many of the family as I could get to meet and with feedback from the people working with me to help the family, a picture would begin to emerge. Often very important connecting pieces were provided by people who might begin by saying, 'Well this is probably unimportant, but . . .' and suddenly a light was thrown on another mystery so that things began to make sense.

As the clock struck one, I finally pressed 'save' for the last time, and turned off my computer. I knew I would have trouble turning off my thinking, so I picked up my standard 'light read', kept by my bed for this very purpose. Before long I was able to escape into its reassuring pages over some supper, and then staggered off to bed.

It seemed as if I had only just turned over when my alarm began its ridiculous racket, announcing the start of another day. The clock, a present from my brother last Christmas, was a crowing alarm clock. I was unsure how long this gift would last – one morning I might seriously attack it – but not today: I was rather too weary to be anything but mildly annoyed at its intrusion into my world of dreams.

Breakfast fortified me somewhat and before long I was off to work, wondering how I was going to find somewhere for Martin, my fiery-headed teenager. At least today, thank goodness, I was not on duty so could deal with my own caseload.

The day started well: I found a parking space instead of having the long walk from the multi-storey; I found the right change in my bag, admittedly after a frantic search right to the bottom; and the ticket machine was actually working. I arrived into work feeling 'OK'. That was destined to be a fading emotion! I was met by my senior, Marie Tomlin.

Marie was petite, slim and given her height you might think she would be easy to miss, but no, not Marie – she had brilliant red hair, the colour of deep red autumn leaves. Cropped short it may have been, but its colour was so vivid that she stood out from any crowd. This, in addition

to her larger-than-life personality, meant everyone noticed
Marie. She hailed from the highlands of Scotland, spoke
in a soft lilting accent, and along with her husband and
two young children (both, I was told, sporting beautiful
red hair) spent every spare weekend returning there.
Perhaps it was the hours she spent walking the mountains of Scotland that contributed to her calm manner.

In a well-known and much-repeated incident – repeated
by all but Marie I would add – she had found herself in
Smiths' card department one Saturday afternoon. Rounding
a display unit, she came face to face with the drunken
father of a child she had removed in very acrimonious
circumstances the previous week. To say this was awkward
would be one of the understatements of the century.
Marie's presence was like a red rag to a bull. The father
began to spit venomous comments at her, shouting obscen-
ities at the top of his voice, all definitely untrue, and
accused her of being a child abductor. You can imagine
the effect this had on other shoppers! As he got into an
increasing rage, which did not help his already unsteady
gait, he demolished a stand of books and a magazine
display rack. Then he lost it completely when asked by
security to calm down. In attempting to make a swing at
Marie, he left two security guards very bruised. He was
only finally placated by the strong arm of the law in the
guise of two burly policemen, who, with the help of hand-
cuffs, removed him unceremoniously from Smiths. And
what did Marie have to say about all this? No hysterical
attention-grabbing accounts of her unmitigated terror,
such as most of us, I have to admit, enjoyed occasionally
as a relief from the stress at work. No accounts of lost

sleep, fearful flashbacks or the like. Apparently she was heard to say very calmly to her colleagues, 'My hair makes me rather too easily spotted. Pity.' However, those in the know say she does tend to shop in Denton at weekends now – some fifteen miles away! Marie was extremely calm and a tower of strength when the team members needed her, a real inspiration with an ability to cut through all the waffle and see right to the point.

Marie summoned me into her room for a discussion of the previous day's events. After a quick run-down, plus a copy of the reports, she reminded me that Sarah's social worker, Wendy, was on leave, and she was up in County Hall all day. She asked whether, as I was known to the child, I would mind very much following up on the case today. Marie then paused before her next words: 'Becky, I am going to have to ask for your extreme discretion in what I am about to say, but there is a strong possibility that Wendy will not be returning to work, for personal reasons. As this is the likely situation, I need to ask you to consider taking this case on permanently. I will redirect several other cases I had earmarked for you, as this will be an involved case, with many court reports, plus any other work on placement.' Here Marie paused, and then added, 'How do you feel about this? Of course, if Wendy does return we would review the situation.'

Initially my heart sank. I had so much on in all my cases, yet I knew that there was simply no other option, and I would at least have the satisfaction of seeing Sarah through the immediate crisis, and then working out the longer term for her. After briefly thinking through the situation, I agreed to this and, as I did, realised just how involved I had already become with this small child, experiencing a surge of pleasure at the prospect of sticking with her.

As I left Marie's room, my mind was already in fast forward. I began to quickly run through my essential tasks for the day. I needed to travel the seventy or so miles to Forth Lodge to see Martin, and move him to a new home. This was going to be tough on him, but clearly Forth Lodge was not staffed to cope with such outbursts, and we had pushed our luck there too many times. They had been on the phone repeatedly since this latest outburst – to the managers, to my senior, indeed to anyone who would listen. I knew that Martin depended on me and would respond to me in a way that he would not with an unknown social worker, so I could not fail him. But where would I find time in the rest of the day to liaise with everyone about Sarah's case, hold a meeting with the police, interview Matthew, if I could, and also talk with Sarah's mother again?

I could see no easy way forward. I knew that Marie understood the pressure this was putting me under, but the situations were there and had to be dealt with. They were not 'pieces of work', which could be just left. This was about people's lives, in much the same way that I hope the staff in Accident and Emergency might forgo their breaks and lunch to save my life even if they were run off their feet. I knew this work had to be done whatever the cost. So, I went back to my desk and tried to prioritise, thinking that, if I had a placement lined up for Martin, then I could deal with that after all the visits relating to Sarah.

*

I sorted quickly through all the centres that had been suggested for Martin by the placements team. All sounded
really good, with tons of therapeutic input, but rushed
as I was I couldn't stop a little voice within me which
kept on saying: 'You know Martin. Is this really what he
needs?' I tried to control my desire to rush on and take
one of the centres that were there in front of me, and
then Martin's face came up clearly in my mind. I had got
to know him well over the last five months, and had read
through the copious files recording his life from his very
earliest years, when Social Services had first become
involved with his family.

Difficult as he could be, I really felt for this child; indeed,
I had become very fond of him. He was a tall gangly boy
in his early teens, removed from home when his mother
kicked him out on the street when he was only ten. Why?
Because she found that he was becoming a nuisance when
she wanted to entertain her friends, mostly men, mostly
for money, and mostly to fund the supply of heroin on
which she depended. She had never made any convincing
attempt to redeem herself. Martin was the unfortunate
result of a long-past relationship, and was becoming an
increasingly troublesome part of her life. She had had
enough of him.

I couldn't imagine how that must feel for a child. He
was a bright youngster in spite of everything, and had no
illusions about his past, though he blamed himself for
everything. Somehow he felt that if only he had been
more helpful none of it would have happened, and his
mother would have wanted him. Believe it or not he worried
about her safety endlessly.

He had a hugely open personality and was able sometimes to talk about issues and feelings. Indeed, many of his teachers, prior to his admission to care, had been extremely fond of him. Whenever I visited Martin, the unit's very large and disdainful cat, Tibs, would always be on hand. The two of them had struck up such a relationship that, after a while, Martin had taken on some of the animal's care. He made little of this, but I had seen how he responded to the cat. He adored Tibs and she was usually to be found curled up beside him or on his lap. It reassured me that he still had a real capacity to care and that was a big plus, although surprising looking back on his history. After little but ongoing hurt and rejection, many children became emotionally withdrawn and fail to develop a caring side. Martin had had his full quota, and more, of rejection; was it any wonder he exploded at times?

I had never been convinced that a residential placement was the right thing for Martin and felt that he should have gone into foster care at ten, a more usual choice. It was his violent outbursts that governed the decision, by the placement team and his then social worker, that a foster home would never cope with him, but I still wondered. I had been reading a lot in the journals about specialist foster homes for severely disturbed children, many of whom sounded not unlike Martin. I pulled out my desk drawer and shuffled through the mountain of professional journals lurking there, along with many other leaflets, forms, spare envelopes etc. I pulled out the one I wanted and found the article, plus the details of the few foster agencies that had begun these specialist placements on an experimental basis. The initial results were encouraging, but the carers had to be resilient and able to stand firm and caring through many early ups and downs, mostly the latter. But those who were able to ride the storms found that slowly, many of these children could, even after a lifetime of rejection, learn to trust them and learn how to become a member of a family who cares. I felt my adrenaline running, and with it a determination that I was going to do this for Martin.

There had to be a family out there that could give him what he needed: unqualified love, certainty and boundaries, and that had the ability to cope with the outbursts in the transition. At this point I have to say I added a little prayer. Well, Martin needed all the help he could get, and I seriously doubted if I was enough!

I raced over to find Marie, and told her what I was thinking about Martin's placement. She was very quick on the uptake, and I found she was studying me with that intense look she had, when you felt she was trying, fairly successfully, to read your mind and see if you had really thought an idea through thoroughly. I was pretty sure she had grown to trust my judgement, and I also knew that she had attended one of Martin's reviews last year and been unhappy about what was happening to him. She looked at the costs, and agreed that there was little in it. Anyway, like me, she had a great belief that foster homes were better for children whenever it could possibly be set up.

I had what I needed: her blessing on the idea, and the funding. All I needed now was the right home. Somewhere out there, there must be a family for Martin.

4

Search for a Home

I left Marie's office feeling suddenly so wide awake that my lost sleep seemed irrelevant. I bounced back to my desk clutching the journal with its list of agencies involved in the project, grabbed the phone and without a moment's hesitation began to dial. Over an hour later, with an aching hand from all my scribbling, I had talked through Martin and his needs with a good number of the agencies who had these specialised carers; now it was over to them. They had all agreed to fax through details of families that were both available and seemed a close match; this would enable me to read through them and make a short-list. In the meantime, Sandy had set up an immediate meeting for me to discuss Sarah's situation with the police liaison team. This was also critical, so I had no alternative but to leave Martin's situation in the hands of the fostering agencies. This left me free to see the police team, and then visit Sarah's mother.

Another 'difficult' interview with Julie ensued, and I managed to catch Matthew briefly at his mother's home, which was on the same estate as Julie. I was again very glad of James's reassuring presence during what was a rather stressful interview with Matthew – not a calm man. Any secret hopes I might have harboured of his mother being a restraining and calming influence on her son, of her being a solid, salt-of-the-earth type of mother, were very quickly dispelled in the cold, dismissive and antagonistic face revealed as she opened her door, responding to my introduction with, 'Oh, so you're from the Social. What do you want?' The tone of this question left me in no doubt that even if I had wanted a blade of grass from her neglected and litter-strewn frontage, my request would have been angrily refused.

She lurked in the background while I talked to Matthew about the events surrounding Sarah, and occasionally she threw angry and quite menacing comments into an already very difficult interview. Matthew was extremely resentful of any questions that he interpreted as placing suspicion upon his shoulders and his mother continued with periodic outbursts relating to his human rights and her intention to report us to the MP, the 'law' or the Director of Social Services, to name but a few. As she got into the swing of verbalising her intentions, she began to mention various 'uncles' and 'brothers', who would 'not be well pleased' at the family being 'victimised' in this way! There was also reference to the fate of certain 'other persons', who had 'upset the family' and just how long it had taken them to recover. I struggled to keep a rational take on these threats. They were not an uncommon part of the job, and I knew it was usually just a way of coping and attempting to maintain a degree of control over events. Then again, I did recall times when, for some social workers, the threats had stopped being idle!

It will not surprise you to hear that I was not altogether sorry to step out of the front door into the bright sunshine. At least I had Matthew's side of the story, which needless to say bore little resemblance to Julie's story, but there we are: that was no surprise.

When I got back to the office, I found that Sandy had carefully piled up the F Forms faxed through by the fostering agencies and left them on my desk for me to peruse. An F Form is a detailed account of a foster family, written by a social worker whose task it is to really get to know a family. The report tells the reader about the people within that home, their personalities, likes and dislikes, strengths and weaknesses. It is a substantial and extremely valuable portrait of a family. So clearly are they portrayed within the report that the families almost seem at times to walk off the pages. The work done in compiling these valuable documents takes many months and ensures that only the robust and self-aware continue on to become foster carers. Subsequently, the completed reports are used to assist social workers in trying to match up children to families.

With a coffee in one hand – kindly supplied by Sandy, who had clearly decided that I needed some TLC – I ploughed through the rather lengthy documents. Some I could rule out from the short pen picture at the start, others merited a good read. Disappointingly the first four were just not right; I felt a creeping sense of anxiety. And then I found them: the Bridges family. They had reared their own brood of three children – two boys and a girl, now grown up – lived in a fairly spacious home, along with three cats and two dogs, so a few extra chips would not be noticed there then! But it was something about the way they talked about children in their interviews. They came over as very warm and caring, but also very realistic about the damage many children have to endure, and how this affects them. The father was a sports fanatic, a keen runner, who until recently played for a local rugby team, but in his spare time helped to run a youth club in a tough area of the town. I read on and my heart was definitely beating a little faster with suppressed hope. Mrs Bridges was described as a calm, competent, motherly person, who had worked with teenagers in schools before becoming a foster carer. Reports about previous children they had cared for highlighted their strengths. A story was included of how Mrs Bridges had handled a very distraught teenager, whose response to a disastrous contact meeting with his family had been to climb a huge horse chestnut tree in the school playground and refuse to come down or speak to anyone. Apparently, in the face of such total intransigence, Mrs Bridges calmly settled herself down under the tree, with a vacuum flask and rug, and waited. Eventually, she was able to persuade the boy to accept some sandwiches, which she inventively passed up by means of a long pair of hedge cutters. I believe it took five hours, but something was established there. Someone cared enough to be there for him, a revolutionary concept for that boy. As far as I was concerned, a woman able to display the patience and wisdom shown in this incident was just what I needed for Martin.

As I continued to read, I felt a mounting sense of excitement; they seemed to have so much that would make them a possible match for Martin. I searched back through the form for the contact number and lifted the phone to dial. I was keeping a cap on my feelings but I was hoping. Oh, how I was hoping!

I was in luck, and was able to get hold of the couple's

supporting social worker, Sally, who knew the Bridges very well, having worked with them for many years. We must have talked for well over forty minutes. Sally was honest and realistic, asking me as many questions as I did her. She was clearly very knowledgeable and was not for taking any risks with her carers, or with the lives of any child placed with them. She was someone I felt I could trust and who shared my desire to get this right for all concerned. Knowing she would be their support made this a personal issue for us both.

Sally told me that when this new fostering scheme for particularly challenging children was launched, the Bridges had been really keen to get involved. She recounted how they had enthusiastically undergone the specialised training recently set up to help carers understand, support and cope with particularly challenging behaviour, sometimes ringing her to discuss aspects of the course and debate issues. These courses, which really told it like it is, and demanded serious commitment in both time and learning, had simply increased their desire to try and help children who would otherwise spend their childhoods in institutions rather than experiencing family life.

Sally's voice softened and dropped in tone, 'I would just add, the Bridges are committed in a tough, really caring way. It's not any pink and fluffy sentimental commitment; they mean it. In for the long haul, these two. I want you to see that, Becky.' Yes, I was beginning to see that very clearly, and my hopes rose further.

Finally, we both found ourselves feeling that this was as right as we could hope for; if this couple could not work with Martin, we would have to look a long way to better them. It was agreed that I would talk to them and I found myself dialling their number and dreading them having gone out for the day. But no, they were in – that was a good start. The voice answering the phone was strong, but warm, very human and . . . 'Stop!' I told myself, 'This is too good to be true!' I forcibly reined in my hopes.

I chatted to Mrs Bridges first and then to Mr Bridges. I liked them; they were grounded, expected a tough time, but really believed that, in time, most children could be helped. They had been foster carers for many years and in that time had had children with many difficulties and had weathered countless 'storms'. Many of their now-launched children came back for weekends or visits, or rang for chats, and this couple were passionate about what foster care could do for children, which was why they had been so interested in this new scheme. They listened very carefully to my description of Martin, asked some thoughtful questions, and over a longish chat I felt that they were growing to feel this could be right for them, and my feeling was likewise. They took some time to talk through the implications for all concerned, including Martin, and then rang me back with further questions about him. It was clear from the depth of their questions that they really knew what to ask and that they were fully aware of the task involved in taking on this boy, and also of the responsibility of not letting him down. They said they would consider this further between themselves and their social worker, and read through the information I had sent over about Martin, following which their social worker would contact me. I almost couldn't bear the suspense. They seemed as ideal as anything in this life can be! If they felt this was not right for them, I'd be back to square one and the thought left me drained.

I pushed this thinking to the back of my mind, tackled the outstanding paperwork from Sarah, and arranged to pop over later to see Sarah and her foster carer to catch up. I also took some of Sarah's belongings that I had collected for her, including a small felt mouse she had begged me to bring and which I had finally succeeded in finding under her bed in spite of her mother's annoyance.

I had spoken to Martin earlier. He was well aware that he was moving on, and had known this was the case since the last outburst. Unfortunately, all attempts to persuade the unit to keep Martin even a day or two longer had failed; they were bluntly refusing to keep him any longer. One member of staff had gone off sick after Martin's last outburst. They had another child who needed the place urgently, and they felt we were asking them to keep a child whom they were not equipped to handle. They would not move, and we had little option but to act accordingly. On the phone Martin had sounded in rebellious mood about the whole thing. I told him I would be down to see him later, and would talk to him about his move. Relationships in the unit had, I felt, become unhelpfully negative towards Martin, so that in some ways the sudden move had become more acceptable, even though this would certainly never be my chosen way of moving or placing any child. We had little option.

I was just answering another call about Sarah when Sandy, who knew I was waiting for a call from the fostering agency, gesticulated to me. I asked her to hold it, while I tried to concentrate on my present call. Trying not to appear to be in a rush, I finished the call and then dashed over to speak with the foster agency social worker. As I reached for the phone, could I feel my heart do a little flutter of fear? Or hope? I'm not sure, but this call really mattered to me. The voice of the social worker on the other end came through loud and clear. 'The Bridges are really keen to take Martin. We just need to talk through some details.'

The relief! I could have danced for joy and my smile, about 200 miles wide, said it all to my surrounding colleagues who were well aware of what was happening with Martin. Endeavouring to restrain my feelings of mania, and maintain an appropriately professional response, I made all the arrangements, took directions and rang off.

At that moment I felt like the whole world was a wonderful place to be in; all I had to do now was sell this to Martin.

Time was moving on quickly, and I had managed, by a combination of good luck, hard work and not wasting any unnecessary time, to have pretty much completed all the necessary meetings for Sarah. I had fortunately brought my lunch with me, though in fact eating seemed a bit of a waste of valuable time, so I ate an apple on my way down to the car park where I made a quick, final check of my papers for the rest of the day.

The drive down to Martin's assessment centre was fairly smooth, but my mind was full of conflicting thoughts. I believed this was a chance for Martin to have a real family, and to have a chance to find people who would stand by him, and help him to deal with his own feelings of rejection, guilt and anger. I so wanted to say the right things; I wanted him to give this a chance.

When I arrived, the key worker told me that Martin had been very withdrawn since the decision to move him had been confirmed, and would speak to no one, so they were concerned about him and wondered whether this would trigger another violent episode.

I went through to the room Martin was in, and went over to him. He was sitting huddled up in a large armchair facing the wall, his arms crossed over his chest, his head down, rocking to and fro. The cat was on the floor next to him, which was unusual – she was usually on his knee. I sat down and gently began to try and reach this boy, who yet again faced wholesale rejection.

At first I felt that I was simply not getting through to him, but slowly the rocking became less constant, he began to listen and his eyes lifted a little, fleetingly at first but then occasionally looking at me as I spoke. I had rehearsed my thoughts over and over in the car but now, faced with the reality, I could only try to relate to how Martin must be feeling, and explain how much I would like to help to give him a chance to change things.

I talked about how I had felt for some time that a family would be a good place for him to be. His reaction was initially very negative. He was angry. Very angry. Hardly surprising as his only experience of 'family' was pretty grim. Let's face it, what's so great about families if they beat you or neglect you? If while you starve, cowering out of sight, they drink and drug themselves out of their minds then kick you out without a backward glance?

It would take some convincing to get Martin to give any family a chance, and who could blame him? The only weapon in my arsenal to get him to hear me out was that I had spent quite a lot of time with him, talking and getting to know him and I did think he trusted me. I suspected also, that for better or worse, he knew I really cared and I think that was why, over time, he began to listen to me. We talked about his own family, and again about why they had found it so hard to cope, that none of it had been his fault, and that he should give himself the chance to be in a family that would help him. He slowly began to thaw, just a little, and talked about how angry he felt, and how it all spilled out at times, almost before he knew, leading to these horrendous outbursts of aggression. Again, I tried to reassure him that with a family who could understand all he had coped with, he might learn, eventually, to control these feelings. Strangely, this was something he wanted me to repeat and explain, as if he was frightened of himself and would welcome help.

I noticed his posture had become very slightly less defensive, and he expressed a very reserved interest in 'this family', as he put it. I showed him the booklet that the Bridges family had put together to show to a child, with pictures of them both, the pets, house and so on, and this did slightly catch his attention. Particularly the cats! For two pins, I would have abducted Tibs in my briefcase for Martin, but the existence of three very robust and quite appealing cats at the Bridges' family home made this step probably unnecessarily extreme.

I have never seen myself as much of a salesperson, but

today it seemed to work. Slowly but surely he began to ask tentative questions about the family. That I had chatted at length to them helped me to convey a great deal to Martin, and I hoped he might get a sense of them from my words. Eventually, when weighed up against residential options, and with a throwaway comment along the lines of, 'I'll give it a week; they'll throw me out by then,' Martin agreed to go to the Bridges.

The centre tried to be as supportive as they could in the circumstances; they were adamant that they could not safely manage a child like Martin, and that he was a risk to staff and other young people, and that was that. But they did try to talk positively to him about the future, though I wonder how he could hear these words when all he felt was their rejection. Without a backward glance at anyone, Martin came out to my car, but I saw him reach out to Tibs who was waiting near the front door and ruffle her fur. That got to me, right deep inside, like a stab in the heart.

5

On the Road Again

Once on the road, I had a barrage of comments and questions from Martin, all in quick succession, about the Bridges.

'Why would they want to foster?'

'Haven't they got children of their own?'

'They'll probably change their minds when they see me.'

'Does the father beat the foster children?'

'Where will I go to school?'

'Will I have my own room?'

And so it went on. At times he was quiet and thoughtful, and I worried. At other times he was anxious and questioning, and it was tiring trying to work out what he was feeling and respond in a helpful way. At odd moments he was near to tears about all that was happening and had happened in his past, and I was gutted.

After a two-hour journey, the light was failing, but we were nearly at our destination. Martin became very quiet, and I was desperately trying not to miss my turn, something I managed with only two slight detours. We drew up in the drive of a solid, square, white house surrounded by garden. The outside lights were all on and as we pulled up a couple in their late forties came out to greet us, as did two very enthusiastic hearthrugs on legs in the form of the family dogs. Mrs Bridges was fairly tall, of medium build, with an open, reliable sort of face, brown curly hair and warm brown eyes. Mr Bridges was, well, big, tall and well made, with a relaxed walk and a smile to match. They were the sort of people you quickly feel you might have known a long time.

We all went into the house together; it was rather rambling, with lots of comfy, well-used chairs and a lovely lived-in, warm feel to it. Mr Bridges carried Martin's cases to the hallway, Martin was swept in with me, and before long we were being offered tea and sandwiches to tide Martin over until supper. I could see Martin sizing things up from the corner of his eyes, casting secret penetrating glances around, but he was not speaking. He managed to eat a couple of sandwiches, nibbling at them in a restrained way. I had the distinct impression that he was feigning a level of disinterest in the food that he did not feel and that he was actually starving. It is hard to eat in a room full of strangers, when life is tough.

Mr Bridges took a subdued and totally silent Martin up to take his things to his room, while I went over the inevitable paperwork with Mrs Bridges. After five minutes, a still subdued and totally silent boy came down. Mrs Bridges told Martin in a cheerful and matter-of-fact voice, that his uneaten sandwiches were in the fridge for him if he wanted them, and that it was a house rule that 'the Bridges don't do hungry!' Martin was clearly taken by surprise at this comment and turned to look at her for the first time, his eyes both questioning and somewhat confused. Mrs Bridges explained to Martin that she always kept a good supply of cheese, milk, bread and fruit in the fridge. She added with a warm smile, 'I like you to do justice to my cooking, but if you are hungry, you can eat as much of these extras as you can, make yourself toast or have a bowl of cereal any time you like.'

To Martin this was a completely new concept. He wasn't sure he understood what this meant. Free access to food, anytime, all day, all night even! He had known years of real aching hunger, in fact it had been a part of his normal and miserable life before he came into care. Then he was living in 'homes', where food was available in prescribed ways – not at this time, not at that time or only with permission. Food represented something very major in his existence – it was comfort, security, a substitute for the love he never had. Free, unquestioning access to it was quite a staggering freedom. He put his hand into his jacket pocket, where the now rather congealed piece of bread he had hidden from the breakfast table was to be found. Martin held it like a bit of security blanket. Yes, he liked to always have something handy for a snack, and he was a dab hand at secreting food away from the table, that way he felt safe. He had still not said a word and his eyes still refused to engage. I was feeling some degree of concern for the family, when a pitiful mew announced the presence of a tiny black kitten tottering over from the kitchen door.

'Oh dear,' said Mrs Bridges, quickly scooping up the tiny mite to return him to the kitchen, 'our latest additions to the family: two of them,' she grinned, nuzzling the little creature. 'They were found abandoned in very sad circumstances and, well, what's another two cats in the house, though they do take rather a lot of feeding, still needing bottles.' My thoughts had been momentarily distracted by the absolutely gorgeous kitten but, as I turned to look at Martin, I saw a flicker of the first sign of life, a spark of interest in his face as he followed the kitten with his eyes. I risked it and jumped in: 'Maybe Martin could help a bit with the feeding; he has cared for a cat before.' I knew this could backfire, but just as I spoke the other kitten peeped out from the kitchen and made its unsteady progress across the room, stopping at Martin's chair which was nearest the kitchen. A tiny ginger tabby with huge green eyes, and a look on its face utterly bursting with pathetic appeal, collapsed into a wobbly heap at the foot of his chair, and the little scrap gazed up at Martin. That did it – Martin couldn't stop himself. He scooped the kitten up, and had it snuggled up on his knee in no time. No one commented and we carried on as if nothing had happened for fear of breaking the spell.

We all chatted and dealt with odd things that had to be sorted, but all the while Martin quietly held the kitten, stroking her fluffy baby fur. Mrs Bridges brought their bottles through and gave one to Martin while she had the other and as we chatted two small felines sucked contentedly on their bottles! In a pause in the conversation, Mrs Bridges said to Martin: 'Tell you what, I've no names for these two yet, maybe you could think up some for them?'

It was then, after a very long pause, that we heard the first words from Martin as he looked down into those enormous green eyes, which were now the centre of a contented, milk-splattered little face, and we heard him say, 'Could we call this one Tibs?' I felt momentarily choked, and in my mind was the picture of Martin and his beloved

Tibs 1. This was the only time in my life that I had had reason to be glad that a small kitten had been abandoned.

Before long, it was time for me to hit the road and leave Martin. I always hate this bit, but I explained to Martin that I would be back in two days to see how he was and would ring tomorrow to talk to him. The Bridges came out to wave goodbye but Martin grunted a farewell and remained in his chair with 'his' kitten. I thought that little cat, whose tough start in life brought him to the Bridges, had much in common with Martin, and the two would be perfect for one another. I dearly hoped both would find healing and sanctuary in this family.

As I drove away, I felt as if I had walked out of a home so full of emotion that it was like breathing mountain air to have left. All the issues of the day had taken their toll, paramount being my concern for Martin. I could only hope the Bridges were as good as their reputations. I often wonder if foster carers realise just how much trust and desperate hope we social workers place in them.

I drove off along high-hedged lanes, through tiny hamlets, the red wintry sun very low in the sky, hanging above countryside now only visible in dark shapes behind the hedges. The dramatic scene somehow emphasised all the emotions that the last hours had raised, a mixture of sadness, hope and even a degree of wistful elation.

As the miles droned on – particularly once I was on the motorway – a terrible exhaustion hit me, so great that I decided to stop at the first service station; I simply could not keep going. I bought a large coffee, a sandwich and a bar of chocolate, found a quiet corner of the café and sat staring out; and while I nibbled bits of the sandwich

I allowed myself to stop thinking and tried to relax. The world around me seemed almost unreal, so muted was its emotional content. But then we only see the fronts others choose to reveal, and know nothing of the pits or peaks they may be dealing with. At first, as I sat there, I felt almost a little shaky, but the caffeine and food helped to calm me. The words of the Bridges' social worker came back to me: 'All I can say is, that if they can't help him you'll be lucky to find anyone who can. They've got grit, and they really care.'

Well, I was hanging on to that.

It was at that moment that my mobile rang, loudly intruding into my silent thoughts. It was my senior, Marie, ringing to check on things. Firstly she listened carefully to my account of events. There was then a pause, and Marie said, 'Look, Becky, you must be exhausted, but you've gone the length for Martin, and some. You have done more than anyone could possibly expect, well done, you can do no more tonight. Do try to step back now and get a good night's sleep. It sounds as if the Bridges can be trusted to do their very best, and you really need a rest! Drive carefully, and we'll talk in the morning.'

I tell you frankly, Marie was as supportive a senior as one would ever get. I really appreciated that call; this could be a lonely job at times, left alone so often to cope with some wildly difficult emotions. It was nearly 7 p.m. and I still had to make that visit to Sarah at her new foster home. I saw this as a very quick call, to touch base with her, and deliver some vital belongings collected earlier in the day.

It was 7.30 p.m. when I arrived, and I was greeted by

Patty as if it was 9 a.m. in the morning! I had a chat with Sarah, went through the bag of clothes her mother had very grudgingly found, and handed over the mouse, who was snatched up and cuddled by Sarah. She showed me her room, and it was clear she was feeling comfortable for the moment. After a chat to sort out one or two immediate issues and concerns, I was ready to leave when Patty pulled me to one side and told me that Sarah had been very anxious about being left alone with her mother, or even taking phone calls from her. She knew that contact with her mother would be set up straight away, and was concerned. I called Sarah to join me for a moment and, over a cup of tea, we chatted. Sarah was very nervous of speaking again about this, but slowly relaxed enough to say that her mum would be very angry with her, and she was scared of what she might say, or tell her to say. Sarah became tearful but went on to say that if her mum got angry she would make her pay when she went home.

I asked her about Matthew and Sarah gave me a glance from under her eyelids, for want of any other words it was a look of pure fear. 'Mum says I annoy him, but I don't mean to, and . . .' Sarah shifted uncomfortably and there was a silence while clearly she was weighing up how much to say. After a prolonged pause, I leaned forward and quietly said, 'Are you able to go on, Sarah? You were saying you don't mean to annoy Matthew, and . . .' Sarah seemed to summon up some courage, and added, 'Well, Bruno annoyed Matthew.' Pausing for a moment to think, I asked, 'Who is Bruno?' Sarah was sitting on the sofa, her little thin arms tightly crossed over her chest, and seemed unable to get any more words out. At this point

Patty came in from the kitchen and gesticulated to me. Did I want her to stay in or out? I suggested she joined us, and she sat herself down next to Sarah, instinctively knowing that an arm around her shoulders was needed, with a little hug.

Sarah moved slightly up the sofa towards Patty, as if her presence was the comfort she needed to continue. 'Bruno was our dog, he was lovely. I loved him.' At this she broke down in sobs and for some time Patty could only hold her. When she began to calm down a little she continued, with real anger and hurt in her voice. 'He killed him, he kicked him and kicked him, only because Bruno wanted to be with me and had sneaked up to my room.'

The terrifying account Sarah then gave of a man completely engulfed in mindless rage, attacking this poor animal, was one I will spare you. I am haunted at times to this day by the child's description. But her final words sent an even bigger chill down my spine. 'He threatened to do this to me if I don't behave and keep out of his way.' After another pause, I asked Sarah, 'And what did mum do, Sarah?' In a small voice she replied, 'She said it was all my fault. I encouraged the dog, and Bruno had it coming, and . . .' She paused while big teardrops rolled down her face, 'and she said he'd do the same to me if I didn't behave, but I do, I really do try. Still he is always cross and mum gets cross if I annoy him.'

By this time I felt the child was exhausted. Patty and I spent some time talking about less traumatic things, and I told her I would visit again tomorrow, and that with Patty she was safe. Patty said she had some storybooks to read which would help Sarah to calm down. I reassured her that she would not be left alone with her mother. The issues that had come to light raised many serious concerns and I knew that there was a long way to go before I could ensure the long-term safety of this child. How can I describe what I felt? Words fail at times.

I was shaken, angry and upset for this child. No matter how often one hears children's stories giving a small snapshot of their tragic lives, one never becomes resistant to feeling their pain and fear. Never. Perhaps if that day ever came then that would be the time to resign, and quickly.

I made my goodbyes when the time was right, knowing that Patty would provide all the reassurance that she could, and walked out to my waiting car. Sinking into the seat was like returning to an old and comforting armchair. Tonight was bitterly cold, the streetlights cast a dull glow, and I pulled the collar of my jacket up around my ears. No matter how many times I had heard stories along these lines, I never got over that feeling I now had – a sort of shivery churning. Was it fear, having pictured the horrors that this child had been through? Was it anxiety, that I might not be able to put together a case sufficiently convincing to ensure this child was freed from her nightmare existence? I knew that unless I did my job carefully and prepared clear reports that truly reflected the issues, the court might not accept the child's words. Was it anger, that this couple had hoodwinked the department, the schools, and many others for so long? I suspect a mixture of all of these. The chill night seemed as cold as the tale I had just heard.

I drove down the road until I was out of sight, then

stopped, pushed back my seat, got out my notebook and wrote, for probably over half an hour or so, trying to note down every detail that Sarah had revealed. I knew that if I left this until the morning – or even later tonight – I would forget some of the details, some of the very telling expressions and movements which had accompanied her words. There was no way of knowing whether this would be only the beginning of Sarah telling us about her life or whether, at some contact session with her mother, the supervisor might be momentarily distracted and a threat whispered in Sarah's vulnerable ear by her mother would ensure that she would not speak again, for fear of the consequences. I couldn't take the chance. Before I drove off, I gave Patty a quick ring and asked her to do the same. I asked her to be sure to note down in her diary everything she had heard, and to write it tonight and date it, lest some clever barrister tried to say it was written when the facts had become blurred by time or other experiences.

I always believe that the best and most accurate accounts are written at the time of hearing, before one has had opportunity to process the information, which might be when slight changes could occur. Written much after the event, it is hard not to add some of one's own colouring to the picture. My senior would be signing this report first thing in the morning, so there could be no questioning the time of writing.

I turned on the engine and put the heater on full blast. Sitting in the car, engrossed in recording the events of the evening I had simply not noticed that my feet had turned into blocks of ice, and I was generally turning blue! It was with great relief that I set off for home.

Home always seems doubly welcoming when you have had a really tough day. I let myself in and leaned back against the door, almost as if I was reinforcing the sense of shutting out the world. My little hallway seemed cosy and pleased to see me. A meal eaten in front of some puerile rubbish on the box, and I began to feel that all I wanted was a hot bath and bed. Less than an hour later I fell into a deep, exhausted sleep, not stirring until that crowing alarm clock dragged me into consciousness.

6

The Guardian

I knew that there was plenty for me to do the next day. I had some court reports to look through and check for any errors. I had to meet the new guardian for one of my families that was going to court fairly soon. I had work to chase on Sarah, I had a family and professionals meeting for another case and on top of all this I had offered to cover two hours of another social worker's duty session so she could go to a hospital appointment.

Typical, then, that the day started badly. The boiler service man was due at 8 a.m., and didn't arrive until 8.30, which put me in a rush to try and get to work on time. As if that wasn't bad enough, the traffic was dreadful and so I decided to take the short cut along the country lanes. This usually cut some ten minutes off my journey at busy times, so I was confident that I would make up some much-needed time. Some hope! Today of all days, six young bullocks had squeezed through a fence from a field adjacent to the lane, which delayed me another twenty minutes.

By the time I finally reached the office, my phone was already ringing. It was from reception, to say that the guardian I was due to meet had arrived and would I come down to collect him? It was then that I suddenly remembered that I had, due to the hectic events of the last week,

forgotten to book a room for our meeting. A simultaneously hot and cold feeling overwhelmed me. This was a
serious oversight; we only had four rooms available for
meetings, and they were often booked well in advance. I
felt slightly sick. This was not a good way to meet with
a new colleague, we had nowhere in the offices that was
not open plan and extremely noisy.

I grabbed the booking file from our admin support girl,
and so wished there was someone who could take this
from my shoulders – I didn't need a tussle with rooms
just now. Unfortunately Sandy was away, as she would
probably have helped me in a crisis, and the young girl,
Simone, who covered in her absence, was very clear about
her job description: it did not cover what she had often
been heard to describe as, 'Running after social workers
and doing their work for them.'

Simone had her own set of priorities, which often
included long chats on her mobile to friends. When she
arrived in the morning she would not pick up a phone
until exactly 9 a.m., her official start time, and at ten
minutes before her official home time, heaven help any
brave soul who dared to ask for any help. A tyrant, challenged by no one, so like all tyrants she grew stronger by
the day!

In a utopian parallel universe, social workers would be
relieved of the endless bureaucratic hassles so they could
actually spend any time they did have doing their job properly. Further, while many of these 'tasks' seemed small to
others, even insignificant in themselves, added together,
the sheer number of them became stressful and immensely
time consuming.

I thumbed through the book – no obvious spaces – so I made a couple of calls to the various individuals responsible for this endlessly harassing process. No go. Then one very helpful girl suggested to me that I could just try the conference clerk – not ideal, she said, but better than the car park. Hmmm, very true. I quickly dialled reception, and asked Rhona to apologise to the guardian for my delay, get him some coffee and generally smooth things over. Rhona was another Sandy; I knew she would do this for me, willingly and well. She was amazing and I so appreciated her!

I dialled conferencing, my heart by now in my mouth, my blood pressure through the ceiling; if this failed I didn't know what I would do. A rather officious sounding lady whose name was Barbara answered. I explained my dilemma and she asked how many people I needed the room for and waited for my answer. I hesitated. I realised that a room for a conference was not usually booked for two people, and I was just having a last desperate thought as to whether I should invent another ten people to make my request logical. But before I had had time to think Barbara prompted me sharply with, 'Well, don't you know how many?' I came clean, explained my problem and told her, 'Two.'

'Two!' she retorted. 'Two!' her voice growing higher with indignation. 'Well, I can't book this room for two people. I have the capacity for at least forty people and I cannot possibly use it for two!' I felt that I had dealt such a mortal blow to her sense of the right order of life that I would not be forgiven this preposterous request any time soon, indeed perhaps ever. My hopes sank, but I had to try . . .

'But it is free, isn't it, and I do need it now, I would be so grateful.' Grovelling was not a pleasant step to take, but hey I would have done many things to simply win a room. Barbara continued, 'Well this room is free now, but not for two people, that is simply ridiculous. You should have rung first floor rooms.' Endeavouring to maintain a calm and pleasant front, I replied, 'I did, but they have absolutely no spare rooms until three o'clock.'

'Well then try second and third floor.'

Again, I mustered calm from a pool I must have developed in my years as a social worker, and replied yet again, 'unfortunately they have none either, and someone suggested you.' There was silence at her end of the phone. What she was thinking I cannot guess; she was clearly thrown by this procedural aberration, two people wanting to use 'her' beautiful conference room.

'Well I'm sorry, but I am not allowed to let it out willy nilly, it is designed for conferences.'

I hesitated, feeling almost beaten, but desperation gave me renewed drive. I thought briefly and then asked her, 'When is the next conference?' She came back, 'This afternoon, a child protection conference.'

I think the strain of my call had finally taken its toll as she suddenly lapsed into a fit of the most appalling coughing, sounding more like the inmate of a sanatorium than someone who should be at work. When she had calmed down, I immediately said, 'Good grief, that's a dreadful cough. Are you alright, you shouldn't be at work with a cough like that.'

There was a silence, she was clearly shaken by the outburst of severe coughing and could hardly get her breath.

'I've had bronchitis, really badly. I am supposed to be off work.' She was clearly feeling very unwell, and her voice changed as she responded to my concern. She sounded quite different, depressed and anxious, and in spite of all that had passed between us, I felt sorry for her. After Barbara had told me how it was that she had gone down with bronchitis she paused again, and suddenly said, 'Oh well, if it is just you and another worker, and not a bunch of thoughtless individuals who leave crisp packets lying about, then you can have it.' I was so relieved, I thanked her profusely, and made a mental note to pop in and see how she was later in the week.

I had my room, all I had to do was calm down, collect the files and go down to meet the guardian!

My guest was waiting expectantly and rather impatiently by the doors. He was a tall thin man of probably about forty, and had a rather cold and serious expression. He introduced himself as Will, and smiled as we shook hands, but there was no warmth behind it. Although we had to work together he didn't need to like me, so I dismissed this. I ushered him through the security doors into the inner sanctum, from where we walked some considerable distance to the conference rooms. The walk gave us an opportunity to establish a level of connection with one another. However, Will was very reserved and we moved little further than a polite exchange of facts.

I appreciated his reserve was probably simply a function of the sometimes difficult relationship between social workers in the local authority – who are hands on – and guardians, who are appointed by the courts to represent the child and need to remain detached, able to take a position more removed from the hurly-burly of day-to-day casework. They are employed to take a fresh look at the case from the child's perspective, review decisions and perhaps challenge one's thinking. This is a very vital and useful role, critical to ensure that all possible steps are taken in the best interests of any child. For me – and indeed most social workers – the interests of the child are our starting point, our main menu and our end target. It is central to all our thinking but we are always at risk of over-involvement, which could cloud our judgement. So I can see that a guardian's detachment is necessary, but too much detachment could prevent them really getting to grips with many of the issues that would only be illuminated by an open and frank exchange of views. It is important that we, as the 'hands-on people', listen carefully to the guardian's views and thoughts, and allow ourselves to be challenged by these. Equally it is important that the guardian listens to our thinking and concerns, which spring from the hours and hours of contact we have with our clients, leading to a deep understanding of any family. All I can say is that, in my experience, some guardians are brilliant. One can work with them, have mutual regard for our respective points of view – even when they differ – discuss difficult areas, and still maintain a professional and courteous distance. Others, however, come in with an almost adversarial approach. It becomes 'us and them' from day one. There is no interaction, indeed it can begin to feel like a struggle and the outcomes are not considered or thoughtful. Differing views between local authority social workers and guardians should lead to healthy and valuable discussion, because this is about a child's future, and both sides must be pre-pared to consider challenge to their understanding of any situation. It doesn't always happen.

The Mullen family, whom we were meeting to discuss, threw up many concerns. I had held this case for a while now, and felt I was getting the measure of both the mother, Clare, and the three children: Jade and Jasmine, twins of six, and Jordan aged three. Will had met the family only in the last month, but had spent time with the files, and had visited Clare on several occasions.

I had read years of reports by the many social workers who had supported Clare over the time since the twins had first come into care, initially at six months of age when they were found by a neighbour screaming and filthy next to their comatose mother. By the time the twins were eighteen months old, Clare had moved into a 'good stage' and had the children returned to her. They remained with her for the years up to nursery school age, by which time she had had a second pregnancy resulting in Jordan, who was born with some degree of Foetal Alcohol Syndrome as a result of his mother's drinking in pregnancy. As a result of concerns about the mother's drinking, the children were removed again, but after a time it was considered that things were acceptably under control and the mother more together. As a result, the children were allowed home, and within nine months the case was closed.

Unfortunately the pressure of new cases flooding in sometimes caused seniors to insist on closure of any cases which seemed to be 'OK'. Sadly, these were often only OK because no one had the time to investigate them in any depth. This is just a sad fact of life; if many new high-priority cases flood in, something has to be done, and there will always be limited resources.

The twins' school, however, had ongoing concerns but nothing could be proven. They had many deprived children and felt unable to conclude that anything was happening to these children over and above others. Matters came to a head when Jade and Jasmine returned to school one night at about seven o'clock on their own, and were spotted wandering in the grounds by a caretaker who had gone in late to check the boilers. When the police took the twins home, Clare was found to be comatose, the house was a public health issue (I believe it had to cleared by public health, and fumigated) and the children's sleeping arrangements were found to be a corner of one bedroom with only two old blankets, soaked in urine, to cover them. These practical issues, dreadful as they may sound, were doubtless of far less significance than the emotional damage inflicted on the children by the neglect and in-difference they had experienced on a daily basis. It had not made good reading.

This time, we had begun proceedings and believed that long-term care for the children – ideally adoption – would serve their best interests. These children had been messed about, had serious issues and needed stability. Their mother was an alcoholic and their father had mental health issues and was off the scene altogether. There was an aunt in the background who surfaced from time to time but had never wished to take the children on, and she was none too stable herself anyway. Clare had recently been going through a long 'good spell', said she had stopped her heavy drinking and was asking to have the children home again. This had all moved towards a court case, which was coming up soon, and at which Social Services were asking for these children to be finally freed to go to a permanent home, instead of being constantly at risk of a further relapse by their mother.

The guardian's duty was to review all the evidence and come to his own conclusions.

Clare was, in spite of all she seemed capable of inflicting on others, a very likeable young woman. She had long dark curly hair, attractive green eyes and a soft Irish brogue. She was a reasonably bright girl, and somehow endearing. However, when drunk she was very aggressive and became completely unaware of the needs of her children for days on end. She was clearly an alcoholic, although she would still insist that she was only a social drinker. When she was sober she was well dressed and fairly articulate, and had the insight to know exactly what she should be doing, and saying!

People tended to like Clare; she knew this and used it. I had developed a theory that because of her likeable personality, over the years she had won over countless social workers, who all fell into the trap of wanting to help her, because that is how one felt with Clare. Somehow she brought out all one's protective traits. She had, when sober, a gentle, vulnerable face and it seemed so easy to fall in with the belief that if only she had enough help she would make it. I increasingly felt that this was why she had managed to convince people, on several occasions, that she would turn over a new leaf in order to get her children back home. She was, quite simply, very credible. You found yourself 'wanting' very much to believe her; it was as if she managed to home in at an emotional level and have this effect on us all. I knew she had made me feel like this many times, and I would return to the office after a long chat with her, sit at my desk and wonder whether if I did this, or if I did that, maybe she would pull through. And then I would have to shake myself and look at the children. This wasn't about Clare, needy as she was, and however much she claimed to love her children, and however much I might wish to help her. It was about three young children who had experienced the most harrowing existences, broken relationships and disruptions to their young lives, and this was what I hung on to.

There is a difficult dilemma for social workers. We go into the profession to help people and perhaps our personalities home in on need in others. When confronted with a likeable parent, who on the outside so clearly needs help, we can be lulled into a state in which we turn off our critical faculties. Then we are at risk of getting sucked into a scenario in which we find ourselves supporting a parent who is simply taking and not actually changing. But this can lead us to be so bound up with the parent's needs that we fail to recognise the ongoing serious and cumulative damage and risk to any children involved.

Will drank his way through two liberally sugared cups of coffee as we discussed the case, and munched his way through at least six rather nice-looking biscuits which were there in a tin. I mused briefly, as he bit into the fourth one, on the injustice of life. He was of that tall very skinny build and clearly would never gain an ounce no matter how many luscious biscuits he consumed, whereas most of us . . . ah well. I stuck to three glasses of water!

One factor that Will had homed in on – and felt was very significant – was that Clare had recently asked her mother to come over from Ireland to help her out, and that her mother was now established in Clare's home. I had met her mother on the first week she was over, and she had – in the privacy of Clare's little kitchen when her daughter was elsewhere – made it clear to me that she was well past wanting to take on three young children every time their mother went on a bender and, anyhow, she had a 'relationship' back in Ireland and needed to return to him. However, I noted that she made no reference to this viewpoint when Clare returned to the room. Somehow I think she was scared of Clare. The mother only told me this once, and these plans and her relationship were not repeated to me or to anyone else again. I suspected Clare had told her what to say to us, and perhaps more importantly what not to say to us!

Will resumed the discussion, continuing with an enthusiastic flourish. 'Well I have had several very in-depth discussions with Clare Mullen. She seems a very intelligent and thoughtful young woman and I really do feel quite optimistic for her future. Did you know she was now going to Alcoholics Anonymous and also her mother has come over to stay and Clare says that her mother will support her to get back on track? That has to be an enormous support for her and I feel this is critical for Clare.'

I felt my heart sinking. Clare had worked her spell on Will. He continued, 'I think she is beginning to feel that with support from her mother, and possibly her aunt sometimes, she could have the children home and get herself sorted. She said to me that the children are her focus, and she really loves those children, you know.'

Oh, I did know she loved her children, that is, when she was sober. When she was drunk, she could be either very aggressive or unconvincingly sentimental about her feelings for the children, who never seemed to feel the benefit of her expressed emotion! I had read the file accounts from her last social worker, who recalled sitting with her, when she was slumped on her sofa surrounded by empty gin bottles, crying about how she had let the kids down and was no use to them and how much she loved them. Sadly, these sentimental claims to love a child do nothing for that child. Love has to involve far more than words and feelings if a child is to benefit. It isn't enough to claim to want to do better and say you will stay sober for your children: you have to actually do it, whatever the cost. This is a much, much harder call, because all that matters to the child is the reality of a sober mother there for them at the end of every day. Rearing children is a full-on responsibility, and society fails to recognise this at its peril.

I let Will talk on, and he raised the possibility of special programmes – which were available and that the mother had agreed to attend – and the importance of family ties. I too had enormous respect for the benefits of family ties. Strong families can be the support network that makes all the difference. Strong families are what children need but don't always get. I also had a vast experience of children who have been removed from their families after serious neglect or abuse and had seen them fare extremely

well within a new family, be it adoptive or foster, although
the former has the huge added-value factor which is important to most children – commitment for the long haul.

I could see that Will really believed Clare could do this.
I remained unconvinced. The history of this case was
whirling in my head. Had he read the files thoroughly?
How should I approach this? Then Will stopped talking
and looked right at me. He had read my early court sub-
missions and knew that I believed (as did my seniors) that
these children had suffered enough and needed some
stability before it was too late. The look he gave me was
challenging and to my eyes read, 'OK, that's my position,
no discussion!' I wanted him to say, 'Now justify yours.'
That is what was usually said or implied when there was
disagreement, but he didn't. Neither did he seem to want
to hear anything that was said. I could see that our working
relationship was not going to be easy and I didn't want
that. I was clearly going to say what I believed to be right
in my eyes, but I also knew that I had to listen and heed
Will's views, because if the court took his stance those
would be the plans I would have to work with.

I began, 'Well, you have clearly given this much thought
and I am glad you can see these positives. You know we
have considerable concerns, so it would be good if we
looked at these to be sure we are both addressing the same
issues.'

We had a long discussion, during which I tried to explain
the reasoning behind our thinking, the past history and
problems. We discussed the grandmother and the fact
that I did not believe she really wanted to care for the
children or even remain in the country. We also discussed

getting Clare to agree to allow us to monitor her AA attendance, and the risk that Clare would become pregnant again, which would be another huge pressure. Will maintained that this had been discussed in one of their meetings and Clare had responded confidently that she would ensure that she did not become pregnant at this point. I thought back to Clare's previous casual relationships – often embarked upon when she was drunk. I had discussed with her about six months ago the benefits of the long-lasting contraceptive injections, which would free her from the added stress of an unwanted pregnancy, but she had been adamant that she was taking care and would not get pregnant. Although I had raised this several times over the months, she refused to accept that this was a problem. I could do no more, and explained to Will that I had hoped she might accept this help, suggesting that perhaps he could include this in his next meeting with Clare. Perhaps she would listen to a new voice. If she would only take this step, no matter the outcome of the case, at least it would prevent another child being born into this chaotic family set-up.

Will held very optimistic views of Clare. He had accepted at face value Clare's confirmation that the grandmother's presence would be permanent, which was what Clare told him, and he felt that now the children were older Clare would find it easier to get back on track. When the grandmother met with Will, Clare was also present, and the grandmother had agreed that she was staying in the country, and would support her daughter for the long term. He remained convinced that she could succeed in turning her life around now if she kept off the drink. The Social Services department had a different view-point. We understood and accepted that Clare was hoping to have her children returned. She said she loved them — an easy thing to say — but would that be enough? If love involves putting someone else's needs above your own, then I would have to suggest that Clare might have loved the children, but was incapable of that level of care. I rationalised all my thinking to Will. He may have heard the words, but I remained convinced that he had already made up his mind and was not prepared to take on board any of my concerns.

7

Clare

Will and I had closed our discussion at that point, noting the date of our next meeting in our diaries. The Mullens' problems were far from resolved and I am going to jump forward in time in order to tell the full story.

Following our conference room meeting, Will continued to visit Clare, and seemed to become more and more convinced that her children should be returned home. I haven't so far really mentioned the children. At first sight they looked like three little angels: each with their mother's startlingly green eyes, framed by masses of blonde curls, they looked incapable of any misdemeanour. Sadly, this was a long way from the truth. They had all been placed together with one foster carer, and had been there some time. When they were first admitted to care on the most recent occasion their behaviour was extremely challenging and the carer often struggled to cope, particularly with the twins. She had managed to work through some of these problems, but the older two were prone to very violent outbursts and had some serious difficulties with other children. The carer told me that she had done nothing else in the last months apart from deal with the children, because they were so demanding. The younger child, Jordan, had learning difficulties, was hyperactive and needed additional help and patience.

Yes, the children had benefited immensely from a good, motivated carer but how would Clare cope with all this? And to what would she turn if the strain proved too much? Clare was an alcoholic and would always be an alcoholic. She had never coped well and I felt the strain of three young children and all their issues would be the straw that broke the camel's back. Will believed that the grandmother would be the support Clare needed – and indeed this is what the grandmother had promised to do – but I feared that she would quickly disappear back to Ireland once the children were safely installed at home again. I felt worried and concerned. I saw a lot of the children and knew they had come a long way but were still very needy. But I could do no more.

This case rattled on, many options were examined and I spent many long hours with Clare and her mother. Nothing I heard or saw gave me the desire to change our recommendation to the court. The hearing was prolonged and difficult. I sensed that the judge had concerns of his own about the case; it was not an easy decision for him to make and the questioning was long and in depth. I spent long hours on my court reports, arguing our position as logically as I was able. We monitored Clare, and she managed to get through the period leading up to the court hearing, with only a few slip-ups. One could see why someone might be hopeful on the evidence of the present, but the history remained.

In the end, Clare presented as a very good witness, the guardian stuck passionately to his belief in Clare and her family support, and the judge decided to rule that the children should be returned back home. I felt tired, beaten and troubled. This was such a risky decision. Over the previous months, I had rationalised my arguments, thinking through every point I was making and grilling myself to see if I could see any other perspectives on this case. I still believed in what I had said in court but now my job was to follow through a rehabilitation plan for the family, which would see the three children back at home with their mother.

This sort of situation is always very difficult for a social worker. Being required to follow a plan which you have concerns about is tough, but you just have to decide to do all you can to minimise any risks, and give full support to the family.

Initially I think Clare, who clearly knew we would not have opted for her children to return home, was a little suspicious of me and thought I was out to prove her incapable. Had I felt unable to follow through the court decision, I would have had to have taken myself off the case, but the fact that I knew it so well made it wise for me to continue. I wanted the best for the children. I had no illusions about the problems Clare now faced and would do all I could to enable her to care properly for her family. I encouraged her with her AA visits and made sure she could get to meetings, the Family Centre provided support and training for her in parenting and dealing with behavioural difficulties and she even had home care workers to support her in the early months. I encouraged her to join a local mothers' group to make new friends who would be a support for her – and an alternative to her old drinking friends – and I visited her frequently. We built up a good working relationship, and the weeks went by.

With the increased support we had put into the family, Clare seemed to be doing quite well. Her mother had gone back to Ireland just once, but returned within the week, along with her boyfriend, Fergus. Fergus in fact proved to be a real boon. Just at the point when we were having to begin to slowly reduce the level of support, he stepped in. He was easy-going, pleasant and full of seemingly endless energy – playing with the children, reading to them – and was generally just what Clare needed.

He was an older man, the eldest son of a huge, apparently very stable family and it sounded as if he had helped to raise the younger ones when his father died rather young. He seemed to love children and was proving to be an enormous help. His presence in the home had signalled many changes: the home became more organised and he even helped with the cooking! I noticed that he was also making an attempt to teach Clare to cook and to make routines in the home. I began to hope that I had been wrong and that Clare was actually going to fight her way through, with Fergus by far her greatest source of support, while her mother seemed to be more likely to be sitting about rather than active in the home!

It was about a year after the court case that I made one of my regular visits to Clare's home. We were approaching a time when questions were being asked about closing the case and I had begun to feel that, against the odds, Clare was getting back on track and just perhaps might be able to make some sort of a job of things. I knocked and waited at the door. Usually Clare answered quickly but today she was slow to respond and I wondered if she was out. After a third knock, the door opened slowly and Clare asked me in. I went through into the living room and in a chair was Clare's mother, clearly in a bad way. She looked as if she had been crying for hours – or days – her face puffy and swollen. She seemed to be beyond caring who saw her. I asked her what was the matter and she said, 'He's only gone and upped off back to Ireland, the filthy swine. Says he's had enough of being a babysitter for a bunch of wild animals. Wild animals! I ask you, who does he think he is? Anyway he's gone. That's it.'

'How long have you been together?' I asked.

'Too flaming long if you ask me! On and off for two years and now this. I can't believe it. Says he's done with children and wants a rest from their squalling and shrieking and arguing! Well, I don't need him! We'll be OK without him, won't we, Clare?'

I glanced at Clare, and noticed that she was looking somewhat anxious and unusually silent and thoughtful for her, but she nodded in agreement.

After a rather prolonged visit, I returned to the office in pensive mood. Indeed, so deep were my cogitations that I walked straight past Hilary and Ginny in the car park! Hilary turned and shouted after my fast disappearing form, 'Hi, Becky, you look a bit preoccupied. Check on your computer, I've pinned a note from the Mullen children's school to ring them.' I came to, registered Hilary's words and wondered what this was about. As the Mullens were fresh in my mind I thought I would clear this query quickly so I could move on to my other work.

The sound of the school secretary, whom I had now

grown to know well, was a little serious, with none of her usual pleasantries, and she put me straight through to the head, Mrs Spencer. She sounded relieved that I had returned her call but her words did not have a correspondingly good effect on me.

'Becky, I needed to speak to you. I'm rather concerned about the Mullen children. They've been quite punctual and fairly well presented until the last few days. But this week, well the last few days they've come to school late, very late, hungry and somewhat dishevelled and their behaviour is off the wall. We've had special support in class all day. I don't know if it is of any significance, but in view of their history I felt you should know so you can keep an ear to the ground. I can't imagine what has changed, but I feel better that you are aware of what is happening.'

I sat considering her words. I replied, 'Well, I may have some ideas, but please let me know if you have any further concerns and I will check out what has happened here. Thanks very much for this; I'll be in touch with you.' I put the phone down, leaned back in my chair and thought, 'Fergus'.

You could hardly blame the man. He had, after all, been dragged right into the fire and must have found that the novelty wore off after months of unrelenting responsibility. I felt it was highly probable that his leaving would throw the whole family into chaos. I needed to help Clare and her mother sort themselves out again and organise a Fergus-free routine. And that was exactly what I endeavoured to do.

One alternately depressed or angry granny, and Clare

seeming a little lost, was not an easy pair to work with.
I asked for Homecare to go back in to bridge the melt-
down in the home and warned the Family Centre to be
extra alert to their needs. I also spent time ensuring that
Clare did not lose her focus on the need to keep up her
AA meetings, as without those we would be on very
dangerous ground indeed. I set this all in place, jiggling
my caseload to accommodate the extra time I needed to
spend with Clare, and after a couple of weeks felt that
just maybe things might be getting back on track. Then
two things happened.

I arrived at work one morning and checked my folder
for post. Among the endless forms and procedural guides
there were some actual letters. One was a handwritten
envelope in bold, black childlike writing. Needless to say
I opencd this first.

I pulled out two sheets of lined paper and looked immediately for the signature, as the address – from County
Clare – meant nothing to me. The letter was signed Fergus
O'Malley and the contents were very revealing. Fergus
wrote that he had grown fond of the children but simply
couldn't stay, because he was past all this twenty-four-
hour childcare and anyway Clare's mother was impossible
to live with. She was even violent at times. He couldn't
take any more and reckoned she wasn't the full shilling,
so he had returned to Ireland, for good. He told me that
he was writing because he couldn't get the children out
of his mind. He wrote, 'And terrors as they are, they have
had such a dreadful time it's no wonder. Those two women
know bally all about raising children. They have no idea;
I did everything when I was there. Clare watched the telly

most of the time; I even had to put the children to bed, and sometimes get them to school. You don't grow up in Ireland and not know what drink does to people. I saw her 'fluthered' a couple of times when she fell off the wagon. I made sure that girl went to AA. I even took her myself sometimes. Then she met someone at the meetings so she went regularly, and it was better. I am writing to warn you, please watch out for those kiddies. They're not safe with those two. I'm sorry I had to leave them, but I'm too old for this. And those two are just full of guff.'

I folded the letter and sat back. This answered some questions. Fergus had left me his telephone number and I would speak to him in due course. The difficulty here was that when relationships break down there can be no limit to the vindictiveness of the spurned partner. But Fergus had not been spurned. He had freed himself of this family and was well away. What provoked him to write? The most logical conclusion was that he was genuinely concerned – and so was I. There was little I could do today, but this latest revelation merited serious extra monitoring to keep this family on track.

Over the next week I visited them daily, clearly not mentioning Fergus, but there were always reasons to visit if I needed them. I saw the children at home and at school. On one occasion, when Jade told me that his mum had been very sick, I popped in to see if all was well on my way home. Clare maintained she was OK and made a comment about children and the nonsense they talk. It was the following day that my phone rang and it was Clare. Her voice was trembling and she was clearly in tears. 'Becky, please can you come. Mum has gone, I don't know what to do.'

I told Clare I would be up as soon as my next two meetings were finished. I am not sure I heard some of the discussions at these meetings; my mind was full of Clare, Fergus, Ireland and three vulnerable children.

In due course I was back at Clare's home, waiting for the door to open. Finally, a tear-streaked Clare answered the door and I went inside with her. We sat down and Clare began, haltingly, 'She went last night, got the night ferry.'

'Why, Clare, did she explain?'

'Oh yes! Do you know what she said to me, her own daughter? Said I was lazy and she was tired of running round after me. It's not true! I do my bit, but I get tired.'

I looked at Clare, and suddenly realised that, yes, she did look tired, far more than normal. She was almost white and had little specks around her eyes where tiny capillaries had burst.

'Clare, are you drinking again. You look like you've been very sick?'

Clare looked up at me and said, in such a defiant voice that I was completely taken aback, 'Well, you might as well know, you'll know soon enough. I'm pregnant.' My heart sank. This was all we needed. She was going to have her work cut out with the three children. No Fergus, no mother, add another and . . .

By now, Clare was crying. 'I don't know what to do. Ma said get rid of it, but I can't.'

I took a long silent breath and we talked and talked. I had less confidence than I portrayed to Clare, but in my experience, where there is a will there is a way. For everyone's sake I had to help Clare get through this. She had never agreed to have the long-acting contraceptive injection, which would have seen her through a couple of years safely and given her time to get on her feet. She had been adamant that she would go on the pill and be careful.

When I left Clare's home I felt a weariness that was beyond anything normal. It seemed like I had a weight on my shoulders and could hardly move. I felt that I had wasted months of effort trying to get her back on track, only to have all this happen. And I didn't know if there was any way to salvage things and stabilise life for the children. I knew the children would be having a really tough time now and I was too tired to think straight anymore. Actually, I felt thoroughly depressed and just wanted to get home to the familiarity of my own little house and garden.

I doubt if I was particularly safe on the road going home that day but I made it, pulled up at my house and staggered wearily from the car. Carrying my briefcase, which suddenly seemed to have assumed leaden qualities, I struggled to get my key in the door, pushed the door with my hip and almost fell inside. I wandered through to my little kitchen and stood there, where it was still and quiet and peaceful. I liked to think it was pleased to see me after a day spent all alone and just standing there in the silence – no phones, no voices, nothing – was sheer bliss. You can hear silence, and it is very therapeutic!

After I had soaked up some calm, I returned to the task of finding something that I could eat, in five minutes flat. I did little else that night; I was just too tired. The thought of the work ahead of me was daunting. I just felt a sense of 'where do I begin?' Luckily I slept, and in the morning, feeling just about human again, I drove off to work, aware that things were going to be hard, but blissfully unaware of just how hard.

There was to be no respite for me at the office. It felt as if Clare's situation had collapsed like a pack of cards overnight. I was busy catching up with things in the office until about 11.00 a.m. and was just heading out on a visit, when Sandy called me and asked me if I would take a call from Mrs Spencer.

I went back to my desk and picked up my phone, to hear a worried voice tell me that none of the Mullen children had arrived at school that morning. I replaced the receiver, only for the phone to ring again. This time it was the police. They reported to me that they had attended an incident that morning and that a woman in a seriously inebriated condition – clearly Clare – had attacked a neighbour in a fight about a boyfriend. Goodness knows what this was about. The police were very concerned, over and above the affray, because of the presence of three young children.

The terrible weariness of the previous night hit me briefly but then it was replaced by something more positive, the energy to get out and sort this. I thought about those poor kids stuck in the middle of this completely messed-up family situation and somehow that gave me fresh energy. I made some calls to cancel my visits and went to try and catch Marie. I probably managed to achieve all this in fifteen minutes and was leaving with one of the trainees, Lucy, very shortly after that. Marie said she would flag up the fostering team for me in case a place of safety was needed.

It didn't take me long to drive to Clare's home. When I arrived there were two neighbours, two policemen and Clare in the front drive. She was very drunk and was making aggressive threats to the police and neighbours – and swigging gin from a bottle. I went in to look for the children, who were cowering in an upstairs room, terrified, and when they saw me the younger one began to cry. I tried to re-assure Jordan, and Lucy and I brought the children down. Lucy kept them inside while I went out to speak to Clare. I tried to calm her down, and after a time she listened, as far as she was able, and seemed able to understand the need to get the children to safety. She agreed to allow them to spend the weekend with foster carers.

There is no happy ending. I only wish that there was. Clare took to the bottle and completely lost the plot, her mother was never seen again and Fergus's prediction was proved right. Clare couldn't cope: as soon as her props had gone she had no reserves to fall back on.

She was rarely sober for more than a few days at a time over the next few years and her children remained in care. She gave birth to her baby in due course, but was in no state to care for the child and, the last I heard, the predictions for the baby's health were not good. Clare's heavy drinking had again taken its toll on a child.

By the time the children came back into care, their behaviour was off the wall. They trusted no one, were aggressive and antagonistic at school and no matter how hard we tried, there was no normal foster family able to cope with the older two children's rages, violence and seemingly total disregard for anyone around them. They had been rejected, neglected and rejected yet again. They had been bundled from pillar to post, never in one place long enough to grow firm roots. Every time they managed to form a new bond, it was broken. They had experienced no continuity, just endless short-lived relationships. They trusted no one. Why would they?

And why all this? So that their mother could have another chance, and another and another.

Jade and Jasmine finally had to be placed in a special fostering home for severely disturbed children because no normal family could have coped with the level of disturbed behaviour that they were increasingly exhibiting. What an unnecessary tragedy. Jordan was placed with carers who seemed able to cope with his difficult behaviour and his problems from being born with Foetal Alcohol Syndrome, a double load he carried at his mother's hand.

We all hoped that the older two might settle enough to one day go to a more normal foster family, but that remained to be seen, and the sad truth is that it was unlikely they would survive all this without carrying the legacy of their early life into their futures. The facilities at the home they were placed at were amazing and there was considerable intensive therapy available but that was all you could say. This was the last port of call for children so damaged by the worst that families are capable of inflicting on them that there was nowhere else to go!

Three lives wrecked. I could only hope for a miracle some day.

8

Staring Down the Barrel of a Gun

The day following my first discussion with Will, the guardian, I woke to a glorious, bright sunny world. It was very cold, but the sort of weather that makes you feel totally alive and alert. There was still a slight frosty sheen over the roofs, which gave everything a truly seasonal feel. I drove into work along the old high street. Somehow, the 1960s' town developers had missed this beautiful Victorian street with its quaint olde worlde cottages and it had survived that savage age unscathed.

Christmas was becoming ever higher on the agenda, windows were decorated and any day now the tree would go up in the square. I would have to see if I could find my tree in the attic – or perhaps this year I would treat myself to a real tree, smelling of Christmas, and of course clogging up the hoover repeatedly. Maybe I would nip out in the lunch break and treat myself to some new Christmas tree baubles. It had always seemed to me strange that everything seemed to pause for Christmas, but not in social work. It seemed odd somehow; shouldn't there be a truce in family traumas to match everything else? But no. Relentlessly, the struggles went on for so many families.

Indeed, Christmas often brought added stress for many. Contact arrangements between parents and their children who were in care could potentially be a source of height-ened tension and disappointment. For families, the sheer amount of time spent cooped up in the house with too little to do – and too much alcohol or drugs – tended to highlight problems that otherwise would go unnoticed in the rush of working days. So often, the silent victims were the children, who saw much, said little and learned early on to keep their heads down and make themselves scarce when mum or dad had had too much to drink, or had lost themselves in a haze of drugs. So many of these children learned to survive from an early age, feeding themselves and sometimes their siblings, while their parents lay wasted on the sofa. Sadly, that was the reality of life for too many of the children I met.

I arrived promptly at the office, the traffic having been light and good humoured, as if the Christmas spirit coupled with the sunshine had brought out the best in everyone. Today would hopefully turn out to be a more 'normal' day, whatever that was. I had some scheduled meetings, and some serious follow-up work on Sarah after the disclosures from two nights ago, but perhaps I would leave on time, which would enable me to catch up with some of life's vital tasks, like shopping for food!

The office seemed more cheerful. Two of the admin team were struggling to put up some decorations which had definitely seen better days but, nevertheless, the overall effect gave the office a sense of the season. What health and safety would have said about all the perching on wobbly chairs and desks I am not sure. Well I am, but hey, the end result was worth it, and everyone survived!

I hung up my coat, and actually had time to make a quick coffee to start the day. Signing up for the Christmas lunch was the next essential step of the morning. This annual event was a rare chance to chat to work colleagues whom often one only saw when speeding past them in the endless endeavour to catch up with work, visits and so on. I sat back and took a moment to try and decide whether I would tick for turkey, fish or the vegetarian option.

I was deeply considering these tempting alternatives, not greatly helped in my decision by the various comments being thrown around the office by the usual harbingers of doom reminding us all of last year's disastrous choices, when my phone rang. I quickly ticked fish, and thrust the menu list onto the next desk. That was that. I picked up the phone.

One of the health visitors was returning a call I had made a few days ago to discuss a shared case, so I was pleased to hear from her. The health visitors were at least as elusive as the social workers, so this was a precious conversation. We were able to have a good discussion around our respective findings and thoughts on one particular family.

Half an hour later, I put down the phone rather heavily as it was clear that she and I shared similar fears about one of my newer referrals, and I needed to pursue a number of avenues of enquiry with some haste. I had planned to visit the children this week, but they had just shot up my list of priorities. Following our conversation, I now felt that I had to get to see these children very quickly indeed.

I made a few calls to set all this in motion, and all of a sudden my watch was screaming at me. Having thought I had tons of time, I suddenly realised my 10.30 a.m. meeting at a nearby military base was looming. Two quick gulps of my now-cold coffee, a snatch of my brief-case and jacket, quick sign out, and I was away.

The base was within our area, though somewhat removed by being out in the countryside, a lovely drive through rolling hills and greenery. Sadly it was not without its own social problems. It was full of families separated from their familiar support networks, husbands – or indeed wives – serving away on duty, lonely partners and some-times extreme experiences of life and death. None of this was ideal as an environment for young families. Furthermore, the experiences of real bloody and violent war are traumatising, something that the eager young recruit could have absolutely no concept of at the outset. It can be these very terrible experiences, which the young recruits have to learn to adjust to, that create an addi-tional stress which may make it hard for a young person to easily settle back into 'normal' life, with all the demands of family and home.

As I drew up at the gates of the base, my ID was checked by the guard on duty. As he studied my card and asked me some basic questions, his gun, which had been slung over his back, slipped down and to my consider-able discomfort it ended up with the barrel pointing straight at my head. The guard seemed totally oblivious to this situation! Worrying thoughts about loose safety catches, faulty mechanisms and horrible accidents crowded my mind and the final question asked of me was met by silence. My brain ceased to register anything but the barrel of his gun. I was terrified that I might trigger any sudden move by the guard, as by now I had rehearsed in my mind all possible outcomes. In as calm and as quiet a voice as I could muster, I asked the young man if he could reposition his gun, as I was feeling rather uncomfortable. With the dawning of realisation and a big grin, the offending weapon was moved and I was waved on my way. With a sense of great relief, I wended my way to the meeting hall, and parked.

Before I left the car, I took a deep breath, sorted out my papers and focused in on the meeting ahead. I had found that this was the only way to cope with the endless plethora of meetings and discussions about so many different families and situations, all coming at you pretty much simultaneously. I went through the names of all the main family members and those of the other professionals. I then reviewed in my mind the most important issues that had to be addressed, checking the list I had drawn up earlier, and adding one or two extra points to ensure that we achieved what we set out to do.

This was a relatively new case for me and I was not yet sure where we were going, neither did I have any clear picture of the family. With very new cases it was so easy to forget names and confuse people, or the other professionals involved, but to the family concerned this could give the impression of a lack of interest or commitment, so my strategies were essential fall-backs.

I made my way to the meeting – finding my way through the corridors – and walked into the conference room. The atmosphere was frosty in the extreme, so it was good when everyone had arrived and we could begin. It wasn't long before the meeting was in full swing, the introductions had been made, the coffee handed round and off we went.

The small son of the family concerned had sustained a 'mystery' injury and full-scale marital warfare had been unleashed between a quiet father – who on the surface seemed totally innocuous – and his partner, a thin rather pale girl of about twenty, whose drug addiction had done nothing to stabilise her input to the care of their child.

If I told you this began as a stormy meeting, that would be an understatement; tropical typhoon would be nearer the truth, and this blew up within minutes of the start of any discussion.

How some apparently quiet, ineffectual people can become raging and unstable in an incredibly short time has always troubled me, and it bodes badly for any child in their uncertain care.

The father seemed to be of the opinion that the louder he shouted the greater his chance of getting his own way. Doubtless this was his usual strategy, the classic 'bully' mentality. His partner crumbled under this treatment and became helpless and tearful. Every minute that passed it seemed that the father felt increasingly that he was able to take control. I could see that we now had a slightly better measure of the mechanics of their home life; it was useful to see how their normal interaction operated but now what was needed was some control and some rules.

I called a very firm halt to the discussions, and momentarily everyone was rather taken aback by my sudden precipitous intervention, but it gave me an audience. I then explained that we were going to have set rules and that I expected everyone to abide by these rules. These were all very much the usual: no interruptions, everyone to be heard, no abuse, no shouting, everyone to have their say.

In this way I managed – not without some intense initial opposition – to get all parties to talk more freely about the situation and to listen to each other and hear my feedback.

After a very exhausting hour and a half, it was agreed to meet again the following week. It had been a hard session, and the look on the father's face as he looked at me, clearly spoke volumes. I would not be on his Christmas card list!

I have little doubt that we all came out exhausted, and there were times when the rules had had to be 'clarified' anew, but discussion we did have and ground rules we had established. It was particularly good to see that the usual relationship pattern – of bully versus passive bullied partner – was, at least in this session, stopped. It was a small step, and had freed up the young woman to speak a little.

One of the strange things about working with people and their often-confused lives, is that it is sometimes seemingly very small changes – facilitating new ways of interaction, getting people to talk about their concerns – that can lead to much bigger changes in a situation. Sadly, also, no matter how much input and support we put into some families, there is no moving on at all, no change, and for the family unit no hope of improvement for the children.

As I left the base, past the guards and out into the open country, I decided to grab some lunch en route, and pulled up in a quiet spot off the road. Winding down my windows, I took a big gulp of crisp fresh air. The sheep in the adjacent field stopped grazing and looked at me with curiosity while they chewed their last mouthful. As I got out my exciting spread of crispbread, celery and nuts, I could feel the tranquillity of the silence, broken only by the odd baa-ing of the sheep or the calling of circling birds. I sank into my seat, drinking in the peace and quiet. The venue had the effect of making my meal into a positive banquet and I briefly closed my eyes, enjoying the feel of the sun on my face, albeit a December sun. By the time I set off, some fifteen minutes later, I felt refreshed and calmer, ready for the rest of the day and, leaving my woolly friends behind, I drove off back to the urban world.

Back at the office, I had a great deal of paperwork to catch up with, including this morning's meeting notes and a pile of reviews for another family, so I was grateful for an unusually quiet office. I switched on my computer and did a quick perusal of my emails to see if there was anything critical needing my attention. A few speedy replies, others needing some factual confirmations and the rest looked as if they could wait until later.

I needed to talk to Marie about Sarah, but as she was in a meeting I looked through my reports and checked that the chronology was up to speed, adding the events of yesterday. I could not afford to have any delays in my recording in such a critical case and knew that I would need everything ready for both Marie and legal to peruse.

I gave Patty a ring to ensure there were no problems and contacted the fostering team support worker to brief her, to ensure she could be available for Patty if things became hard to deal with. I knew that Patty was experienced and competent but in a case such as this, she needed someone alongside to ensure she handled things as wisely as possible, and that she was supported emotionally.

At about 2.15 p.m., Marie came back to the office and I was able to grab some time with her to discuss Sarah. She, like me, knew that we needed legal in on this pronto, to ensure that Sarah's mother could not try to reclaim Sarah if she suspected that she had been talking to us about her home life. There and then we fixed up to meet with our legal team and, as luck would have it, one of the solicitors was at the office later in the day and squeezed us in. I was relieved that at least all the paperwork was up and ready so we could move fast.

9

At the Office

I returned to my desk, my mind buzzing with the issues that Marie and I had talked through and clutching my notebook with a now-even-longer list of 'to dos'!

Before I did anything else, I gave Patty a ring to see how things were. Sarah was playing in the garden with the dog, so we were free to talk briefly. Patty told me that she had had a great deal of trouble settling Sarah for the night, as she seemed to be accustomed to staying up until the early hours then drifting off as she felt like it. Having got the child into bed, Sarah insisted that all the lights had to be left on for her and, when she did finally fall asleep, she woke frequently in the night in a terrible state from nightmares.

Food-wise, Sarah had announced that she would only eat pizza. Patty was accustomed to this and had lots of clever ways of making vegetables more exciting! She was always happy to produce the inevitable pizza alongside the rest. What Patty was capable of creating with a carrot was something that would easily win a space in the Tate Modern and, more importantly, it looked seriously tempting to eat! She also specialised in some very messy joint cooking sessions, which seemed to encourage even the most reluctant appetites.

On a general front, Sarah seemed to accept her situation

so far and appeared to be enjoying being with Patty, following her everywhere. Patty commented that if she wasn't careful she was in danger of constantly stepping on the child. It was, she said, like having a shadow. The dog gave Patty her only respite. Sarah had taken to cuddling up to Bumble, Patty's canine hearthrug on legs. While Bumble may never aspire to a degree in psychology, or a psychotherapy qualification, she seemed to just know what a child needed. She tolerated all the cuddling and hugs of many a troubled child, almost as if she understood their need was of such an order that the occasional overly heavy-handed treatment could be forgiven. I used the word 'almost' there, in describing the dog's empathy, to fall in with any somewhat cynical readers, who may not accept an animal's ability to pick up on human emotion. It is, however, my own strongly held belief that we, in our human arrogance, grossly underestimate the rest of the animal kingdom. Indeed, I truly believe that many animals can sense our emotions in a way that makes most of the human race appear emotionally blind in comparison. Perhaps we are so obsessed with our own preoccupations that we have lost the ability to read and sense the feelings of others!

After my chat with Patty, I had a string of calls to return to various people involved with my other cases. I also needed to put together all the paperwork for our meeting with legal later in the afternoon. In the middle of all this, reception rang up and said that Sarah's mother and Matthew, her mother's boyfriend, were downstairs demanding to speak with me. I told Nan, who was reception secretary, that I would really like to have security on

hand as there could be 'issues'. This meant William. We
all loved William; he was an ageing former rugby prop
row forward, now well past his prime but, my word, if I
saw him coming down a rugby pitch even today, I would
put the ball down and run hell for leather . . . in the opposite direction! He was enormous, as broad as he was tall,
hailed from the Highlands and had the firmness of character to match. He dealt with all-comers: outbursts of
screaming threats, intoxicated individuals hurling metal
bins about, drug induced fits of paranoia, and once we
had a client who pulled a knife on his worker screaming
like a banshee. William was totally calm under fire, no
raised voice, just, 'Come along now, laddie, we'll be having
none of this,' and somehow he always appeared fearless
and in charge. I think this may be what communicated
itself to the offenders. William knew, without a shadow
of a doubt, that he would be able to 'sort them out'
should the need arise, and somehow they picked up on
his confidence. The result was that they fairly quickly
crumbled under his handling. Those who did not get the
message fast would be transported outside by William,
with an ease that would make anyone envious, and there,
among the bushes in the shrub garden, William stood over
them until they gave up the struggle or the police were
summoned to take them for a somewhat longer period of
cooling off! In spite off his size, and his abilities with
some of our very violent and menacing clients, he could
be as gentle as a lamb and very kind. I had seen William
comforting a very new social worker who had completely
crumbled after a particularly aggressive incident in which
he had had to intervene. I saw him supplying her with

tea in the office and helping her to put things in perspective and not feel diminished by her perfectly natural reaction. I hope that he may recognise himself, and understand just how much we loved and appreciated him and how much his support helped us in our, at times, very difficult work. It was with his support that the futures of many children were helped to change, their social workers not being intimidated into compromise.

I felt it was important to have him on hand when I met Matthew and Julie. The warning on Sarah's file was always in the back of my mind and assault, far from an unheard-of occurrence, was not what I needed! Notwithstanding this concern, I jumped at the opportunity to see them. I felt much safer in the office, rather than on a home visit, and urgently needed to discuss contact arrangements and to lay down ground rules.

I walked into reception and could see them across the waiting area. Matthew was pacing up and down with a face like thunder and Sarah's mother was downing a canned drink while looking about with a thoroughly aggressive expression. She greeted me with a very hostile stare, while Matthew announced to everyone on the ground floor exactly what he thought of me, leaving nothing to the imagination. I was, he announced, a child snatcher, a liar and a few other labels that I would probably prefer not to put in print.

I tried to appear totally calm, which was far from how I felt, and opted to speak with them in an open yet private area near the stairwell. I had at first to allow Matthew his rant, until he calmed down enough to listen, then I tried to bring him into a slightly more positive mood. I emphasise 'slightly more' because it was touch and go whether he lunged at me or listened to me. It was extremely reassuring to see that William the security guard was casually 'doing his rounds' and, while tactfully done, I knew he was aware of my situation.

This was not an easy interview; Matthew seemed to be 'on something', I felt sure. His eyes had an unusually bright look; he seemed very agitated, restless and far from reasonable. But by a combination of carefully chosen words on my part and the distraction provided by a rather glamorous and scantily dressed client waiting close by, Matthew didn't seem to manage to concentrate on the issues long enough to remain worked-up. Julie, needless to say, was both abusive and angry with me and later also with Matthew, once she pinpointed his wandering eye! Oh yes, it was a very interesting meeting! We did at least manage to draw up a contact agreement; well, they pretty much agreed with the format I had taken down with me.

I went back up to the office and straight into a meeting with legal. Sandy had helped me find all the old files for the family and with her help I carried all of them to Marie's room. Anna, one of our in-house solicitors, was waiting with Marie and enjoying a rare and brief chat. Anna was a slightly built young woman with a mass of blonde curly hair and sparkly blue eyes that seemed to miss nothing. She was very bright and committed, moved at the speed of light and thought equally quickly. She had her head round the issues in no time. Together, the three of us trawled over the situation and clarified what we would do next.

Clearly, Sarah had to be kept in care until we were clear

what had been happening. At no point had either Julie or Matthew come up with a plausible reason for Sarah's injuries. Both vehemently denied being responsible for them in any way. While the probability was that they or one of them were responsible, we had to collate enough evidence to justify taking more permanent steps, while we investigated the family situation. The police knew both parties. Matthew was on the police records for serious assault on a neighbour at a previous address and a variety of other offences, many of them of a very violent nature. Julie had on record one violent altercation with a member of staff at the benefits office, a record of a serious fight with another woman in a club, plus several shoplifting offences. Both of them had been caught some years ago in possession of class A drugs, and they were under observation at present because it was suspected that they might be involved in a drug-selling ring along with Matthew's brother. So, a colourful history. I was setting up an assessment of the family, so would be seeing much of the couple, and I knew I would have to be extremely careful. Clutching the mountain of files (Sarah had been known to Social Services for years), I staggered back to my desk.

I couldn't help but think, when I stacked all those files up on my desk and looked at the very ancient and dog-eared early files, what was this all about? All this work, and what had we really done to protect this child? Endless meetings to discuss this mother and, over the years, her various partners. Multiple concerns expressed and noted on the file. Endless broken promises by the mother that she would get the child to school and ensure the child was not left wandering the streets day and night. Concerns expressed by health staff, even, on one occasion, a local take-away shop manager!

Fortunately, Julie had not had more children because of a complication at the birth of Sarah, so there were no other children to consider. Well, that was something, but I had a lot of work to do and I was determined to get to the bottom of this child's life. I sighed and mentally shook myself. Coffee, that was what I needed. And some chocolate, yes that was it! So – off to the kitchenette and slot machine to refuel!

When I reached the kitchen, well more of a deep cupboard actually, Paula, one of my fellow social workers, was leaning against the wall. I greeted her cheerfully. I liked Paula, who was kind, supportive and very committed. I was surprised to get a muted response. Putting it down to her preoccupation I carried on hunting through the cupboard for a coffee jar which actually had some coffee inside. Triumphantly finding one with a few grains left in the bottom, I had to squeeze past Paula to reach the kettle, and only then noticed her hasty attempt to cover up a tear running down her cheek.

'Paula what's wrong?' I asked. She didn't answer immediately, but took a short breath and said, 'No, nothing really. I'm just being silly, ignore me, bad night.' I let her comment stand for a moment, and then said, 'OK, exactly how bad? Come on.'

Paula took a deep breath and I was unsure whether she was going to reply. Then she continued, 'Well, several bad nights actually. It's . . . the Bagley children. You know, the two older ones were here last week and there's the little one. I'm in court again this week for the mother's appeal

and, well, I think the court is leaning towards agreeing
to give the mother another chance. Her barrister is brilliant and frankly he could talk up my Ikea kitchen table
and sell it for thousands at Sotheby's. The mother is
saying she has given up the drugs, has changed her lifestyle
and wants the children back. She can be a very convincing
witness. It's hard, Becky. I think the mother probably
believes she can do it and she may be off the drugs at
present. But in the long run? I really think that for her to
both weather the usual storms of life without the drugs
and cope with taking back her three children, all of whom
have issues as a result of the past, is unrealistic.'

Paula fell into silence, her anger having given way to
deep thought, then she continued, 'She's given up the drugs
before on two occasions, once for nearly a year, and then
as soon as something went wrong, or changed – a boyfriend
left or financial difficulties reared their head – she relapsed.
That is how it has been for over ten years . . . She can
always pick up the pieces of her own life, but those children
just accumulate more and more damage.'

Paula stopped and looked at me and I could hear the
frustration and emotion even in the low, flat voice in
which she continued, 'I removed those children from their
home; I sat with the foster mother and heard the accounts
of the children's appalling emotional state. I carried those
pathetic little bundles, half starved just like bags of bones
and absolutely filthy, out of that house. I saw with my
own eyes the room they had been locked in for goodness
knows how long, the baby had maggots in her cot, and
the smell. I've seen how hard the foster mother has worked
to begin to bring those children out of their terrors and

withdrawn behaviour. It's been a long hard year and a half. Those little kids are well on the way to being adopted and we've a lovely solid family lined up to take them, all three, desperate to adopt them. If they go home . . . well it's such a gamble. I don't think we have the right to take that risk with children's lives.' I could feel the anger mounting again in her voice, strange for such a calm and serene person. But she then continued, 'Honestly, Becky, who matters most? The mother or the kids?'

At this point Paula stopped and with one finger traced the pattern around the top of the mug she was holding in a vice-like grip, her knuckles white. The anger was tangible, and now I was there with her. We'd all met this family and followed the ups and downs of the case and we all knew that the particular judge sitting in court for this case was heavily inclined to let parents have 'yet another go'. Oh yes, we shared Paula's frustration. I also knew that when Paula believed that a parent who had 'messed up' really could make it with help, then she would go to any lengths to ensure they got all the help they needed. Paula was open-minded and supportive as well as prudent.

She took a deep breath — anger had driven away her tears — as she launched into a further tirade.

'Whose rights are we protecting? Take it further, Becky, it feels like no one really cares about the children; they continue to be damaged. Children are not commodities, a must-have accessory; they are vulnerable little people, the future of this world, who need all the protection they can get. That is why I came into social work. Don't the children have rights? Don't they deserve a decent, secure childhood?'

Paula paused, then she leaned back against the wall again. 'You know, Becky, I love this job, but I don't think I can go through this again. The same thing happened to the Riley family. They were returned home from a really good foster home and after about two years of barely adequate care it all broke down again and the children were left in the middle of the devastation of their mother's addictions and lifestyle, once again. They were pretty much destroyed by this last event. OK, I managed, eventually, to get the younger two into an adoptive home but I believe there have been terrible problems. But the older two, well, we just couldn't place them, it was really too late; they were so damaged, poor kids. They are now in a special community home for children with severe behavioural problems. Same judge sitting on that case too. I'd like to take him to see what a mess he has made of those children's lives, to show him how that decision may well have ruined any chance of a stable future for them. I'd like . . .'

Paula stopped, took a breath, closed her eyes and breathed out slowly. 'I'm sorry, Becky, I'm really sorry. I'll stop, I know you're run off your feet too. That's the way it is. I will just cope.' Paula and I talked for a little while longer until I felt she was calmer. I suggested some options but in fact she had done all she could and more. It was one of those cases in which the particular judge really appeared to believe that, no matter what the history of neglect showed, a child is always better off with his or her own parents. I felt deeply for Paula. The whole team were convinced these children, already very disturbed, needed an extremely stable and permanent family to help bring them through the worst of their problems.

We ran dry of things to say. Paula was really low, so I suggested that we get together later that evening (in my case after I had raced around Sainsbury's), with one or two others from the team. I knew she would feel supported by the team and I couldn't bear the thought of her going home alone to dwell on this. Support is essential for social workers, but the reality is that the whole department was just too busy.

When I finally returned to my desk, I realised that I had forgotten the chocolate and had to go back for some. I have to admit that by now I felt rather low myself, but I had a long list of jobs, and soon became preoccupied in my work. I knew my next task was to phone Martin and his carer. I had tried not to dwell on his situation, and my busy day had helped, but in truth I was desperate to know how things were going on.

My coffee was a life-saver and the chocolate the boost I needed, so I dialled the Bridges, Martin's foster carers. My heart was in my mouth and I knew I was tensely listening for the tone in Mrs Bridges' voice, but when a cheery voice answered in a relaxed tone I felt a touch of hope.

'Hello, its Becky speaking, how are things?'

Mrs Bridges immediately reassured me. 'Oh fine. Martin has been great helping me with the kittens. Such a help, actually, he takes his kitten pretty much everywhere he goes in the house. Becky, those kittens have been life-savers; they have given me a real link to Martin.' After a pause she said, 'Look I know there is a long way to go, but we both feel very positive about Martin. There's just something about him. Anyhow, we can cope with some thunder and lightning. It's school tomorrow. That will be a big step for him. There'll be a few ups and downs there, I expect, but we'll be there with him. Today, we're sorting out his uniform and a few other clothing issues. Look, I'll shout for Martin so you can have a chat. Oh, and I've some paperwork here I may need to talk to you about. Anyhow, Martin has just appeared. We'll speak soon. Cheerio for now.'

I had a short chat with Martin, who managed a few words about the kittens, grumbled about the vegetables he had been encouraged to eat and made an off-the-cuff comment about Mrs Bridges. The words didn't sound very polite but the tone told me much, much more. Martin sounded as if he grudgingly had some time for Mrs Bridges. Good start.

When I put the phone down I felt such a relief. I so wanted Martin to have a chance.

I was glad it was home time. I was tired; it had been a busy day with a satisfying end and I was off to Sainsbury's!

10

Past and Future

Christmas was now a distant memory, long since come and gone. I had enjoyed seeing my family and playing endless games of snakes and ladders and hide and seek with nieces and nephews, while weary parents benefited from a bit of a break. It often struck me how different the lives of these children were from those I worked with every day. They were loved and valued; there was little their parents would not do for them even if they had to sacrifice time and energy to achieve whatever that was. They had the childhood that children should have, and the contrast made me sad.

Until I became a social worker, I suppose that I took 'having a family' for granted; after a few years in the job I realised just how important it was to have people who really cared about you.

I never appreciated what it meant to have a family history until I had met people who had none or very little. We cringe when we hear the opening lines of one of those familiar tales we are repeatedly told by our parents about what we did when 'we went to Uncle James's house when we were three,' or what we did when the family went out on the river, or how we let the guinea pigs out when we were four and gave the family a hunt lasting some three hours as a consequence! But what if we had never heard anything from our childhood, knew nothing of what comprised those early years which were the foundation of our present selves, had no one to remind us of all those small incidents? What then? That is the situation of so many people who were in care as a child. Today, great emphasis is placed on keeping a treasure/memories box for a foster child, and it is one of a foster carer's responsibilities to ensure that photos of outings, keepsakes, even rail tickets and entrance leaflets, are kept for a child. But that didn't always happen. It is even more important for a child coming into care, who was removed because his or her parents could not parent them. Many will, as adults, wonder about their past – what they went through as a child – and for a long time now, such people have been allowed to read their files still held in Social Services departments and to learn for themselves the secrets of their troubled pasts. Many will not want to go there but others may feel their life story is incomplete without this knowledge.

One day, I was approached by Marie and asked if I would sit with a young woman, whose name was Rosie, while she read through her old files. Rosie was now in her late twenties, married with a young son, and she was one who had had a particularly grim childhood before she was removed from home at an early age, along with her twin brother Ross and two sisters.

Although the actual work on the file was to be undertaken by a student, there were real concerns that the level of deprivation suffered by Rosie as a child – and which the records would certainly reveal – were so great that it might be very hard for Rosie to handle the emotions this could engender, and it seemed unfair to ask a student to manage this. This probably meant up to four sessions of a couple of hours each but it was worthwhile and fascinating work and, as I already had some knowledge of the family, I agreed.

I first visited the young woman at home to discuss the process. Rosie, Ross and their sisters had experienced a level of neglect that matched up with the worst. Her sisters, some three and five years older than the twins, had struggled all along to stay on track after their damaging beginnings. I knew that they had not been as successful as Rosie and Ross. The eldest girl was now a registered addict and well known to the department; life was very hard for her. They had been through so much in their early life and the scars showed. When I arrived at Rosie's home, a tiny cottage on the edge of town, I knocked and waited. Somewhere in the distance I heard a radio and voices, then the door opened to a neatly dressed, smiling young woman, who invited me in and introduced me to her husband, Tony.

Tony stepped forward to shake hands with me and looked me straight in the eyes with a friendly smile. He had no issues with social workers, then. That was nice for a change. Sometimes I felt the whole world had issues with social workers, not least, most, if not all of my clients!

I was asked if I wanted a coffee, which Tony made, and we chatted. Rosie told me her story: 'I think Ross and I were about five when we were taken into care, and the four of us lived with foster carers about thirty miles away. Actually, they were great. We still see them, don't we, Tony?'

Tony stuck his head round from the kitchen where he was making coffee and added, 'Yeah, they're amazing. Had endless kids since then and keep in touch with them all . . . fantastic.'

'We all get together in December for a big Christmas party,' Rosie continued. 'There must have been, oh, thirty-odd last year! The din! There were all ages, from my sort of age to young children. One big extended family it felt like. I don't think my sisters gave them an easy time. Actually, they went to other carers after a while. Ross and I were younger and although I was a real pain from all accounts, and Ross was pretty wild, we weren't as bad as our sisters! Anyway, Tony and I were talking, and he was telling me about his childhood and I realised I knew nothing about my really early history, so Tony encouraged me to talk to someone. That's when I was told I could read my files. A bit of me is scared silly about it, but I have a child now and want to understand. Does that make sense?'

She looked at me questioningly, with doubt, uncertainty and some level of anxiety in her eyes. My response seemed to reassure her when I said, 'Look I think it's the most normal thing in the world, and lots of people decide to do this. If it feels important to you, then it's something that can help you to come to terms with your past.'

Rosie smiled, looked hard at me and said, 'I know I had an awful childhood. My sisters remember things they don't talk about, and have occasionally said tiny things. But actually, they don't like raising the past. I'm not sure what it is – embarrassment, horror or something – but they say virtually nothing about it.' Rosie sat back and thought. 'It's odd really, a strange thing, but I know nothing. If I ask them about it, they always say they've forgotten or something.'

Tony came in at this point, and put a small tray with three mugs and some biscuits on the coffee table. He'd been listening and said, 'Maybe it's like those men who were in POW camps in the war. I remember talking about them in history at school and apparently most of them never mentioned the horrors they'd been through. Never – weird. Maybe it's the same as that.' 'Hmm,' said Rosie, 'I don't know, but I want to do this.' Tony added, 'I'm so lucky, my parents were brilliant. Oh yes, they were really strict and we couldn't have stepped out of line or heaven help us but, you know what, I think I was so lucky. They were a typical Italian family. Lots of food, loads of relatives always stopping by. They ran a restaurant close by to where we lived, so mum was always about.'

Rosie laughed. 'Yeah, they are something else. I thought they'd hate me, 'cos I'd been in care, but they more or less adopted me.' Rosie turned to Tony, and said, 'I'm sure your mum feels I'm in need of extra care. She mothers me almost more than she does you, and that's saying something!' Clearly Rosie loved Tony's mother and revelled in her attention. 'She's always popping by and leaving me huge great meals, enough to feed an army. She's taught me to cook, spent ages with me, but I'm pretty good, aren't I, Tony?'

'Yeah,' he grinned. 'Actually you're brilliant, almost as good as me.'

I sat there watching the warm exchanges between this couple, who had been together for over ten years now,

and married for seven of those. Rosie told me that she
had never thought of getting married, but her mother-in-
law made it very clear that this was what happened to
'her sons', and then took over the whole event! I quietly
wondered how Rosie had felt about this, but she answered
my question in her next words, saying, 'You know what,
once I got over the shock of the idea, it was great. We
had the works, and held the reception in the restaurant,
and I felt part of the family then. It all seemed just perfect.'

She leaped out of her chair to reach for the wedding
photo standing proudly on the windowsill and thrust it
in front of me. Encapsulated in that picture were a glow-
ingly happy-looking couple, surrounded by a huge family
group – so many I could not distinguish the individuals.
As she held this out for me to look at, she looked over
at Tony. Her smile at Tony was warm and loving, a
sentiment that made a refreshing change from many of
my visits!

I'd have loved to have caught a glimpse of Tony's mother,
but even without that I had in my mind a warm, caring,
lively and emotionally expressive lady, capable of mother-
ing a ship-load of children and capable of steering a
whole family! How lucky was Rosie to land this lady as
her mother-in-law; it was indeed exactly what she needed!
She had a family now.

The couple had a son of five, who was at school. Rosie
told me very proudly that she had decided from the start
to be the best mother she could, and turn history on its
head. She said to me, 'There is no way that my son will
ever have the sort of life I had. I decided from the start
to only have one child, or two at most, so I could cope

and make a really good job of any child I have.' I listened
to Rosie: this was such a refreshing case, to meet a child
from so troubled a start in life, but who was so determined to change things for her own child. The determination was writ large on her face and all around her in
that neat little cottage, with reading books, colouring
pictures and photos that were testaments to Rosie's success. We arranged to meet at the office the following
week, and meet thereafter regularly until she had had a
chance to get through her files.

I had one visit to do before we met, and that was to
Rosie's mother, whom I knew to be still alive and living
in the area. I had to ask her about the release of certain
documents. Where I was going to get the time to fit this
visit in, I had just no idea. I managed eventually to get
hold of the mother and fixed to see her on my way home
from work one evening at about 6.30 p.m.

It had been a hectic day, with endless meetings and a
great deal to write up. By 6.00 p.m. I was still knee-deep
in work but had to put it all on one side for the morning.
Some of the notes I could do at home later. I set off for
the estate where Rosie's mother lived. It was a veritable
maze of streets, with some very peculiar names. Then
some clever soul had had the brilliant idea of having
Hugo Road, Hugo Close and Hugo Crescent all within
a short distance and as some of the road signs had been
partially destroyed there was an element of inspired guess-
work in knowing which of the three roads one was actually in. I would add that my inspiration was clearly lacking
on this occasion. Well, after several wrong turns, I found

Hugo Close. I wondered who Hugo was, and would he have felt it such an honour, had he seen into the future and been able to witness the sad deterioration of 'his' road. There was no green to be seen; any that had existed was now obliterated by the presence of various dilapidated vehicles parked on any space, some so rusty that I doubt they had felt the wind on their screens for many a long year. Rubbish blew about in the sharp breeze that had blown up with the evening and the only people to be seen looked at you sideways, if they looked at all, as if they expected you to be a threat of some sort.

I parked my car carefully to avoid the broken glass, hid anything of value in my car and stepped out onto the pavement outside number twenty-two. Well, I had calculated this to be number twenty-two, by counting down from the only house which still sported a number. I wondered how the postmen managed here, but I expect they had their systems. Anyhow, that was not my problem at the moment, and I found my mind reviewing what I knew of Rosie's mother.

She had been, when last on the Social Services radar, living alone and still quite a heavy drinker. From our brief conversation on the phone – well, extremely brief, because she clearly did not want to speak to me at all – she still lived alone. I had had difficulty persuading her to allow me to visit but she had eventually agreed to a quick visit.

I walked up the path to the door, only to find that I was actually on the neighbour's path. So, retracing my steps, I tried again, with more success. The house looked neglected: the net curtains were not grey, as once they might have been, but were now nearly black, and the door looked as if it hadn't seen paint since its very first entry into this world.

I thought about the files I had read. This woman had been responsible for starving, totally neglecting and regularly abandoning her four children. The descriptions of the home and children on the day of their removal made shocking reading even to a social worker, though not a lot shocked me nowadays. Human beings seem to be capable of sinking to a level of degradation that robs them of the ability to care, feel or function. Having said that, the tragedy here – as with so many, indeed the vast majority of our cases – was that alcohol and drug addiction had ruined any chance of this woman functioning better. Tragic.

I knocked and waited. Within seconds of my knock the deafening racket of a dog barking frantically and scrabbling at the other side of the door set up, as if to say, 'Just let me get through this door and then I'll show them!'

'Oh no, here we go again,' I thought. What would it be this time? I couldn't imagine that an older woman – somewhere in her fifties – would have much more than a small terrier, or some small cross breed, all bark but no menace. Or maybe a poodle, I thought optimistically, though on reflection I decided that a poodle was a dog that needed serious pampering, and that didn't fit.

The door was opened by a stooped woman and a young pit bull rushed out, hurling itself at me in an enthusiastic welcome. As the dog rushed round me, panting and woofing and seemingly wanting to be friends, I relaxed a little and looked at the woman. Her skin was the colour of grey paste and her eyes were cold and hostile. I guessed she was in her early fifties but she looked about seventy.

'You the Social?' she asked. I replied that I was, accepting as inevitable this odd label for my job, which made me sound like a mix of the benefits department or some local charitable organisation.

'You'd better come in.'

As the door shut behind me two men walked out from the kitchen. They had swarthy complexions, black hair and glittering angry eyes and spoke in broken English. They were not happy. The very presence of someone from the hated and despised Social Services department seemed to be enough to set them off. I don't think the department was generally 'hated and despised', but the level of venom that they poured out at me over the next half hour led me to suppose that this would be an extremely tame way to describe their feelings towards it. They launched into a wholesale attack on the department; I got the lot. I cannot imagine what experiences had resulted in their feelings, but past imagined insults must have festered long and painfully.

I stood in the hall, faced with the men; the woman had now wandered vaguely off to lie down on the sofa. They ranted and they raged; they shouted and they bellowed; they told me how they would plan to burn down the department with every one of 'its rotten staff of villains in it'. They screamed at me that the staff were all crooked and useless, and alluded to events in the past when social workers had treated them badly. And wasn't I paying now! While they embarked on this savage tirade, the dog, seemingly unaware of the significance of their raging, continued to wag his tail at me, fuss round my legs and look to me for attention. He had clearly taken to me, which made him the only one! Clearly he was a traitor to the cause and this was really aggravating one of the men particularly. He stepped forward, grabbed the dog by the collar, yanked it across the hall and threw – and I do mean threw – the poor animal out of the kitchen door into the garden. I heard a yelp of pain and shock but had no time to dwell on the dog's fate. I had problems enough of my own.

The door was firmly shut behind me. I could not escape without provoking an attack and these men were seriously aggressive and for all I knew might also be 'on something', which would aggravate any sense of injustice they might feel. My mind was working overtime, and I concluded that all I could do was listen with as much of a semblance of concern as I was able to muster. I endeavoured to genuinely understand what it was that had upset them so much and expressed the view that clearly they felt really angry about everything that had happened. There was no way I could reason or discuss. When someone is that angry it would only seem as if I had not understood their feelings. There are times when all of us feel misunderstood and just need others to recognise that. However, I was horribly aware that one wrong or unintentionally inflammatory word and I would probably not be as lucky as the dog: I would probably be hospitalised, if I ever got that far!

This ranting continued for about half an hour. Very slowly they began to shout less and even the ranting became less aggressive. Suddenly, one of them said, 'Of course you weren't there when all this happened, it's not actually your fault is it?' After a few more minutes in this vein of thinking he turned to the other man and said, 'Look, we've said our piece, let's go down to the pub for a (another) drink.' With that, they went. The door slammed and I just wanted to run out into the street, get in my car and drive, as far away as possible. But I didn't. I then took the opportunity to talk to Rosie's mother.

She lay still on the sofa, the floor around it littered with empty alcohol bottles of many sorts. She was truly not really all there and I suspected she had been drinking all day already. I explained what I needed to get her permission for, though honestly I wasn't sure she really understood all I was saying. She showed no interest at all in the children; they were a part of her history that was of no consequence now. Her life was a tragic and endless search for the next bottle and the money to buy it, and probably other substances as well. What an existence. I thought of Rosie – bright-eyed, smiling and ambitious to give her child the best she could, living in a happy, loving family. And here, her mother, aged and sick with a lifetime of drinking, eyes devoid of feeling, her face starved of any soft expression and lying day after day on a filthy sofa in a similarly filthy room. As wasted lives go, this was very high on the list. But perhaps . . . perhaps it wasn't all a waste. Her life had resulted in Rosie, though she had not seen her in many a long year, and Rosie was making a tremendous success of her life.

Rosie arrived for her first meeting at the agreed time a week later and I had booked one of the quieter rooms for us to meet in. Rosie looked apprehensive and slightly nervous. She told me that she had wondered whether to bring Tony, but had decided that she had to do this alone. I brought a drink for us both and we settled down to the task.

I talked to Rosie first, and discussed how she might feel if the contents were to be very graphic. I think she had an idea about the contents and accepted it could be hard. I told her that if she found the contents disturbing she might want to take a pause for a while, or even not continue. The ball was in her court and I would support her in whatever she decided. I also told her that I would see her during the week between sessions if she was struggling with the previous session.

With the preliminaries dealt with, we sat with the first file. I explained how they were organised and Rosie began to read. I had looked in depth at the file and knew what she was going to face.

The file began long before the children were finally removed. The children had been in and out of the eye of the department until the day when they were finally removed, a move triggered by the discovery of the older two girls found wandering one night, at about 1.00 a.m. in a deserted local shopping precinct, looking for food. A police patrol fortunately picked them up and drove to their home, when the true extent of the family problems were revealed. The house was basically a drinking and drugs den being used by many unsavoury characters. It wasn't fit for human habitation. It transpired that the children were locked in their rooms for long spells, starved, neglected and beaten when the mother was not too drunk to be incapable of violence. The older two girls had looked after Rosie and Ross, who were quite a few years younger, and had even hidden them when there was a risk of beatings from a violent boyfriend. It didn't make good reading. Rosie read on.

After a silent time while she digested the circumstances of the report she was reading, she turned to me and said, 'Ross and I wouldn't be here now if it wasn't for my sisters. They kept us alive. They fed us and protected us from people.' Her eyes were full of tears as she continued, 'You know what, I've been a right cow to my sisters, and they did all this. When I think about how I have been with them. I never understood why they were so cagey about the past, like they'd shut it out. And they didn't want to know when I told them I was going to read my records. In fact, they were really cross and agitated about it.'

We talked about her sisters, and she talked about how she might raise the past now. I warned her to remember that everyone copes differently, and not to go blazing in and open up a vast number of issues that her sisters had so far chosen to 'put in a box'. But perhaps knowing what she now knew about their part in her early life might make a better relationship with them possible. Rosie listened intently to me at this point, and nodded.

'I owe them so much; they were amazing and were only little kids themselves.' She hesitated, and then said, 'You know, I am going to tell them that I am sorry for being such a cow with them over the years, and understand a bit more, and really try to make things up with them. I am, I'm determined!' She continued to read on, and fell silent. At one point she pushed the file away, looked up and said to me, 'What kind of a mother does this to her children? How could she?'

This was the point at which I decided we needed to have a long talk about her mother's addictions and the effect these would have had on her behaviour. Rosie didn't move in her judgement. 'You know what, if she had wanted to, really wanted to, she could have kicked the drink and brought up her children. She was a waste of space.' In a smaller voice, she added, 'How could I have a mother like this? D'you think it was something to do with us kids?'

I now knew a great deal about her mother's history, as I had read through it the previous day in preparation, and I asked Rosie to read through her mother's Social History report, which was on the file from all those years ago – now on yellowed and crinkled paper not unlike the face of the woman who had once been the subject of this report. The story was grim but tragically familiar. Rosie's own mother, reared in utter poverty and deprivation in an industrial area of the Midlands, had been sexually abused from an early age by her father and uncle, and her own mother had mental health issues and had never functioned well, later on turning to drink. There was nothing positive in this account so I'll spare you the details. The point has to be that for her mother to have escaped this background unscathed would have been nothing short of miraculous. Rosie needed to understand that, for her own sake, so she could absolve herself from any possible feeling of blame, which is a common response of children in this situation.

Rosie went very quiet and was clearly thinking. Then

suddenly she blurted out, 'I wonder if I would have turned out like that if I had been left with my mother. Would I have drunk and neglected my son? I just can't imagine it.' I suggested that we stopped at this point as I could see this was enough for Rosie just now. I closed the file and we talked. Rosie talked and talked. Her final words that day to me were, 'I simply could not have imagined this. I am so lucky.' There was a long pause and, as if she was gradually coming to a clearer realisation of the situation, she looked straight at me, and with much feeling – which seemed to be a mix of incredible anger and deep sorrow – she said, 'I was lucky, wasn't I? And my mum was left to rot. I escaped, didn't I?'

Rosie later told me that she had gone home and talked to Tony, and that had been good. I was glad, as I felt this would help her in time to lay the ghost of her past if she could share it with Tony, who seemed very grounded as well as compassionate.

Over the weeks that followed, Rosie worked her way through her files, laughing at some of the incidents, becoming very serious when reading other sections, sympathising with some of her old social workers from her teenage years and repeatedly, when reading about those teenage years, bursting out with comments about her foster carer. 'How on earth did she put up with all my nonsense . . . I was awful to her!' '*Oh no!* How could I have said that?' 'What on earth possessed me?'

It was one of the tales recounted in the file about one particular misdemeanour, which her then social worker, Mike, had dealt with, that caused her to nearly choke on her coffee and say to me, 'I can't believe I said that to him,

I was such a lying little toad. You know I'd love to meet that social worker. Do you think he's still around? He did such a lot for me and I was awful to him most of the time.' It so happened that Mike was still working for the department, no longer a lowly social worker, now very senior, usually to be seen in a quick glimpse through his open office door surrounded by massive piles of paper and always head down peering at the computer screen. I wasn't at all sure how Mike would react to meeting Rosie after all these years, so I told Rosie that I would make enquiries.

I approached him, later that day, with some degree of trepidation because I knew how extremely busy he was, but he didn't hesitate. He seemed genuinely excited to hear all about Rosie and even more delighted to hear about how well Rosie was coping with life. Not only that, but he recalled the case very clearly. Mike asked me to sit down for a moment, and wanted chapter and verse of Rosie's story. He leaned slightly forward in his chair as he listened to every detail, as if he didn't want to miss anything. Mike had been in the department for a long time and there was little he had not seen but as I finished speaking, and indeed answering his questions, his eyes turned away, not really seeing me but, I think, drifting back to those years in the past and the times he had spent with Rosie and many other young people like her. I know I saw the slightest glimpse of a sparkle in his eyes – there were tears lurking there, well hidden but there, and I knew why Rosie remembered him so well, Mike had really cared. His mood had softened from the busy, focused, now office-bound Mike to something else. His words when they came were said quite emotionally.

'Thanks for fixing this, Becky. I've had a terrible week, drowned in mostly pointless paperwork, and I've been wondering what on earth I am doing. The likes of Rosie are the reason I came into social work and to hear that she is doing so well is the best thing I have heard for a very long while. It's made my week!'

I heard from Rosie that she and Mike went out to a quiet coffee shop and drank their way through several cups of coffee while they exchanged memories of those difficult years. Difficult they may have been but the two of them had some good laughs over some of the incidents and I believe some tears were spilt by Rosie when they discussed things that Rosie had never really understood as a teenager, but could now see. I think this meeting was very therapeutic for Rosie and the next day I had an email from Mike stating simply, 'Thanks, Becky, that was great!'

Mike, much to everyone's surprise, left the department about four months after this meeting, and the day he was leaving I happened to bump into him on the stairs. I wished him well and Mike turned back from his progress down the stairs and said to me, 'You know, meeting Rosie reminded me why I came into this job. I've taken a job working with troubled teenagers, in a very tough setting, and for the first time in ages feel excited and that I have a sense of purpose. I never wanted to shuffle papers, it's not my thing, but it paid better, and I had to get my two through university without going bankrupt myself! Well, they're through now. I have choices and I've chosen. So think of me!' With this he set off down the stairs with a huge smile and the appearance of a man with a real sense of purpose; even his face looked different. And yes, I would think of him. Everyone said he had been a brilliant social worker but he hadn't set eyes on a client for many years. It was my guess that many more young people would be helped once Mike got his teeth into his new job. I was glad for him, very glad. Thanks, Rosie.

It is one of the questions that people sometimes ask – do you ever think about the cases you had in the past – and the answer is yes, definitely. How can you live, breathe and lose sleep over a child, worry about them a great deal and then forget them. You don't. Sometimes you find yourself wondering what they are doing and hoping that they are getting on with life and coping. On very rare occasions you do hear about past cases in various ways and, if the news is good, then it is as Mike said, 'really great', because they are rarely forgotten.

At our next meeting, Rosie was full of her meeting with Mike, telling me lots of things that had cropped up between them. After a while of chatting she became serious and said, 'I did think he'd aged rather a lot, though!' Hmm, he probably had. No wonder!

I I

Duty Day

It was my duty day and I needed to be in work extra early to tackle some of my paperwork, so I was hoping for a clear run to work. Today I had it, so I arrived with time to sort out my emails before I had to man the duty desk.

Once we put on our 'duty hats', it was a serious transgression, a big, 'No No' to even look at one's own caseload. This had to be so because, quite simply, it would be impossible to deal with the duty calls and try to fend off one's personal caseload at the same time, so all incoming calls to the social worker on the duty desk are diverted and logged for future reference. So, after a quick run through of my emails, I gathered my things and moved myself, both physically and mentally, to the duty desk.

The job officially began at a quarter to nine and lunch was covered by another worker, though in truth there was rarely an opportunity to indulge in luxuries like 'lunch'! I often wondered why the teams were not all very slim. I think perhaps there was a 'famine mentality' among us, so when there was time to eat the temptation was to eat far more than was needed to stock up for times when one couldn't!

At one minute after a quarter to nine, the duty phone rang. It was the Family Centre ringing to see what had happened to the contact supervisor for a family who only had 'supervised' access to their children. When children are removed from a family for reasons of abuse then all contact has to be supervised to protect the children from the risk of harm or possible threats by parents who may not wish their children to reveal some of the events that led up to their admission to care. A family centre worker will remain with the children literally at all times if there are any concerns that harm could befall them. In addition, the observations which can and should be made during these sessions were critical to the assessment of the relationship between parent and child. In this case the allocated contact worker had not appeared and there were no staff in the centre to cover it, the family was kicking off and the foster carer who had brought the child for contact had other children to take to school. Deadlock. I couldn't contact the worker concerned – goodness knows what had happened to her – and this case was at a very critical point, as it was going to court in three weeks and was having a very rough ride. The last thing we needed was the parents making false claims that we had not maintained their agreed contact with the children.

After ages spent on the phone, I got hold of a worker we knew of from one of the agencies and arranged for her to get over to the family centre pronto. I put the phone down with huge relief.

As soon as the receiver hit the telephone cradle (if not sooner), the phone rang again. It was Rhona from reception this time, bright and breezy, cheerful as always – it really did make calls from reception more of a pleasure

– and she asked me if I would see a young man who had come in and wanted to see a social worker. He had a loose link with one of the social workers but that worker was away. So I popped down to see him.

The young man was sitting alone in reception. He was leaning forward with his head resting in his hands, staring at the floor. He looked tired. No, I think perhaps weary would be a more accurate way to describe his demeanour. I went over to him and introduced myself and he looked up at me. His eyes had that blank, negative look of someone who doesn't expect any interaction with others to have a positive outcome. There was no cheerful smile or greeting, only that offhand, slightly defensive, slightly aggressive expression born of years of standing alone, with no one to turn to, no one who cares enough to go the extra mile, no family, no real friends.

I took him through into one of the interview rooms that was adjacent to reception and we sat down. I don't know why, but on this particular morning the room seemed particularly depressing. Little natural light penetrated the small window, making the drab, grey-painted room seem darker than usual. The floor was a speckled grey colour and in the centre of the room was a damaged coffee table and four very tatty chairs. The red emergency button standing alone on the wall was testament to the outbursts of rage that this room had witnessed over many years. There were no pictures, because of the propensity of people in a temper to throw anything convenient; so, granted, pictures were not a good idea, though I often wondered why we couldn't have some calming scenes painted on the walls by local art schools, and grey, for goodness' sake, who was responsible for that choice of colour? Still, that was how it was! I couldn't change the world; I could only do my bit in a tiny corner!

The young man was called Rob and he had been taken into care in his early teens. After a very tough childhood, his foster placement had not been successful and he had walked away many years back and was now alone. He needed help to furnish a room he had just acquired. Until the previous weekend he had lived with a friend. However, the friend had kicked him out when a new girlfriend came to live there and didn't take to Rob. Had the room, tiny as it was, not come available through work, he would have had nowhere to go.

He was a tall, gangling young man, with a head of limp fair hair hanging about his shoulders. He was quite aggressive at first, demanding his old worker, grumbling about his ex flat mate, grumbling about the receptionist and then having a go at me before I had barely spoken. But this young man had no one, no relatives (in a fit state to help him), no friends able to help him, nothing, so wouldn't you feel angry at the world? What else was there to feel to cover over all the hurt of years of being 'no one to anyone'. It was almost unbearable to imagine how that must feel. Not a soul, literally, who really cares if you live or die. For a short moment I had allowed myself to dwell on what that must be like. I had to stop because it hurt so much to put myself there.

I let him rant and grumble for a minute, then asked him where he was living at present. Rob replied, 'Well, I've been kipping down on the storehouse floor at work since I was kicked out of my friend's flat. If my boss knew he would probably kick me out of there but I wouldn't feel safe sleeping on the streets.' There was a mixture of awkwardness and aggression in his voice. I could sense that he didn't enjoy having to ask, and why should he. He had more sense than many kids, because he had had the sense to ask, but where else would he go? He was just that bit too old to access the usual provision but I knew we should be able to find a way to help and he could certainly use some.

We talked a bit about his job, which was in the restaurant kitchen, and no sinecure that's for sure; he worked long hours, jolly hard, and his boss was, it seemed, of very uncertain temperament. But it did seem the other staff were an OK bunch, of all ages, and it rather sounded as if they had taken Rob under their wing at work. He had kept the job for over six months now, which was fantastic and showed this kid had grit. I told him so and for a brief moment he looked up, clearly unaccustomed to any form of compliment; it was as if he didn't quite know if I was being serious. I was; jobs did not grow on trees and hard work was not always something youngsters were prepared to keep up. I said to him that there were a great many people who simply wouldn't bother to keep on working when it was hard going and I repeated that he really was showing that he had 'grit' and I wished more of my teenagers had it.

I suddenly noticed that for the first time he fell silent, listened intently and appeared to absorb every word I said. I was sad to think that he probably so rarely heard any good of himself that this small comment I made to him was a rare and important input for a young man whose self-esteem had rarely had anything but savage undermining.

He settled a little and began to talk more about his life, and I listened. Not because I had lots of time – I didn't! I knew the calls would be stacking up but I felt this kid merited my time, far more than many. Life had dealt him a bad hand, but he was trying and deserved some meagre bit of encouragement. He was struggling to deal with the cost of furnishing – well, basically he had no money after the tiny rental for the room and simply didn't know what to do. He told me that he had left his foster family after a big row some years before and managed to live with his friend. It was a great shame that the new girlfriend had fallen out with him, such that he had been forced to go. However, he had managed to find this flat. Well one room, with a sink and gas ring, rented out by his employer in the restaurant where he was working.

I listened; the flat sounded grim but it was a roof and Rob needed everything: a bed, bedding, kitchen bits etc. Fortunately, we had a charity in the town to which people gave all sorts of unwanted stuff, some of it in brilliant condition and all of it very serviceable. I also said I would contact another group I knew of, who might consider giving him a small grant in kind, i.e. not money, but items, to help him through. What I didn't say, but knew, was that this charity, in contacting people who could do with a hand for a while, often offered some friendship support as well, which I felt Rob needed as much as the rest.

Rob looked at me and assumed 'the look', and then said, 'I don't want no help from do-gooders, I'd rather be without . . .' I looked straight at him and said, 'Rob, do you honestly think any of us can get through life without occasionally needing other people and some help from them? If I tell you that I happen to know that some of the people who are helping with these two groups have themselves needed help in the past from similar organisations, will that stop you talking nonsense to me. What's more, you have managed to get a job and keep it, you are trying to sort yourself out. People respect that you know, and I will make sure they know that! OK?'

Rob looked up at me. I was, I admit, in feisty mood but I believed he needed to understand that this is not a stand-alone world. Try getting sick and needing a doctor, then you will realise. Money will not pay for everything we receive in this life.

His eyes looked more open and he said thoughtfully, 'Do you really think they will respect the fact that I have a job?'

'Yes Rob, and even more the fact that you are trying so hard. And I will tell them that, so they jolly well do know.'

He grinned at me, and put up an arm as if to protect himself from my rant at him. 'OK, OK, I take your point.'

'Look,' I said. 'On a more practical level, how are you going to get any furniture up the stairs?' I knew the furniture charity just delivered and didn't have staff to carry heavy weights. Often it was much older, retired men who drove the vans and they couldn't have carried it up three floors. I asked him to ring me when he had some furniture and knew when it would be delivered, and then promised to get James to give him a hand installing it in his new room.

It was hard for youngsters who had broken the link with both their birth families and their foster families. How many young people at the age of eighteen, nineteen, twenty or even twenty-one years would manage easily without any support, both emotional and practical, from a family behind them? It's a tough call and frankly many of the most stable young people have benefited from years of ongoing support. Isn't that what families do? So how youngsters who haven't even had a stable start in life are supposed to cope is an interesting question.

Rob left, and on his way out he looked at me and smiled. I had done very little, and felt nothing but inadequate that all I had done was access furniture for him and spend a very short time chatting. But in spite of all his blustering, he was a likeable young man and I so hoped that he would be strong enough alone to cope without falling victim to the many perils he would certainly meet, if not now, in the future.

I walked back up the stairs to the office, deep in thought. But my reveries were sharply interrupted by the brisk ringing of the phone (again!). It was reception.

'There's a Mr and Mrs Patel in reception with their teenage daughter and family, asking to speak to a social worker. Could you see them please?'

'Yep I'll be down.' I quickly grabbed a coffee, which I topped up with cold water so I could actually get to drink it immediately – I downed my coffee at record rates – and set off downstairs again.

The couple and their daughter were sitting looking very stressed at one side of the waiting area. Next to them was a very elderly couple. None of them were speaking, and the girl was looking down at the floor as if determined not to be part of things. Mrs Patel and the elderly couple were dressed traditionally, and Ria, their daughter, was dressed very fashionably in typical teenage clothes, with dangly earrings and a few streaks in her hair.

I walked over to them and invited them into an interview room. They all trooped in. Mr Patel introduced his wife, daughter and parents, explaining that his parents spoke no English. I asked whether they all wished to be present, and a considered look fell over his face.

'I wonder whether my parents might be happier waiting outside.'

I took this to mean that he felt he would find this easier, so I suggested to him that we could take them over to the comfy corner, as we called it, which had a drinks machine and loads of magazines to thumb through. We installed them there and Mr Patel bought them both a drink, explained what was happening in Gujarati and left them with a quick wave. As I closed the door and invited them all to sit down, I could sense the icy atmosphere and I suspected we were all in for a difficult time. When we had all sat down I looked at them and said, 'Well how can I help you?'

No one spoke. Mrs Patel, gripping her bag as if her life depended on it, looked down at the floor, with tears brimming in her eyes. Ria looked sulky and defiant, and sat with her arms crossed firmly across her, looking determinedly sideways at the floor. Mr Patel sat on the edge of his seat and seemed to be wrestling with how to begin. It was finally he who broke the silence, suddenly and without any preamble.

'She's out of control. We don't know what to do and someone suggested we come here.' He clearly wasn't happy to be here but he looked at me and what I saw was desperation. Quietly I opened the conversation with, 'Well, perhaps you could tell me what it is that has been causing you all such a lot of worry. Then we can talk about it.'

Mr Patel began to relate their story. He and his wife had lived in Britain for a long time, though they were both brought up in India. His parents had come to live with them about three years ago. When their daughter Ria had been born, it all seemed so perfect as they had waited a long time for a baby and had begun to wonder if they would ever have a child. She was very precious. He made great play of just how 'good' a child Ria had been, not an ounce of trouble, lovely friends, bright, musical, always very obedient. Then she had moved up to senior school and things had slowly got worse and worse. Mr Patel continued, 'The girl's out of hand, she's out all the time, won't speak to us, won't tell us where she is going, stays out all night sometimes, is always on the phone to goodness knows who, and has shut us out totally.'

He paused to take a breath and looked almost confused, and then he threw in, 'And just look at her clothes and what she has done to her hair. She's behaving like a street girl!' At this, Ria, who had listened silently, never lifting her eyes from the floor all through her father's monologue, leapt to her feet and made to run out. Before she got to the door, she turned and shouted at her father, 'How can you say such dreadful things? You know nothing about me. I don't talk to you because I can't talk to you.

Your minds are closed; you want me to be locked up by six o'clock, not have any fun and be different to everyone else. I don't do half the things that most people in my class are doing.' She paused briefly and appeared to be thinking, which in turn seemed to refuel her anger and she continued in an even louder and more infuriated tone, 'I don't smoke or do drugs. I don't even drink . . . and most of my friends do. You just think I'm wicked because I go to parties, see my friends and go off on a Saturday to the shops with them.' Her voice rose to an hysterical crescendo, which I think would have been heard five miles away. Tears were now streaming down her face.

'You're living in the past. You're not in India now. I've got to have friends; what do you want me to do? Sit at home all day. And Nan makes it all worse, constantly telling you I shouldn't be doing this and shouldn't be doing that. I don't stand a chance. I'm completely suffocated!'

She took a sharp intake of breath, and screamed at her parents, 'I may as well be dead as live like this. In fact I wish I was. That or living anywhere, literally anywhere, but with you two.'

She made for the door, but I called, 'Look, Ria, please stay. We really have got to talk about all this. Please sit down.'

She turned and looked at me and in her face I saw the same desperation that I had seen in both her mother and father. This did not look or even sound like a seriously off-the-rails teenager; this looked like a case of huge culture shock for the somewhat older and overly protective parents of a lively, sociable, normal teenage girl, raised in the UK and expecting to have friends and a social life. When denied this, she had reacted with defiance and increasing rebellion, which was leading her into behaviour that could indeed end in the very things her parents, in their concern, were seeking to prevent.

She had halted mid-flight and continued to look at me. I wondered if she was trying to work out whether there was any hope. I appealed to her again and she remained standing there – a sort of, 'I'm not caving in, but I'll reserve my judgement' position. So, with Ria standing stock still ready to bolt, her mother sobbing audibly and uncontrollably now and her father sitting with his head in his hands rubbing his forehead, I decided that now I needed to act.

I asked her to please sit down, politely but firmly. The fact that she did, admittedly with a slightly surprised expression on her face, rather supported my view that this was not a wild child scenario, rather a difficult cultural and now family issue. Further, the father looked genuinely devastated, rather than angry. So perhaps . . . perhaps there were grounds to be hopeful.

I told them I would be back in a tick. I shot out to the water machine, poured four chilled waters out, grabbed the tissues from reception and, using one of the old tin trays kept there, I carried this all back to the room and offered it round. I allowed the three of them time to compose themselves a little and then suggested that we were going to talk, listen and discuss. I picked up my pad and pen and explained. I told them we were going to allow each one of them to express their feelings about all this, but that no matter what was said no one had to interrupt anyone else. Every one had to be heard.

I could see Ria showing just a touch of interest, watching my face intently as I spoke. Her mother looked at me with that same look of desperation but perhaps the very slightest flicker of hope, and the father seemed to be prepared to go along with anything now; he looked defeated and out of his depth. We began.

Their home life over the last nine months had been little but a battleground. Endless rows with Ria, because she was going out, and the more they rowed the less she responded and the more determined to go out she became, until now she was barely communicating with her family. Ria had stayed out all night with some of her girlfriends, which had seriously worried her parents, and she had even recently threatened to run away. Her terrified parents no longer felt these to be idle threats; they expressed their fears for her future and the dangers she faced, and so it went on, for a good while. Mrs Patel managed to verbalise her fears in a shaky voice, saying she feared she had lost her daughter and was simply desperate. Tears prevented her from continuing.

Ria was then encouraged to speak. Her parents respected our agreement, and listened intently. Ria talked about her restrictive life, losing friends because of her parents' attitudes, being unable to be normal and so it went on. There was a moment when all paused and the room fell silent, yet was almost buzzing with unspoken concerns. The silence lasted for a few minutes and I said nothing – it was as if the moment was needed for everyone to process what had been said.

It was into that silence that suddenly Mr Patel finally stopped just talking, and really said what he was feeling.

He was clearly not a man used to dealing openly with emotion. I think he had said that he worked in the computer field, and computers and expressed emotion were not always comfortable bed-fellows.

He began to speak, 'I just want . . .' he managed these two stumbled words, and then stopped. Then there was a crack in his voice as he began again, and he was clearly struggling to keep his emotions under control. After the first few words it seemed as if our presence had become almost irrelevant as he said, 'I've worked all my life to give my family everything they need. That was the whole reason we came to Britain in the first place, to make a better life for ourselves and any family we might have. I've worked so hard; we own our own home, everything is good, but the only thing that really matters – Ria – hates us, because we don't want her to wreck her life.'

At this point, tears began to run down this proud man's face. I noticed Ria looked up at his words and when she saw the tears the absolute horror that registered on her face said much. I very much doubt if she had ever seen her father cry. From that point on, I noticed her mood change from anger to anxiety. She could be angry with the immovable strong figure, but when that figure crumbled, she suddenly realised that she was on her own, making her own destiny, fighting paper monsters. Her father was the strong authority figure, the one who said, 'No,' not someone who cried and suffered like herself or her mother.

Mr Patel continued, 'I am so afraid. I know Ria thinks I know nothing about the British culture but I understand more than she thinks. I go to work, I hear how the other fathers talk and, worse still, I hear the youngsters in my office. They seem like really nice young people, I don't know what their parents are going through, but I hear the stories on a Monday morning. About the drunken parties, the staggering home and what goes on, and they laugh about it as if it were funny. I hear about the drug taking and how lightly some of them take the whole issue. I also hear about the abortions . . .'

At this, both Ria and her mother reacted very violently. Ria's posture became extremely defensive; she had her arms wrapped about herself and couldn't look at her father at all, staring down at the floor as if her life depended on that little patch of flooring. She looked to be in an agony of horror that her father was aware of – and worse, even talking out loud about – issues that would simply never be discussed in her home. It was embarrassing and terrifying all together; all her preconceived ideas were being shot down and she was afraid. It was all too much.

In contrast, her mother moved very sharply in her chair; her eyes went from confused to angry and horrified and her body language making an amazingly violent and sudden change from the passive, distraught mother to something else, very different. It was as if, in those few words, her husband had destroyed the comfortable, albeit false, assumption that they could just continue as they had always done, hoping that their child would live and grow up as they had done.

She looked sharply at her husband in absolute disbelief that seemed to say, traitor, what is happening? How can he talk about all this so openly, has he lost all sense of himself? Then there was fear. Fear of having to change, fear of accepting the unacceptable, fear of losing all she held dear. I felt for her; this was extremely painful for her, but sadly necessary for them all to move forward.

But Mr Patel continued. I don't think he noticed anything in the room; it was as if, now he was really saying what was on his mind, he felt some sense of unburdening that was freeing. Not that it made him feel good – he was far too distraught to feel anything like that – but perhaps it was cathartic. 'After all we have been through, I don't want my precious daughter to come home pregnant after a drunken night out or get caught up in drugs. Goodness knows, I saw enough of the addicts on the streets in India. Or . . .'

He paused, and with emotion cracking his voice completely, added, 'I can't stand the worry, I lie awake imagining things. I . . .' He stopped; he had no more he could say. His family had now heard him; their strong father and husband had shown just how vulnerable he was in the face of all these unknowns and it left them both shocked into a paralysed silence, in which none of them could now look at the others – all remaining alone in their individual nightmares.

I let this run for a short time; they needed time to process the fact that their world had been shaken at the roots. I rather suspected that for Ria and her mother it felt as if their worlds had been destroyed, left like a bomb-site with the future now looming ahead as nothing but a terrifying chasm.

I saw Mr Patel reach for his water; his hand was shaking so much that he spilt a small amount. I sat forward, and looked at them all in turn. I put into words just what I could see: a loving family who felt their world was being destroyed by their fears of a new culture that they perceived to be full of dangers over which they felt defenceless. I then talked to them. I pointed out that the majority of young people did not fall victim to their worst fears, that there were things all teenagers needed to be aware of to protect themselves and we needed to look realistically at their new life, and what could be done.

Bringing them out of their present mood was hard at first, but I asked them to tell me what they liked about this culture. With thought, all of them came up with more and more positives and Mr Patel also added some comments about India and the many things he disliked there, and that he had been happy to leave. Ria slowly joined in, and spoke openly about her love of the freedoms and opportunities she felt she had, and said a surprising amount. She began to talk herself into a more positive frame of mind.

Getting them to see some positives was helpful; we then went on to talk about setting standards for their own family, and Ria setting standards for herself, which might not be exactly the same as theirs, but still equally valid. We also looked at understanding risks and ensuring that Ria, and they themselves, knew enough to avoid them. I think talking about drugs and dangerous behaviour in an adult way was hard for the couple, although Mr Patel coped more easily. Ria seemed to feel a sense of relief at discussing openly issues that had simply been unspoken 'elephants in the room', and left as such. It was a moving moment when Ria effectively took the floor and said, 'You know, I have ambitions for myself. I'm not a child. I decided last year, after a talk at school, that I want to train to be a physiotherapist. And my teachers say I could do it. I'll need good grades but I've even looked at colleges that do the training.' She seemed calmer and more adult, and then added in a slightly irritable voice, 'There's no way I will get those grades if I get pregnant, take drugs or start to drink heavily; its not an option. I don't want to end up on the scrap heap.' Her voice was suddenly more adult. It was like listening to a young woman, who knew where she was going and, better still, how she was going to get there. I could see that her parents were utterly stunned at her words.

Mr Patel finally said, 'Ria you've never mentioned this before. I didn't know all this.'

Ria's reply was short: 'Dad, you never asked. You were too busy worrying about me. Too busy trying to keep me in and arguing over everything I did. You never talk to me about careers; nor docs Mum, so I just got on with it.'

He sat back in his chair, clearly trying to digest the fact that his little girl had already devised her own life-plan without his help or interference, that she was already on her way to being all he had ever wanted, a successful young woman in her chosen field, but without his help.

Her mother had listened to much of what was said up to now with a shocked expression of disbelief on her face, suddenly growing into interest as Ria revealed her thoughts for the future. Ria's mother had broken her hip the previous year and had much physio in hospital, and she chipped in with a comment about how amazing the physios had been then.

Ria butted in, 'Oh yes, I know, they were amazing and so nice with you and you were so difficult. Do you remember, you moaned all the time about doing those funny side-kick exercises! But the physios were saintly! It was partly them that started my thinking about this, and then the careers talk at school.'

Ria's mother looked up, shocked at her daughter's honesty about her behaviour, and was about to say something when Mr Patel, a slightly amused smile on his face at last, said, 'Come on, you were, you know. You must have driven them mad, and you pretended you couldn't understand when you didn't want to do that dreadful exercise with your leg!'

Mrs Patel clearly thought that silence was the most dignified option here. But this tiny, somewhat light-hearted interlude had changed the balance in the room. Ria was finding that her father had become an ally, albeit briefly, someone who perhaps might understand in time, and her mother could see she would have to adjust, even if only a little. Slowly, I got them talking. When they had all had their say, we began to look at some boundaries we could agree. Taking it in turns, each had to say what they most needed the others to understand. As the conversation progressed, the couple began to see that they had actually been having a negative effect on the situation. In spite of all their efforts, Ria was still going out and intended to continue to do so. Indeed, because of their antagonism to her friends and lifestyle, they were almost driving her away. But they had heard the very adult way that, in spite of all, Ria was looking at her life, and suddenly they both felt that here was someone who demanded to be listened to, indeed had to be listened to. But on the other side, their fears had some basis and Ria needed protecting; she was still young and there were risks out there, but they felt at sea and frightened in a culture which differed so much from the one in which they had grown up.

After a good while discussing compromise, agreeing boundaries that they could all learn to accept and looking at realistic ways to keep Ria safe, Ria gradually joined more and more into the conversation, becoming more assertive. It felt as if she was taking her place back in the family, no longer just as the child but more as an emerging, strong-minded young woman in the making. She even began to suggest ideas, such as allowing her a mobile so she could ring home to let them know where she was and the time she would be home. She dared to suggest also that if her mother also got a mobile, she could text her directly, but she said that this meant her having to learn how to use a mobile. She said this with a rueful look at her mother, which I took to mean this was not likely to happen. She then seemed to gain strength, looked challengingly at her mother and asked, 'Well, will you do that? Then I could let you know just what I was up to without my friends knowing I am checking in to home all the time?'

I saw the measured look her mother gave Ria – an 'Is she serious, can I wriggle out of this?' look.

Mr Patel chipped in, and said, 'You know, Jagitha, that would be good. I think you should. Perhaps it's time we both thought about becoming a bit more in tune with things. Everyone uses mobiles now and it would be good to be able to keep in touch!'

I could see that his wife was not thrilled about this. I got the feeling that with only one child and a clearly very devoted husband she was perhaps accustomed to remaining unchallenged about most issues. I stepped in and pointed out to her that I understood this would seem alien to her but would show her commitment to improving things and making things easier for Ria. I added, 'If you have a mobile, even if your husband is at work, Ria can contact you if she needs to. It's a safety device.'

I looked at Mrs Patel very deliberately and said to her, 'It is really important for you to show willing if we are going to move forward and keep your family intact.' An echo of agreement from her husband, and a louder one from Ria, cut the ground from under her. I hoped she was beginning to get it: words and tears were not enough; after them must come change, and this meant all of them. I worded this sentiment to her and she looked up thoughtfully at me, anxiety and vulnerability overwhelming her eyes and expression. I think she was realising that she was being left behind and would have to move. I also knew that she really loved Ria; I could also see that in her eyes. She sat up straight, took a deep breath and said, 'OK, how hard can it be? You know I used to always be top of my class at school in Maths. I can do this.'

Ria looked admiringly at her mother, saying, 'You never said that before. Were you really?'

Her mother seemed to grow a little and her words were interesting. 'Well, I didn't tell you all. You all think I'm only good for cooking and cleaning. I do actually have a brain!' Both of them looked at her now, as if seeing her with new eyes.

Ria's father was clearly a thoughtful man, but had just so many fears for his daughter that he couldn't relax his demands upon her. As we talked, he began to see that he was driving her away and could see he had no option but to compromise. Ria, while firmly stating that she was not giving up her freedom, agreed to help her parents to adjust and to indulge their anxieties somewhat by being careful to keep in regular contact when she was out. Between us we agreed some acceptable ground rules for both Ria and her parents, such as when she was to be allowed out, until what time and how that differed on school nights etc. But in these rules were freedoms for Ria that were now agreed by everyone. It was at last give and take, talk and agree. It was far from smooth progress, but slowly they began to discuss all together.

I felt that things were as yet incomplete. The family grandparents were now living with the family and I wondered how this was affecting things. So I asked, 'How will your parents cope with these changes, Mr Patel?' From the now-fluid flow of conversation that we had been having, this question elicited such a total silence and an exchange of meaningful looks between all of them, that it felt as if someone had slammed on the brakes at eighty! No one spoke; Mr Patel couldn't prevent an involuntary clenching of his hands and his face was a picture of conflicting emotions. The silence continued for a painful time and then suddenly Ria burst out, 'Well, let's be honest, they will nag you endlessly like they always do . . .'

Horror crossed Mrs Patel's face and Mr Patel looked very uncomfortable – embarrassed and unable to look up. Mrs Patel began to speak in Gujarati to her husband, and

I was fairly sure she was really upset. I asked Mrs Patel what she had said, and she just looked. It was Mr Patel who responded, 'Well, my parents have very traditional views, and they have, I admit, been making it worse for my wife by going on about Ria's behaviour. It is hard. Very hard. They mean well, but it doesn't help.'

I thought for a moment, and asked him what he felt he could do about this. It was Mr Patel's turn to think – for quite some time – and I could see the struggle going on. I also saw his glance up at his daughter and wife, both of whom were by now watching him intently and expectantly. In the silence, the clock on the wall seemed to tick very loudly and the sounds from outside penetrated the room. Even I felt the tension building up inside the room.

Mr Patel shifted his position in his chair, nervously drank some more water and then took a deep breath. 'If I listen to my parents' view of life, I could lose my daughter and all that is most dear to me.' His wife nodded at him, and he continued, 'Therefore I have no choice but to explain to them that this is what we are going to do. But,' and here he sounded very uncertain, 'they won't take this without comment.'

I thought some more, and suggested to Mr Patel that we invite his parents to join us in the room and explain to them what had been decided and why. I asked Pritti from reception if she could spare me some time to translate. Mr Patel agreed, clearly with some considerable trepidation, but it was no good them all going home and finding the grandparents lacking any understanding of events.

Pritti came across and sat with us, while Mr Patel's parents came through to join the group. They looked puzzled and a little worried. It was hard for them to leave their own country so late in life and adjust to a new culture. Like many older people who make big moves, they might never really settle, but I hoped they would understand a little of what we were trying to do for the family. I had a brief word with Pritti so she knew what to expect and she in turn had a brief word with the grandparents and then we began.

Mr Patel launched into an explanation of things to his parents, who looked very unimpressed. There was considerable fairly heated debate between them, and this continued for some while. Pritti gave me a running commentary. Mr Patel had spoken in very gentle terms to his parents, whom he clearly cared for a great deal, and this continued for some time, with exchanges and debates. His parents found it hard to understand the freedoms that Ria had, and was going to be allowed, and struggled to move on this issue. The conclusion came as Mr Patel began to get really quite angry, but still controlled, and apparently told his parents that he did not intend to lose his daughter, and this was what was going to happen in the future. His parents were stunned into silence, looking for support from his wife and Ria. None was forthcoming, and they sat back more quietly. In some ways Mr Patel was forced to choose between his daughter's future and upsetting his parents. His decision to put Ria first made her feel a sense of support from him that she felt she had lacked before and she knew how hard this step was for her gentle, caring father.

Mr Patel turned to me and said that they were his parents and he would make certain that they learned to understand things or at least accepted them. It seemed there was a somewhat uneasy truce but it was a start. It was hard for all sides, and again I could see that the grandparents cared a great deal for Ria; it was just such a big culture shock and might take a long time to adjust to. After all, even grandparents who are of the same culture as their grandchildren irritate their children and grand-children with frequent references to 'things they would never have been allowed to do in their day'. There was much talking ahead.

Towards the end of the time, I noticed Ria reach out to hold her mother's hand, and as they were leaving her father put an arm around Ria's shoulder and gave her a little hug. She was a much-cherished child but they all had a lot to learn. We parted and I suggested that they try to work on all we had discussed; they had a photo-copy of our combined agreement plan and I suggested that they came back in a month to discuss their progress and to ensure they kept on track. Mr Patel seemed to jump at this, as did Ria. I think it all seemed too fragile and they felt in need of some extra outside support to make sure it all happened. They were much more relaxed, although they all looked drained. I felt that a small step had been taken and if they could keep on walking they might well get their family back on track.

I watched the little group leave and walk down the path at the front, and saw Ria slipping her arm into her father's. It looked promising. I really hoped so.

I walked back upstairs in a bit of a daze. This had been

a very intensive interview session, unexpectedly ending up as a fairly heated family conference. The satisfying thing was the hope that this might, if all went well, prevent a crisis that we might later have had to pick up and deal with. So much better and easier to help in preventing a broken situation, rather than dealing with it once it had actually broken, always much harder.

As I walked into the office, Lou looked up and commented, 'You've been ages! There are several messages on your desk – one is urgent. But they all came through to me, as admin seem to be busy reorganising the filing system again.' She pulled a face, dropped her voice and said, 'You know what that means. We won't be able to find anything for weeks, files will go missing and nothing else will get done in the interim. Great. Ah well, what's new.'

Normally I'd be agreeing with her wholeheartedly and entering into her irritation with yet another administrative change, but I was exhausted and craved for some peace and quiet. I put my notes down on the desk, to finish in a moment, and made for the coffee, which I took out of the office into a small area with a couple of huge, badly cared for palms, but it was quiet, as people rarely came this way. There was some greenery, some quiet and a window. Enough. I leaned on the windowsill and gazed out at nothing in particular; I just gazed. As my coffee cooled a little, I began to sip it and standing there – looking out over the enormous variety of buildings, some having stood since Victorian days, others now derelict, then some new build – I could see green gently rising beyond the town, with a promise of fresh air and freedom. It gave me a much-needed mental break.

The day progressed; I never did get any lunch. There was a case conference to attend for an absent social worker, the usual mountain of referrals not even looked at from previous days and two conversations with schools about concerns they had about children in their care. In between all this, I had to make sure that all the recordings were updated so nothing was left until the next day. The hours whizzed by and I found myself glancing at the clock and seeing it was nearly four thirty. Duty stopped at five and I might just have time to clear up some issues on my own caseload after that time, but I had to get all these reports written up on the people I had seen that day.

I tried to concentrate even harder and not waste a moment. I was getting on well when the phone rang. It was reception. 'There's a Mrs Arnold here, and she would like to speak to a duty worker.'

I put down my pen, picked up the standard referral pad for duty, took a quick drink of my very cool coffee and stood up slowly. I hoped this would be a simple issue. I really was feeling shattered, and still had so much to do.

I walked off down the stairs – it was my new resolution to avoid using the lift as much as possible, but going down was the easy part! I went over to the reception desk, and asked where Mrs Arnold was. Pritti pointed to a very elegant lady sitting in the corner, looking through her handbag.

I walked over to her and introduced myself. I had the choice of duty rooms, so was able to pick the comfy one with a nice big window, and before long we were sitting down together.

Mrs Arnold was beautifully dressed; indeed, she could

have walked off the pages of an exclusive fashion magazine. She was immaculately made up. She was of Asian
descent, and her hair, glossy and dark, hung in a shortly
styled fashionable bob. I was horribly conscious that I
had not had time to look at, let alone brush, my hair
since I got dressed this morning. She was, without exaggeration, simply stunning, and clearly very expensively
clothed.

I was aware that she had been watching me, as if trying
to assess me, but as we sat down, she immediately asked
me whether I was local. I told her that I lived some fair
distance away and asked her how I could help. My response
seemed to reassure her. She fell silent, and then became
rather agitated. She then paused, took a long breath and
spoke, 'I don't know how to begin,' she said. 'It's my
daughter, well, no, it's my husband, well . . .' She stopped
and seemed to be thinking hard as if she was psyching
herself up for what she had to say. I said quietly to her,
'Look, take your time. There's no hurry.'

She glanced up at me and then began to speak, jumping
in as if from a springboard. 'Well, you see, my husband
hits me, always has.' She rolled up her blouse sleeve to
reveal some old bruises on her arm and they weren't a
pretty sight. 'He began within months of our marriage
and that was twenty years ago. I was very young and there
was always an excuse. I ruined a meal or he was tired and
something I said annoyed him. If I wasn't at home to
cook before he came in, he would fly into a rage. If he'd
had a bad day at work, and he often had, the slightest
thing and he would fly into a rage. If I said the wrong
thing . . . Oh, I could go on and on, but I came to believe

fairly quickly that it was all my fault. He always said it
was. I had annoyed him or upset him. I really believed
that I was a hopeless wife and, although I hated hiding
bruises, I didn't even tell my friends because I was too
ashamed. He was clever; he rarely hit me where it would
show. Oh, we have an enormous home, with every possible luxury, but I have lived all the years of our marriage
in fear of upsetting him.'

She paused and looked hesitant, then continued, 'He
never touched my daughter, until last month. My daughter
is a young teenager and I know they can be irritating, but
. . . well, she was very rude to my husband and that was
it: there was an almighty row and he lashed out horrendously at my daughter. I decided that this was a one-off
and told my husband he must never touch her again. He
was always very sorry the next day, either that or he
denied that he had done anything much. He always had
an excuse, but would never take responsibility. That time
with my daughter, he excused himself on the grounds of
having had a very difficult case that day. So we moved on.
But it has happened twice more and last night my husband did it again: he beat my daughter. I thought he was
going to kill her. It's one thing my stupidly choosing to
live on and accept this behaviour, but no way will I allow
my daughter to suffer as I have done.'

She stopped and looked straight at me, continuing in
a quieter voice, 'I don't really know what to do. I have
no family apart from my elderly mother, whom I can't
bring into this as she is not well. Whatever the cost, I am
going to make it on my own. I am going to leave him.
My daughter is with her school friend at the minute and

I am going there after this meeting. My husband thinks it will all be forgotten but this is one step too far. But I don't know how to handle this, I . . .'

At this point I watched this woman move from perfectly composed to completely distraught within seconds. I am not sure if I ever recall such an appallingly fast transition. I think that her self-control had been so tightly holding her in up to that point, that as soon as a chink came in her defences, the floodgates opened. She broke down and sobbed. She cried for her own lost years, the end of her own dreams, the end of her marriage, her now-destroyed hopes, her own stupidity as she harshly described her own leniency towards her husband – it was desperately sad. At one point she looked up at me and said, 'You know this will destroy my husband. He is a notable surgeon in the Midhaven Hospital region. He won't live this down if it gets out.'

Slowly, she began to calm down a little, so we could talk through her options. We talked about what action she wanted to take, about women's refuges if she really felt unsafe and legal advice, which she certainly needed, and we talked about her husband and his behaviour. She needed to know that all this was her husband's responsibility, that she was not to blame. Violence had been his chosen way to control things and people around him; it was his choice and he alone was in a position to take action to resolve his problem. She listened with interest to my words and clearly found the view that it was not what she had done that had led to the problems quite transforming. That all his words and violence had been the work of a bully was a thought that really hit her because she replied, 'The advice I always knew about bullying was that one should always stand up to them and that is what I need to do.'

There was a stronger note to her voice. She had a tough time ahead – her husband would doubtless beg her to return and then she would have a difficult decision to make: stand firm and force him to deal with himself, knowing he might never do that, or return to a lifetime of uncertainty and bullying.

Eventually she sat back and I could see this had cost her so much. In exchange for financial security and a good life she had lived with fear and abuse, accepting, as so many women sadly do, that the beatings were provoked by herself, that she was to blame and therefore if only she had behaved differently, the violence would stop. No, this is the myth put about by bullies – people who choose to use their tempers to bully others. It is often their partners they bully but it could be others. Experts say that this is learned behaviour and that over half of offenders had violent fathers. They saw it work so use it as a strategy. Other men just learn that shouting and violence work in their need to control or dominate.

The one thing, and perhaps one of the most important, that women need to understand, is that it is repeated because it works. The anger and violence is quite simply a tactic to intimidate and take control and get their own way. Unless there are consequences, they continue to use this strategy. Some men do not need to resort to physical beatings; they will use psychological tactics, engendering fear by banging violently on walls or doors, breaking things or driving recklessly or destroying their partner's self-esteem with negative put-downs or name-calling. It is common for such behaviour to move on in time to more hands-on physical abuse.

It was tragic to think that this woman had waited until her own daughter was bullied to take action. On the other hand, now she had made her stand I could almost see something in her grow, her self-esteem, knowing that at last she would stand firm against her lifetime of bullying.

As Mrs Arnold left, clutching the standard leaflets that we had cause to hand out all too often in a week, we shook hands and she looked at me, saying, 'Thanks for listening, and for your advice. I know it's me that has to act now and I don't think it's going to be easy, so wish me luck.'

She made her way out. Her next call was A & E to get her daughter checked out, as I had told her to ensure she was seen as this would be evidence, if necessary, aside from the need to check for hidden injuries. It would be hard, but I so hoped she would find the strength to do what she needed to do for herself. The police would deal with her husband; they most certainly knew how to cope with bullies.

12

Settling In

Martin began to fall into the routines of his new home. I spoke to him frequently, visited as often as I possibly could and got to know Mrs Bridges (Kathy) very well. She rang if she was puzzled or needed to talk through things that arose. I talked at length with her when Martin was 'throwing up issues', and tried to give her the support and encouragement she needed in these early days. For the non-social-worker reader, I would just add that 'throwing up issues' in Martin's case was a varied activity. On occasions it meant silent withdrawal, sometimes for long periods. On others it involved sulky, uncooperative and plain rude behaviour, or complete and uncontrolled loss of temper, accompanied by stomping, raging, abusive language and sometimes, the hurling of anything within reach when the mood struck!

When the object in question was a large sports bag containing most of his school books, which he hurled with enormous force across the sales floor of a well-known clothing shop, Kathy confessed to be in need of a long quiet sit that evening. And, oh yes, she has made a mental note not to 'grace' that particular retailer with her custom for some time. Fortunately, she told me, there is a high turnover of staff!

Will and Kathy were experienced in helping youngsters

who had never acquired the techniques to calm themselves down. Martin was as unable as any raging toddler
to restrain his anger outbursts so Kathy had to employ
all her skills to help him. She worked constantly, and
deliberately, to reinterpret the world to Martin, slowly
helping him to see other perspectives and interpretations
to things that would otherwise prove to be overwhelming
for him. They endlessly encouraged him to put his anger
and rage into words and, once he was calmer, helped him
to see other ways of dealing with his jumble of feelings.

A particularly good illustration of this, which Kathy
had related to me in great detail, occurred at school.
Apparently Martin had become convinced that another
boy, a generally quiet and innocuous boy from another
year up, was 'always staring at him'. One day, Martin
finally challenged the boy in the playground and the boy
denied ever having even set eyes on Martin before. Martin,
of course, thought the boy was 'having a laugh, at his
expense' (Martin's words) and saw mockery and derision
in the boy's response. So Martin exploded, leading to a
dramatic playground fight – delighting all the boys, who
fell into a primeval circle to chant support (despite having
absolutely no idea of what was happening). Not surprisingly, none of this went down too well with the teacher
on duty – fortunately, the games master – a gentle but
very firm giant of a man, who hauled the two boys unceremoniously to the headmaster. The boys were made to
wait while parents were called in. The school nurse admin-
istered plasters and before long the headmaster's study
was full of all the individuals involved, including parents.
A prolonged debate ensued in an attempt to make some

sense of this event, but to no avail. They say truth is often stranger than fiction. This was.

Oliver (known to his friends as Ollie), the victim of Martin's misconceptions, had been completely stunned at being set upon in this way, was unable to see how he could possibly have provoked Martin's rage and was completely at a loss to understand why it had arisen. It so happened that his best friend had been called in as an independent witness and, unusually for a teenage boy, he had listened carefully to what was being said, processed it sensibly and suddenly a thought occurred to him. All of a sudden, he spoke up, saying to his friend, 'You know, Ollie, you do tend to have a habit of staring at people. I've noticed that, but I always thought it was just one of those things, or perhaps you thought more than the rest of us!' The room fell silent; everyone looked at Ollie, who clearly felt extremely discomforted by this revelation.

It was the headmaster, Mr Hanson, who spoke next. 'Oliver, do you have any problems with your vision? Can you, for example, read that notice by the exam room out there?' Ollie looked out of the window in the direction of the building pointed to, and everyone watched while he increasingly screwed up his face in a vain attempt to focus on the building, looking rather confused and anxious. Slowly, all the participants in this small drama (except Martin that is), began to latch on to a revolutionary insight. It was Mr Hanson who put an end to the boy's suffering by gently saying, 'You can't see the notice at all can you, Oliver?' His mother immediately jumped in with, 'Oh no, that explains a lot. How could I have missed this?'

It transpired that Oliver had become very short-sighted

over a relatively short period of time and, in fact, had never knowingly set eyes on Martin, let alone made him the focus of any campaign of mockery. He had doubtless gazed blindly on many a boy in the school, unaware of the fact that his gaze might settle for oddly long periods of time on someone's face, giving the impression of 'staring' at them.

Martin was utterly shaken by this and took quite a while to comprehend the whole situation, almost as if he was reluctant to lose a grip on his own sense of having been wronged and then have to grasp the knock-on implications for his own behaviour. Kathy had slowly helped him to understand that this, like most of the frustrating and unpleasant things others may appear to do to us in life, are not really deliberate but have lots of other reasons, often unknown to us, so don't justify a response of rage – indeed, they don't justify a response at all. It's a tough lesson for a child reared on contempt and mockery, to learn not to read the world as always 'out to get you' at every opportunity.

I was told by Kathy that the whole incident had been handled really well by the school. Ollie, who was a really decent kid, ended up becoming on quite chatty terms with Martin – once his bruises had healed and he was sporting a smart new pair of glasses! Ollie's resilient attitude greatly helped Martin too; it certainly challenged his outlook on life!

Kathy and her husband, Will, knew this would be a long job, with many setbacks, but every time Martin lapsed into rage they helped him to calm down. Then they got him to listen to them, think through his own reactions and see things differently. They knew he was learning strategies that would, one day, enable him to cut into the angry feelings himself, before they got out of control. Will was always there in the background. He involved Martin in lots of sport, which is a brilliant way to burn off excessive angst and learn how to co-operate with others. On Saturdays the two of them would usually be found making off for the match in town. It quickly became clear that Martin had both a gift and passion for football, which was great.

I was never too busy to talk to Kathy; she was the sort of person who makes social work worthwhile. She was coping with Martin, and he was settling. There were bad days, some very bad, and when Kathy rang to update me about a particularly bad time, I often feared that this would be the one that would break their commitment. But they kept on saying what was true – that problems had to be expected and that they were working their way through them.

There were problems at school with another boy. New boys usually have to take some flak before 'the pack' let them in, but this was extra tough for Martin because he was already riddled with insecurities and low self-esteem. Inevitably, Martin wasn't going to find it easy to cope with some rather unpleasant attempts to bully him and, on one particular day, he exploded in truly dramatic style. His reaction terrified both the young woman staff member dealing with the incident and, I understand, the perpetrator too! Kathy and Will went straight into school and helped to calm Martin down. They then managed to get to the bottom of the problem and, more importantly, showed Martin that they were there to support him and that there were ways to deal with unfairness without exploding.

The head was unusually wise, and tough, and he had worked with Kathy and Will before and knew them well; between them there was trust and respect, which helped greatly. He had the offending boy into his room and insisted that he apologised to Martin for the bullying, and the boy received a meaningful punishment. The head also spent a long time with Martin and talked at length about controlling anger and what to do if he felt like this again. Martin too had some reparation to do for his lost temper. Indeed, lessons were learnt all round. In fact, the headmaster went out of his way to establish an open door for Martin in the early months and gave him small responsibilities to feel more a part of the school.

It had been a deeply considered decision on the part of the head to accept Martin into his school, for which all of us were very grateful. Most of the schools I had approached had found reasons why they were unable to take him. Some, I'm sure, were quite genuine. Others – well, Martin was not an easy child to take on board, definitely high risk, so I understood their reluctance. He was unlikely to do much to enhance their league tables, in the short run anyway. Several past teachers had commented that they believed Martin was actually a very bright boy and that it was only his seriously neglectful background that had caused him to be so unable to cope with his schoolwork. He couldn't cope, no kudos there then, so he chose to 'muck about in class' and be a generally disruptive influence. Sadly, his very poor school performance had seriously contributed to his poor self-esteem, further exacerbating his problems. There was only one way to get over this: he needed help, and a lot of it.

Kathy was great, and made helping Martin with his work a priority, but he needed more. I looked about and found out what was available. I managed to get funding for Martin to join in with a special Saturday group which provided extra help in Maths, but working at the child's own pace and level, to build up their confidence. After two weeks of complaining about this group, Martin began to 'just go' and, after about six weeks, Kathy told me he actually came out with a quiet smile. It was the first time in his life that he had managed to successfully 'do' any Maths. For him, this must have been a gigantic step.

Also, the school decided, after much discussion with me, and of course Kathy, that Martin should take Maths lessons with a younger group until he had gained some mastery of the subject, rather than struggle in a completely dispirited way in his year group. We all appreciated the help of this school. Kathy and I talked through Martin's educational problems and she shared my commitment to helping him at school. She bought tapes to teach him tables, sat with him through taxing homework and read with and to him in an evening before supper. Yes, he was thirteen years old but he had never been read to in his life; he had never enjoyed hearing stories or had poetry read to him. Well he was now! Kathy was seeing to that!

Regular reading is something I have always believed to be particularly important for foster children, apart from any educational benefits, books, perhaps more than anything else, introduce new ways of looking at the world and gaining empathy, something many foster children have not developed in their lives, and which they need so much.

Martin's kitten became his devoted friend, slept on his bed, met him at the door from school, followed him around and comforted him when he was not happy with the rest of the family – which sometimes he was definitely not! I used to call Tibs the Second, 'therapy in fur'. Oh yes, serious therapy: always patient, always loving and always there for him, totally devoted to Martin alone. Who needs more than that?

I knew that Kathy and Will were growing increasingly fond of Martin, but Kathy would sometimes say how hard she found it that Martin would never allow her to so much as pat him on the shoulder, nor would he look her straight in the eyes. I just kept on encouraging her to spend time one-to-one with Martin, take him out for odd treats at his favourite eating places, and sit, talk and listen, just work on building up the bond between them. She would try to involve him in things she was doing and make him understand that he was both valued and impor-tant – something that was an entirely new concept to him and hard for him to believe or accept.

What I relate now was on one morning some seven months or so later. I had rushed into work early to finish off some court papers and was knee deep in files when my desk phone rang. My immediate response was, oh no, not another problem, but when I picked up the receiver it was Kathy.

Her voice was strange, and she said, 'Becky, I just had to ring you. Martin has just left for school so I can talk. You need to hear this.'

My heart missed a beat and I felt immediately tense with anxiety. What had happened? Had it all broken down? What was it? Had Martin done something really terrible? Before I had time to continue with my fearful thoughts, Kathy launched into her tale.

With a somewhat emotional voice, rather unlike her usual calm self, Kathy told me that last night Martin had come in from school and seemed different – agitated, restless, seething with suppressed excitement. Then all of a sudden he came up to her where she was busy in the kitchen, peeling the vegetables in fact, and announced, with a shy grin, that he had been appointed captain of the football first team for the new season. Kathy said she was so proud and excited with him that she had spontaneously hugged him, forgetting his usual dislike of any contact, and for the first time ever he returned her hug, pulled away from her, looked her straight in the eyes and said, 'Thanks Kathy, thanks for putting up with me!'

Kathy was clearly so happy, so proud of his achievement, thrilled that their relationship had moved on to this new level of openness, indeed she was on cloud nine . . . and I could tell she was in tears. If I tell you I too had more than a few tears in my eyes as she told me this tale, I think you'll understand. I have never managed to be totally detached with my neediest cases. We chatted on a little more, then I thanked Kathy for ringing me, and she just said, 'Well, I knew you would understand what this meant to me.'

And I did, I really did. Nothing else that could go wrong that day mattered – nothing. Martin was making enormous strides. Kathy and Will really had begun to transform his chances. There would still be many more ups and downs and I knew that there was no certainty but, my word, to this point they had worked a miracle.

13
Cassie

The day I met Cassie had been very busy. I had reports to submit on many cases, including Sarah and Martin, and various other appointments. Marie had asked me the week before if I would consider taking on two cases which were not likely to become court cases but needed to be allocated. Well, after some thought, I took them, not because I had any time, but because I, like all the team, accepted that some cases had to be checked out and time had to be found in our already very full days.

If this sounds lacking in enthusiasm, then I have misled you. I usually found a new referral challenging and exciting. You simply never knew who you were going to meet and what their particular problems would be. You could always be sure that every family you met would be totally different from every other, that the personalities involved would be new and that meeting them would be interesting and in many cases rewarding. I have never known a boring family – never. Human beings are so complex, so diverse and utterly fascinating. That was why I loved my job – simple as that.

One of the families I had taken on had a mother with learning difficulties and I had been thinking about going to chat with the team responsible for this area specifically, so that I could establish a supportive team approach

to working with this family. However, that would have to
wait for now because the other referral seemed to need
fairly speedy initial assessment. This had come, believe it
or not, from the lady who ran the local post office and
shop, and who had talked to this mother several times and
suspected she was in a mess and rarely got out. The post
office lady told us that she simply didn't know what level
of care the children were getting, but it looked worrying.

Because a fairly big meeting had been cancelled at the
last minute I had suddenly found myself with a slug of
time in my diary for the afternoon and I took the opportunity to ring the mother whom I had prioritised for a
visit. She was both at home and, in a somewhat passive
sort of way, seemed to be OK with me visiting. This was
a good start.

I searched my local map and quickly found the road I
needed. Briefcase in hand, I made for the car park, double-
checked the map, turned the key in the ignition and headed
off for Waterloo Street, which turned out to be a very
long road, lined with old, white-painted Victorian bay-
fronted houses, which in an earlier age must have been
home to prosperous residents. Now, sadly, the houses had
a look of extremely faded elegance. Indeed, the elegance
that had once been was now disguised by the peeling paint,
rotten woodwork and filthy windows. Most of the houses
were now split into flats, with rows of bells at the door
to summon any one of the many residents from within.

After several attempts to spot a number on the houses,
without hitting a bollard or worse, I gave up, parked in
a side road and walked back to the road to resume my
search. After a time, I got the hang of the numbering and

took a now-more-informed guess at the approximate position of the flat I was looking for. Yes, it was just after the next junction before the traffic lights. The triumph of eventually finding myself on the step of number 267 made the selection of the correct flat – a, b, c, d, e, or f – extremely simple in comparison. I pressed the intercom bell and waited.

After a short time, I heard the sound of a child's voice coming closer and then a quiet, slightly anxious-looking girl with long brown hair opened the door and waited for me to introduce myself. She was dressed in a pair of jeans and a rather grubby tee shirt, the standard uniform of most mothers of young children, branded with the sticky marks that probably represented breakfast, lunch and anything in between. On one hip she had a young baby, who looked to be an almost permanent attachment, and beside her stood a solemn-looking little girl with eyes like pools of deep water. The child was regarding me with a serious and thoughtful expression and there was a look of some considerable intelligence in her face. The child turned to look at her mother, and asked who I was. The girl dismissively said I was just a friend, and opened the door wider to let me through. The girl introduced herself as Cassandra, but added, 'Call me Cassie, I can't stand the name Cassandra.'

I followed her through to the rear of the building along a wide corridor, which must have led from what once had been an imposing hallway. The architraves and absolutely beautiful carved cornices along the hall and corridors spoke of an earlier, more affluent period in the history of this house and their presence seemed to emphasise the contrast between the past and present existences of this building. The dull cream paint was now peeling and the walls were laced with cracks of all sizes, running freely this way and that and covering the walls like some sort of asymmetrical and giant grey spider's web. The deep, carved skirting boards, with thick layers of paint from the past, were now – like the rest – kicked, chipped and badly marked.

All this seemed to sadly reflect the fall in status that this building had experienced during the course of the last one hundred years or so. Many families had come and gone under this roof – many tragedies, many joys – and somehow the fabric of the building continued to stand while ever more of the dramas of life unfolded under its watching presence.

At the end of the corridor we came to a door which led into Cassie's flat. It was scarcely more than two rooms. She told her daughter to go and play in the garden. The child disappeared out of the back door and Cassie leaned against the door-post, watching her walk out into the yard area. 'Garden!' she grimaced wryly. 'More like two paving stones with a couple of weeds for good measure.'

She turned to me and in her face I saw the same intelligent eyes I had noticed in her daughter, but in her eyes I also saw pain and anxiety. As she spoke again there was something rather dreamy in her expression and I felt as if she was looking beyond me at a picture from the past as she continued. 'You know I grew up with a real garden: a lawn, flowers, bushes and trees. We lived in the country; in what I guess you would call quite a big house. I ran free for miles with my sister and our dog, had a great childhood, really, really happy. I never imagined I'd be raising my own children in a poky, dilapidated little flat on the wrong side of a grim town . . .'

Cassie shrugged as if to shake off her mood and then looked at me and said, 'Oh, I'm sorry that's just how I feel, I seem to be in such a mess.' She put the baby down on the floor by the chair, and sat down heavily, running her hands through her hair, which fell in straggles about her face and shoulders. I found a space on her sofa, between the piles of washing and bags of stuff, and sat down, Cassie sat opposite me, silent and exhausted-looking. The baby seemed to accept his spot on the rug without comment, and lay kicking on the floor.

I began to speak, and said to Cassie, 'Look, I know you have been having a tough time. Perhaps we can chat about things.' Cassie looked up slowly, and said, 'You know, there's no point. I've so messed up my life, and my kids' lives. I simply don't know how I can cope any longer. I've tried to manage. I look after the children as well as I can, but I'm in a mess.' I leaned forward to Cassie and quietly said to her, 'What is it that makes you feel such a mess, Cassie? Could you talk to me about it?'

A long silence followed this question. Cassie now sat quite rigidly, twisting a tissue round and round in her hand, her head bowed. I noticed that she had begun to cry silently; tears ran down her face. On and off she rubbed her face harshly with her hand as if all semblance of gentleness had become irrelevant in her overwhelming misery. I waited for a little while and then said to her, 'I can see you feel very low. I really do think it would help if you could try to explain to me just how you are feeling.'

Cassie had stopped crying now and was just staring bleakly at her hands. Her daughter had come in from the outside and, seeing her mother upset, had taken up a position leaning closely against her, resting her arm on her mother while looking anxiously up into her face. At one point she turned to look at me and I could see that she was wondering how I fitted into all this.

Cassie finally lifted her head and looked at me. She then said, 'There is nothing you can do. I can't even cope with going out any more. I virtually never leave the flat, only a quick trip to the corner shop and post office.' She stopped speaking at this point, and seemed to be thinking about her words; once again, tears trickled down her face slowly, almost as if they also were lethargic with grief. I asked Cassie if she felt she could tell me about her feelings, and if they were new to her.

She took a breath and continued with an initially very blunt statement, saying, 'It all began at university.' As she said this she looked challengingly up at me, as if to spot any expression of surprise in my face. There was none, as it seemed very clear to me that here was a highly intelligent young woman, who would clearly have been at home in any university. She continued. 'I was always an A-grade student at school and managed to gain a place at a good university to study science, something I loved. My parents were so proud of me. It wasn't as easy as I thought to leave home and make new friends. I often felt as if I didn't fit in – so many of the students were full of confidence and seemed to find it easy to talk to everyone . . . I didn't. I really struggled.'

She paused and thought for a while, and then she continued, 'In my third term, I met another student, Barney. He was on my course and I really liked him and amazingly he seemed to like me, and we began to go around together. It was brilliant. Fairly soon I realised that he was a regular user of cannabis. He seemed to cope and didn't offer it to me, so it was OK. Then, one weekend, at an all-night party, he encouraged me to try some. I'd never done drugs and wasn't really very sure I wanted to, but Barney – my boyfriend – kept saying that I was too uptight and a few spliffs would help me to relax a bit so I would enjoy the evening more. He was quite insistent and I began to feel stupid for not trying it, so in the end I just thought, why not, it can't do any harm surely, so I joined him.'

She lapsed into silence and again took to studying her hands. You hear the expression 'wringing her hands' but don't often see it. Well, Cassie was wringing her hands continuously. Her daughter had squeezed into a crack beside her mother and was looking frightened. The baby still lay on the mat, oblivious to her mother's distress.

Cassie continued, and recalled to me the evening this all happened. 'What happened next is weird, it was terrifying.' She looked at me as if needing permission to go on. I prompted her, with a 'Yes', and she went on, now withdrawing behind her words as she relived that night.

'Well at first, really quickly, in fact, after I had smoked the joint he offered me, the music in the room seemed to become something else, moving, emotional, and even the room looked different, so strange. I felt powerful and calm all at once. I remember getting up to look out of the window and the world just looked so amazing, as if it had been washed clean. I couldn't stop just looking and drinking in the sight of this new world. But then, almost as suddenly, I began to experience a sort of out-of-body feeling, as if I wasn't there and no one could hear me. I began to feel a fear, of such an order that it was unbearable. I was absolutely terrified and was shouting and screaming for help but it seemed no one could hear me. I felt complete and utter panic. I really cannot describe it in any other way, the fear was so awful I thought I would die. In fact, that would have been a relief.'

Cassie stopped for a time, as if the recollection of that night had been too overwhelming for her and she needed to pause to take a breath. She then went on, in a quieter voice. 'As the time passed, I began to think that all the people in the room were talking about me, saying things I couldn't quite hear, mocking me. I began to shout at them but they didn't seem to hear me, and it all continued. All I remember then was curling up in a corner behind a large armchair and hiding myself. I don't know how long I stayed like that, but a long time.'

Again she paused as if there was more, so I didn't speak and she carried on. 'Eventually I came out of this. I still felt really odd but after a night's sleep I felt almost normal, but I had already decided that that was it, nothing on this earth would have made me go through that ever again. Barney dumped me – said I was, well, never mind, but I no longer cared what he thought. He didn't care about me and I knew that I couldn't do weed again. It was a short time later, when I was standing on a railway platform, that suddenly I felt this overwhelming fear come over me, indescribable, just like when I took the weed. I didn't know how to cope; I sat down and froze on a bench. Eventually a member of the staff took me to casualty at a nearby hospital. That happened again and again. I was pregnant by then, Barney's. So stupid of me . . .'

She stopped and then went on. 'It keeps happening, this overwhelming fear. I can't describe it because it's so intense, the most awful thing. Ever since then, I've been crippled by it; I never know when it will hit me or how badly. It's like sheer unadulterated panic and blind fear; my heart races so fast that I think I will die. I sweat, my stomach churns, but the worst thing is the intense fear, utter terror, such awful fear, just awful.'

For a moment she stopped, as if the recollection itself terrified her, then she continued. 'Then I begin to see people's faces, the looks, the comments they make to others they are with, and I know they are talking about me, laughing at me, saying things about me: its unbearable. I feel like I don't want to go out, because I know everyone knows what I'm like, and can see how scared I am. I see it in their faces. I don't want to be stared at or talked about . . . I'm scared enough already. So it's easier never to go out. I thought it would pass off in time; other people said it would. It hasn't.'

At this she turned to me, those intelligent eyes, bursting with fear and terror and desperate appeal. 'My life is over. I can't function and I'll never be able to look after my children.' After a pause she added, very quickly, as if she was afraid to speak out her worst fears, 'I think I am becoming mentally ill. I even wonder if I have schizophrenia. I haven't been to a doctor. I'm afraid of what they will say. Anyway, I haven't got a GP since I moved here. I haven't felt able to go out far, and anyway there's no point.'

Again she stopped, seeming to contemplate all of this, and then said – with such intensity that I found myself shocked to the core by the depths of her grief and frustration – 'Oh God, how I wish I had never touched that stuff. How I wish I could go back.' She continued, 'I've just about coped for a time, and even met someone. I thought that was it and we'd be together, but about nine months ago he just walked out, said I was weird and left me. I was stupid enough to have got pregnant and everything became even worse after I had the baby.'

After this she leaned back in her chair, head down, now slumped in a beaten posture and I found myself experiencing such a mix of feelings that I was having to take stock of my own reactions in order to cope with what had become a dangerously unpredictable situation. Clearly I could not leave her in this state and I had to do something about it this afternoon. By now, the baby had given up on patience and was demanding attention. It was as if Cassie could not even hear the child and the little girl had detached herself from her mother and was comforting the baby, like a little mother. This was not a new situation I was seeing; this child was clearly accustomed to caring for the baby when her mother withdrew. When, without any prompting, the little girl went off and returned with a bottle, my suspicions were confirmed. Cassie had so many needs herself that she really was not able at present to care for the children. She needed help, and now.

I began to ask Cassie about her family, and whether her parents were still alive. She replied, 'I think so. I've only got my parents and one sister, who was living near them. But I'm not in contact with them. They were so angry when I dropped out of uni that I just couldn't cope with it all, and I suppose I did a disappearing act.'

I looked at her face and struggled to read the expression there. I began to wonder – I thought what I saw was longing. 'Cassie, don't you think we should talk to your family?' Cassie jerked her head up, saying, 'Oh no, I couldn't. They were so angry and ashamed when I dropped out. They will never have forgiven me. I couldn't, I simply couldn't.' She paused and continued, 'If you had seen how proud they were when I won that place, and they simply couldn't understand why I dropped out. I felt so afraid and confused that I couldn't cope with their feelings as well.' Again she faltered, and then continued, 'That's why I decided to hide away and not contact them.'

'So you have had no contact since then – in over four years?'

Cassie looked up at me, and in a small voice replied, 'No I haven't been in touch.'

I talked. I tried to get Cassie to understand that her reaction was very much caused by her state of mind, rather than any reality. I asked Cassie how she felt her parents might be feeling not knowing where she was, and whether she was alright. Cassie thought silently for a long time, then said, 'I don't know, I suppose they might be worried, but I am such a failure. My father always respected hard work and success, not someone like me. Look at me; I don't want them to see me like this. They won't want to see me.' At this, she wept tears of agonising misery and it was very hard to listen to; she cried until she was exhausted. I made her a drink in the little kitchen area and encouraged her to drink something. She took a few gulps of tea and then I said, 'Cassie, I think we need to speak to your family. I can do it for you initially. We have to think of the children. You told me you're not coping, and I understand that this is all too difficult at present, but you need help.'

Cassie raised her eyes to my face and said, 'Can anyone help me? Can anything help me now?'

'Look, Cassie, you need medical help. In time, probably with medication and support, you will find a way through this, but you do need support. Would you agree to let me call your family?' Cassie looked beaten and tired; she looked down and very quietly, almost inaudibly said, 'OK.'

I decided not to hang about on this – in case she changed her mind – and I recalled her description of her 'happy childhood'. That sort of parent might be angry or puzzled by a child behaving unwisely but rejecting – I hoped not. I did have active concerns in my mind about her family, in spite of this, and what I hadn't said to Cassie was that in her present state of mind the children needed better care, and if the family could not help then we were into another scenario. I didn't want to go there yet. I told Cassie that I would not be long, and would ring from my car. This at least meant that I could respond to any comments without subjecting Cassie to any further hurt, particularly if her family were not interested.

I dashed off to my car, wishing it was closer, opened

the door and jumped in. With pen and paper to hand, I carefully dialled the number that Cassie had given me, praying that they had not moved. A firm, strong woman's voice answered, 'Hello.' I asked if that was Mary Toon and a slightly quieter, more cautious voice replied, 'Yes, who is that?' As carefully as I could, thinking hard how to say this, I replied, 'My name is Becky Hope. I'm a social worker in Barton and I wanted to talk to you about your daughter, Cassie.' A scream of agony assailed my ears as she replied, 'No, No, don't tell me! Don't tell me something has happened to her! Have you seen her, is she there, tell me, tell me!' And at this the poor woman broke down. I could only hear sobs and a near hysterical voice, and then I heard another voice on the line, a calmer, quietly spoken man, who said, 'What is this? I'm Cassie's father. Is she there?' I began to explain the situation to Mr Toon and before I had managed to get more than a few sentences out a choked voice said to me, 'Just give me her address. Please don't let her go anywhere. We'll be there in about two hours. It's a long drive; we're coming now. Please, please don't let her leave. Please.' He was clearly fighting to prevent himself from breaking down, and I had to repeat the address several times because he was so distraught. I also gave him my mobile number and office number so there could be no mistakes. I wanted them here as soon as possible – they had to be Cassie's best hope. Now I had spoken to them I felt more and more hopeful.

As I switched off my mobile, I just sat for a moment. I felt almost shell-shocked, the emotional content of the last few moments had been so intense. I took a few deep breaths, called round and cancelled all my appointments and then walked back to Cassie's home.

I sat with Cassie and the children for those hours. How long it seemed, how Cassie agonised and I sought to reassure her and talked to her about the future. When a ring at the door finally announced their arrival, Cassie froze and I had to answer the door.

The couple who faced me were about sixty; they were a solid-looking pair but looked completely distraught. Cassie's mother Mary was puffy-eyed and red-faced and her father was clearly extremely stressed. Just as I had begun to speak, a young woman ran up, smiled anxiously and said, 'I'm Cassie's sister, Ellen. Where's Cassie?' I tried to stop them briefly – to talk through the bare facts – but they were unable to hear, so great was their need to see their daughter, so basically I gave up and steeled myself for their shock. I ushered them through to the flat, where two very anxious children and a near-collapsed Cassie sat.

We walked through the door, and Mary gasped, rushed across to Cassie and hugged her like she would never let her go. I heard her say, 'Cassie, oh Cassie, we've searched everywhere for you. We've even hired detectives to find you. We thought we'd lost you,' and then she sobbed, but so did Cassie. There was such lot of crying and hugging that I didn't notice initially that Cassie's father had stepped back because he had noticed the children. Very soon he was sitting on the floor with the little girl and the baby. He looked up at me and asked, 'Cassie's?' His beaming smile to my nodding assent told me all I needed to know, and he added, 'They had to be, the little girl is an exact replica of Cassie.'

Ellen was holding the baby and as Cassie emerged from her mother's embrace Ellen went over to Cassie and hugged her, saying, 'Cassie, please come home.' We did a great deal of talking and finally it was agreed by all that Cassie would stay with her parents while she had treatment for her anxiety state and her parents, and sister, who lived nearby, would help to care for the children. Cassie's mother summed up their feelings. 'We began to think this day would never come. We thought we would never see Cassie again. It has been a long, long nightmare. However long it takes we'll stick with it.' I watched her as she looked across at Cassie, her face so full of love for her daughter, then saw her gaze fall on the children and a warm smile fell across her face. Yes this was good; this was a family at its best.

I left them all to talk and settle down. There were things I needed to raise and warn about, but this was not the time. Before they left in the morning, I called in to take all their details, and I spent time with the family, encouraging Cassie to explain how she had felt and why she had behaved as she did. As Cassie described her feelings of having failed them, her father sank his head into his hands and said that he had never wanted to make her think she was a failure and that they loved her no matter what she did, or didn't do. Her parents were horrified to hear how Cassie felt, and they became very subdued and thoughtful. I think they all moved forward a little and the best thing was the fact that they were all prepared to listen.

As I left, her father shook my hand and said, 'I understand that things will be difficult at times and we have a long way to go in supporting Cassie, but we'll do it. We're not losing our daughter twice!'

I had occasional contact with the family. Cassie was put on treatment and it was actually a long haul to some level of normal functioning for her. The doctors thought that she would probably be on medication for life but at least she was on the road to a form of recovery. Her parents threw themselves into the care of their grandchildren and life continued. The last time I spoke to Mary, she said, 'Well, we had lost one member of the family but now we've gained three! It's great!' In spite of the wonderful family response, this was a very sad case. Read the internet reports on cannabis or accept at face value the words of other people and you may come away believing it is nothing more than a recreational experience. Read the findings that are beginning to trickle through from the very latest medical research and there is another side. What is more, the cannabis on the streets now is vastly stronger than in the past. There is no doubt that Cassie was very unlucky in her reaction after one night's dabbling with weed, but this is a real risk. Usually, such a reaction is only after longer-term use but some people do react like this after a first try and no one can predict who will have a similar experience and who will be lucky. Cannabis messes up the wiring in the brain, which is why it can trigger mental illness, severe anxiety, depression, paranoia, even schizophrenia. Physically, it increases the risk of cancer and heart disease. But no one tells the new users all this because there is money to be made; dealers are getting rich but who is paying the price?

This was not a case I ever recall without sadness. Such a bright independent girl, with such a bright future, all destroyed in a night.

14

Julie

Sarah's situation was gradually moving on. From the outset it was clear to all involved that contact sessions with the mother were strained. These sessions were usually set up in the local Family Centre and a member of staff had the responsibility of 'supervising' the meeting. Contact was important because, when a child has been removed from a family, ongoing family interaction should be maintained until either the child is returned home or longer-term care plans are put in place – at which point contact with the family should be established in a way that best serves the wellbeing of the child.

Over the weeks since Sarah had been taken into care, Julie was often very late for contact meetings and a couple of times she forgot to come altogether. Sometimes it was suspected that she was high on something, at other times there was a suspicious smell of alcohol about her person. It was a frequent event for it to be reported that she had spent her time reading a women's magazine at contact, and often had little time for Sarah at all, just making the very barest of attempts to interact. Sarah said little after these contact sessions but reacted silently with the inevitable wet beds, disturbed sleep and very difficult behaviour at school.

Before her birthday, Sarah was getting very excited

about the prospect of a party and presents and, during contact the weeks before, her mother had made repeated promises in terms of presents, building up Sarah's hopes. Sadly, when the pre-birthday meeting with her mother took place, nothing appeared, her mother arrived both an hour late and empty-handed. The long-promised bike, the puzzle and the skipping rope – all evaporated in vague excuses. Not even a card. Sarah's birthday was low down the list of priorities for her mother. Sarah's behaviour at the remainder of this contact session was of hesitation and confused silence, but later her hurt came out in tremendously angry outbursts and terrifying nightmares, plus some fights at school. This was the culmination of months of disappointment with her mother's disinterested behaviour.

The cynical reader may wonder at the child having any faith in her mother's promises, but children always hope, and rarely give up on the idea that maybe, just maybe, their parent cares about them. Sadly, material 'stuff' assumes a huge emotional importance; it represents all the love and care they have never had.

Patty handled it all well but it was a hard time for her too. There were times when she admitted to feeling really angry with Sarah's mother. But she knew she must never allow Sarah to even glimpse how she found herself feeling, as she stood alongside Sarah through all these hurts. Patty had been a foster carer for a long time and had an understanding of the backgrounds of some of these children. It can be hard for foster carers to deal with the hurts of a child they are growing to love. But the families of these children often live such chaotic lives that all their energies are bound up with their own problems and issues; there is little space to worry about a child's feelings. A child cannot understand this, but foster carers do learn to understand, even though it is hard.

Among the many tasks ahead of me in Sarah's case was to begin an assessment of her mother.

I had spent time with Julie explaining the process, explaining that I would need to talk with her about herself and her life, and I had arranged a meeting. A week later, I arrived at her door at the agreed time and knocked. There was silence; I knocked again, waited, then opened the letterbox and called through, 'Julie, its Becky, could I come in please?' A further silence ensued and then I thought I could hear something. As I continued to stand on the doorstep, I suddenly realised that I was being observed by a small grubby face, peeping through from next door. The child, probably about five, dressed in trousers and top with a short crop could not be identified as boy or girl. I suspected the latter because of the stillness and concentration in the face as I was observed! The child continued to stare at me, so I smiled and said hello. This was met with silence and then, out of the blue, 'it' spoke, clearly establishing itself as a girl! In a confident voice, as if she had been at least thirty-five years old and talking to a friend, she said, 'She's in you know. A bit of a rough night. I couldn't get no sleep for the racket. She's probably sleeping.' There was a pause, more silence. Then the child added most helpfully, 'I should knock a bit harder!' I suspected the child was spot-on in her diagnosis of the unanswered knock. I was saved further thought by the door beginning to creak open, which appeared to be the signal for my newest friend to scuttle very quickly away out of sight.

Julie stood there looking half asleep, but when I reminded her of our appointment she allowed me through. I almost felt that this was easier for her than refusing. She had had some legal advice and I think she had been encouraged to co-operate over the assessment, so perhaps things would become easier. I walked through into Julie's living room. There were clear signs that Julie had just emerged from the blankets on the sofa, though it was very dark in the room and hard to see much. I asked Julie if I could open the curtains, and she responded to this with a vague nod. As Julie was clearly not going to make any attempt to do this, I moved to pull them back myself. Sitting in the dark was not a pleasant way to conduct an interview, though I had been obliged to do so once or twice when interviewing individuals who were so scared of being seen that they literally lived in the dark with every chink of light stifled.

Once the light hit the room, I could then see what can most easily be described as the remnants of Julie's 'rough night'. There were empty cans, bottles and food crushed into the carpet, among a generalised muddle. Mind you, much of this had clearly been there a while. I found myself a seat and sat where I could more easily engage with Julie. She sat huddled in a corner of the sofa, making no eye contact at all. She looked really grim: her skin was grey, her hair hung in tatters and she looked as if she scarcely ate at all.

Slowly but surely I encouraged her to talk a little about herself. Initially her responses were in terms of, 'I dunno, how am I supposed to remember,' or, 'I don't think so,' or, 'Can't remember.' It was clear to me that having someone 'talk' to her, and ask her questions about her-self, was completely alien. I suggested she make herself a coffee as she looked genuinely tired out.

We resumed the conversation. Julie's posture was a little more positive – no longer huddled – but her replies were still limited. I totally understood that I was seen as 'the enemy', the one who came into her life and caused all sorts of trouble for her, and who had removed Sarah. I did understand that she would be angry – she probably hated me – but she and I had to establish some sort of relationship if we stood a chance of moving forward. It wasn't easy. Parents usually came to see that we as in-dividuals were only a small part of the process; they also realised that to help themselves they needed to work with us. On my side, I had to create a workable relationship or I could help neither child nor family.

Julie began to talk haltingly about her own mother; her memories were not good. Her initial comments on her mother were worded, 'I was just a bloody nuisance: she never wanted us kids and she hated me.' She paused and added, 'I didn't care, that's just how it was.' Julie retreated into thought. I remained silent as she was clearly dwelling on something. Julie then spoke again, almost as if I was not in the room, so deeply had she revisited her past, 'Yeah, me mum hated me alright. She was OK with me brother, I always thought she hated me most 'cos I was a girl.' She paused again, adding, 'I dunno really.'

So as not to break her chain of thought, I remained quiet. Julie was at least thinking about things. After another silence, in which I could almost hear Julie's thoughts churning through her past, she finally spoke again, saying, 'You know, me mum used to lock me out all night quite often. Well, you know, if her boyfriends were over I was in the way. I had nightmares, which annoyed them, so . . . I s'pose it was understandable, but I made sure I got meself to school next day, even if I'd spent the night in the old privy. They'd never got rid of it once the council put the inside toilets in, so it was a coal store. Just as well it was there – quite cosy I made it. Me brother would sneak me some bread if I was lucky. The school didn't seem to notice. I'd say I fell on the way to school. I liked school: it was warm, and I always had some food there.'

She paused again, still clutching her hands together and, looking down at them, she seemed to be oblivious to my presence, and then suddenly a slow strained smile crept into her face. 'Oh, and there was Mrs Evans, now she was kind and I think she must have liked me, because she would often give me an extra bottle of milk and a banana from the kitchens. She sat with me and talked to me. I liked her.'

At this point I asked her whether she had ever told the teachers she had been out all night. Her response was matter of fact: 'Naah, none of their business.' As with all her recollections, it was clear that Julie regarded her childhood as not really that much different from others and most of its cruelties as just part of life. To be fair, how would any child know their life was not like others? For most children, what they experience in childhood is normal and they assume others have the same or similar experiences.

Over the weeks, Julie became more open, telling me of

her childhood and then about her life as a teenager, when suddenly her mother had more time for her. Julie talked with pride about her mother's new interest in her and failed to understand that her better position in the family was because she was a young woman whose charms could earn money for the family! I began to feel I was beginning to understand Julie better, and we formed a relationship that worked. She often didn't like things I said and did, and would say so loudly. Fair enough, I still had to do them, but she nevertheless began to enjoy talking about her life.

I secretly hoped that I could help her to see things more clearly, not because I believed she was likely to ever make Sarah a good parent, but because to hear all this and not hope you could encourage someone to seek help for themselves would be impossible. I often left her home feeling a sense of overwhelming sorrow. For whom? Well, for Julie initially, then for Sarah and for all that might have been.

I had known from our records that Julie's parents were known drug dealers, and heavily addicted themselves. But listening to her personal recollections made it all so much more real, and that Julie saw her neglect and abuse throughout her childhood as normal, and a consequence of her troublesome behaviour, was seriously thought-provoking. Although some parts of her story had been known to the authorities in her childhood, no investigations were pursued and nothing was ever acted upon.

I often found myself wondering what Sarah's life would have been like had her own mother been adopted out of the hell-hole in which she had existed throughout her pitiful childhood. By leaving Julie in that home, the damage had been carried onwards to the next generation. Sarah ultimately paid the price, as of course did her mother Julie, whose adult life has been one of endless abusive relationships, addiction and inability to cope.

As I worked for innumerable hours on the court reports for Sarah's case, a picture built up that testified to Sarah's equally tragic life. Neighbours, once they realised that Sarah was in care, came forward, in confidence, for everyone was afraid of Matthew. The neighbours told of hearing the uproars, hearing Sarah screaming and crying herself to sleep. Another neighbour, a decent old chap who lived opposite the family, told me his story, again in confidence. In so doing, among other things, he unwittingly substantiated the story about the dog's appalling end, saying that Matthew had boasted about it one night in the pub.

Unbeknown to Sarah, she had many silent and concerned watchers; what a pity they had all remained silent. It's perhaps a hard, counter-cultural act to report your neighbours, but the cost to the child in failing to do so can be very high – very high indeed. Perhaps everyone thought that someone else would speak up.

School reports showed that Sarah had barely been in school for more than 50 to 60 per cent of the previous three years. Where did people think the child was? Why did they think she was absent? There was even a note on the file from many years ago, saying that a council plumber had rung in because of what he saw during a visit, and his concerns about the little girl in the home.

As time went on, and Sarah felt less under threat about what she said, she began to confide in those around her

– a teaching assistant at her school and, of course, Patty. Little casual comments, matter-of-fact for Sarah, but, to the adult recipient of these confidences, chilling. Nightmare scenarios began to emerge as Sarah innocently alluded to the drugs parties, the violent altercations with dealers calling or, sometimes, when her mother was off her head on drugs and alcohol, of hiding in the dark and terrifying garden shed all night to avoid the attentions of one particular man. She was clearly extremely anxious about this man and didn't want to discuss him; we could only hope she had managed to keep him at bay.

The process for children in Sarah's position was to twin-track our efforts, so we would work with the family and also look at what would happen if the family could not meet the child's needs. There was the assessment and also a very exhaustive procedure involving talking to everyone who was involved with the family. Relatives, health workers, GPs, hospital records, school contacts past and present and a trawl through the usually vast files we had in-house on families who had already been on our radar. Often, old files would, when carefully read, reveal much that had been overlooked and as the months went by a picture slowly began to emerge, rather like a giant jigsaw puzzle.

Clearly, we often suspected that some families were unlikely to be capable of successfully parenting their child. However, one could never assume that. Much could change if there was the will. Undesirable and violent partners could be shown the door, parenting skills could be worked on, health issues could be addressed and supportive family home workers could be provided. The further problem of drug and alcohol addiction, which is present in many of the families we work with, is a tougher call. We always set up counselling with the appropriate agencies but addiction always makes working with these families much more challenging. Not because people cannot get off the drugs or alcohol, but because even when they do get off, relapse is a common event and is hard to predict.

The average person learns coping mechanisms to deal with the stresses of life. Over the years, we slowly find our own strategies and supports, and learn to 'get through' difficult times. When drugs and alcohol have been those very support strategies, as they have for addicts, perhaps from their early teens, when those supports are given up, they are left a very vulnerable person.

This is someone without any of the normal support strategies to cope, and when they feel stressed, as we all do in life at times, without a great deal of support, they will be likely to do what we all do when we are stressed, and crave their comfort strategy. For an ex-addict tragically this can so often be the alcohol or drugs they have turned to routinely in their past, starting off another downwards spiral for them.

Placing a child back with a recently clean addict always carries considerable risk because you are loading stress – the care of often disturbed children – onto someone with poor coping mechanisms, and so increasing the risk of relapse.

All these tremendously difficult issues have to be addressed. At the same time, we pursue long-term care options, adoption or long-term fostering as appropriate.

*

In spite of all I could do, Sarah's mother was simply unable to give up the drugs or drink; she did not attend any of the offered groups. Sometimes she showed up once, and then had excuses for the times thereafter. It was clear that she was a much-damaged person, totally unable to bring her life around to a position in which Sarah could receive any real parenting, basic care or protection.

On the other extremely positive side, Sarah had blossomed with Patty. The school said she was unrecognisable; she was progressing for the first time in her life, learning to read properly, and was happy. Physically, in place of the skinny, wan little waif she had been, she had gained weight, had roses in her cheeks, her hair shone and she no longer fell asleep in the afternoons at school. A smaller but significant change was that she no longer smelt, went to school in filthy clothes or had nits, which Patty had dealt with in the early days, so consequently she was making friends. This was a first for Sarah and made her feel good in a way that she had never experienced. Sarah had always been the child teased and avoided as 'smelly Sarah', always on her own in the playground, always treated as a social outcast. The day Sarah had her very first friend for tea, Patty told me she had been unable to sleep with excitement the night before. Probably no surprise then that she had fallen out with the friend long before tea had been consumed!

Sarah loved being with Patty, but Patty was only a short-term foster carer and was not in a position to take on a total commitment for a child long term. I had been looking into long-term options and the shared view was that Sarah could well be adopted by one of the many families looking for a child. If the judge decided that it was in Sarah's best interests not to return home, and if we could find the right family, Sarah stood a chance of a whole new life with all the opportunities that were available. This was a step that involved a great deal of work, but I was determined that I was not going to have this child languishing in the care system when I knew there were many families out there who wanted to adopt. Sarah had many strengths that would enable her to adjust well to such a change; she might have an opportunity to have a whole new start. I just wanted her to have a chance.

15

Out of Control

I opened my eyes to what promised to be a grey day. Well, the light in my bedroom was certainly grey, but perhaps . . . I prised myself out of bed (another late night had stolen my spring) and walked over to the window, pulling back the curtains hopefully. All hope was abandoned at that point. The grey skies hung menacingly over the world and the clouds were being blown mercilessly across this grey scene. Trees were bending right over, yielding to the power of the wind, rather as if this had become preferable to fighting. As if that was not enough, the sound of the wind was like some clip from a horror film – a sort of moaning howl. I shivered at the prospect of facing this world, and looked longingly at my bed.

But no, the day had begun and work awaited. I jumped in the shower, relishing the warmth this provided and then before long I was checking my briefcase as I got ready to leave. I had worked until late on a court report, and had several files to take back to the office. These I wrapped up in plastic in case it began to rain, and then, checking all was collected up, I went out to the car and began the drive to work.

It was one of those wild days that has the effect of waking everything. The trees were alive, swaying dramatically in the wind, people almost fought their way along the pavements, holding their coats and belongings tightly as they leaned into the wind or pushed back against its incessant bullying propulsion. Rubbish carelessly dropped was lifted almost obscenely into the air; it should have had no place in this wild outburst of nature, nevertheless it swirled around as a testament to human encroachment in the world. The lake I passed on the way to work had been whipped up into a furious scene with waves breaking violently on the shore side. The tethered boats were chafing at their moorings, as if attempting to escape and enjoy an uninhibited dance with the wind, bobbing about and pulling and jerking at their anchors.

Inevitably this was the day that the car park next to the office was full and I had to drive down to the multi-storey. As I stepped out of the car, the wind hit me even in this relatively protected space, I shivered and reached back into the car for my coat and scarf. Bundling myself in clothing I set off for the office. Down and down the grey steps and suddenly, wham, out into the world, in all its fury. But walking out into this wind I felt alive and excited, as if the elements were all out there like raging beasts, as if the world had lost its patience and exploded, hurling abuse and violence all about. It was as if it was seeking to retaliate against some long-held slight it perceived others had inflicted upon it, and at long last it would make its indignity and anger known.

Perhaps this was how Mr Rymer felt. I thought back to the previous day's duty session and saw Mr Rymer's angry face raging and exploding in much the same way. I had been on back-up duty and one of the other social workers in the team, Lou, was on first call and was downstairs interviewing clients. We had had the usual collection of issues: the problems with contact; the concerns from schools; the vouchers for food or other support to be sorted out – but on the whole it had been a much quieter day, mainly throwing up practical issues, which I least enjoyed, and negotiations with benefits departments on behalf of individuals who had got themselves into a mess.

The fact that it had been much less busy than normal had given Lou and I a chance to begin to catch up on the backlog of work left by the last two weeks of duty officers. Indeed, two referrals that I found, when I dared, in a diverted moment, to poke about in the very bottom of the tray, dated back two months. Oh dear. I pulled them out, scanned their contents and agreed silently with past workers' evaluations of the issues, that in the priority stakes, these really were bottom of the pile. So I'm afraid they were returned to the pile with only a red page marker to indicate the longevity of their existence. Next, I began to work my way through a review form for a social worker who had gone off sick with no one to cover her work, struggling to extract details from the files and enter them on the computer form. Not absorbing work, but necessary. But on the whole it seemed a waste of precious time: all this information could have been transferred from a file to a form by someone else, freeing me to deal with some of the issues actually needing a social worker. Too often I felt like a paper-pusher. I knew we all felt like this but we carried on, so I suppose we were all complicit in maintaining the status quo, too busy to actually step back and try to change anything.

I had just reached a critical point in my search for

contact names at a new school that one of the children was now attending, when the emergency bell rang, shattering the air with its urgent appeal for help. Those of us in the office immediately sprang up to go to the aid of whoever had rung the bell. It was not uncommon for the perpetrator of the bell-pushing to be a malicious adult seeking the attention they felt they were not getting, or a downright irritating child who had managed to climb up and ring the bell. In the latter cases the bell was not the only thing we would like to have seen 'wrung', but this was an agency for the protection of children, not their swift dispatch! There was, however, the ever-present possibility that this was a genuine shout for help from a colleague and the rule was, anyone in the office must go to their aid.

There was only me and three other social workers, only one of whom was male. I felt sorry for him because the cultural expectation probably demanded more action from him than from the female workers! We all rushed down to find Lou, standing just outside an interview room which she had clearly just vacated at speed, with Mr Rymer screaming abuse at her from very close quarters as he stood in the frequently seen pose – huge forefinger jabbing taunts at Lou as he screamed. In a voice exploding with utterly uncontained fury, of the sort that causes a surge of primeval fear in anyone hearing it, he was berating Lou for a string of failings the department had, in his eyes, made.

Lou was standing still, with every appearance of calmly listening and even empathising with Mr Rymer. However, I had been in similar situations and I knew that it was a very tough call.

I muttered quietly to Marie, 'Where is James?' Her reply was sobering. 'He's up in the highlands of Scotland on holiday, and we've got some temporary security guard called Ryan in his place. But goodness, just look at him.' Marie's eyes darted over to the main desk and settled on a young man, whose overall appearance would not have reassured a robin in a dispute with a sparrow. He was standing there looking, well, looking absolutely terrified. Marie's eyes rolled very slightly upwards and then she adopted her usual professional attitude. I could see that she felt that she was going to have to take action herself, when suddenly there was a movement from the reception desk.

We had a part-time receptionist, June, who had worked in the department for over forty years. She was often quietly and very unkindly mocked by some of the very junior admin staff for her unfashionable clothes sense, and rather older-generation attitudes to some issues. However, she was worth ten of most of her mockers; she worked long and hard, nothing was too much trouble, but she would neither suffer fools gladly nor tolerate poor work. She was on the plump side, but not fat, wore her hair in a short curly style which fitted her no-nonsense approach to life, and could not have been much above five foot in height.

We had all turned to see what the movement was, only to see June, briskly and very calmly, walking straight over to where Mr Rymer was standing with Lou. Without any preamble she spoke to him in a voice reminiscent of my old headmistress, saying, 'Mr Rymer, do excuse me, but this simply cannot continue. You really are causing a huge

upset in reception and, remember, there are small children here and your shouting is upsetting them. May I suggest you come along with me, and the social worker's
senior to the main office area and have a proper discussion about your concerns?'

She paused only briefly and then gestured to Mr Rymer
to follow her, almost without giving him time to think.
The effect was electrifying. Here was a man who had
always believed that by shouting, threatening people and
creating huge scenes, he could bully his way through life.
Indeed, this is a strategy that had probably worked for
him, because people are too scared to stand up to this
behaviour, and no wonder. Yet here was a woman of
redoubtable character, who did not appear to be even in
the least afraid of him. As we watched this drama unfold,
I have to say some of our hearts were in our mouths. I
think it was sheer shock – at the monumental audacity
of this woman who just treated him as if he was any very
slightly stressed client – that brought him up sharply. He
stopped shouting and turned to look at her in utter amaze-
ment, at which point Marie stepped in quickly, seized the
moment of diversion, picked up from June's cue and got
Mr Rymer to talk instead of shout.

The excitement over, we all filed back to our offices.
As we passed June on the way back to our offices, I
noticed that, like me, most people looked at her and smiled
or made a brief comment of thanks; they must have been
thinking what I was thinking. That woman came out of
a different mould, she was amazing!

I have always wondered quite what we could do if
someone really laid into a worker. I certainly didn't feel

equipped to handle violence. Lou was plied with tea and a listening ear. She was quite shaken, but fairly soon it was business as usual and whatever stress Lou had still lurking in her body, she would just have to cope with as well as she could. Life goes on . . .

But most relieved of all was young Ryan, whose face had to be seen to be appreciated, so great was his relief. But I really do think he should think about a career change!

Pushing thoughts of Mr Rymer to the back of my mind, I finally fought my way to the front doors of the office, where a quick glimpse at the door reflection confirmed my suspicion that I looked as if I hadn't brushed my hair in years: it was matted and tangled. The elements had done their worst. What a wonderful start to the day! I had a visit to a foster carer at twelve o'clock – one of my cases where two children were placed with a foster carer some few months ago. Before that, I had the usual pile of post, then emails and paperwork to complete.

I had some review forms to finish and copy for a family that we were reviewing next week. It was a long and fairly tedious task to just complete the forms, which then had to be circulated to everyone who might be attending the review. Before I had even climbed to the top of the stairs, my mind was working on the tasks ahead. I hung up my jacket and dumped my things at my desk, quickly greeting those of my colleagues who were in the office. Some were on early visits, others were already in meetings and those in the office were already knee deep in files, some had been in since seven o'clock this morning, working on reports.

I turned on my computer, logged in and then quickly made a coffee for myself, as I knew I was in for a long session at the screen. The files needed to be dug out of the filing units. I say dug, because that was exactly what it felt like. The units were kept at the end of the office in a separate room and were so full that to find, let alone access, any particular file was a physical battle of some-times gargantuan proportions. I walked over to the dreaded units and worked my way to the particular files I was looking for. I removed them from their compatriots by dint of a deft technique I had almost perfected, and was quite proud of, whereby you had to push back all the rest of that section, whilst gently and tentatively wriggling out the file you needed. This had to be done at an angle of about thirty degrees. Any less and you would still be fruitlessly struggling when security came round at seven o'clock in the evening to throw everyone out! Any more and disaster loomed in the form of a serious event in which many files would appear to leap suicidally from the shelf at surprising speed, flinging their loose contents (of which there were always some) here, there and every-where – including right underneath the cupboards, where a thoughtful designer had left a small gap above the floor just deep enough for papers but not deep enough to make their retrieval easy, or even possible. The careful manip-ulation required to safely remove a file was a time-consuming process . . . but it worked! Better this by far than the appalling avalanche that met my earliest encounter with this particular office unit, in my very first week. The memory still fills me with horror and I still wince to recall it.

As a then new and unknown quantity, hoping to prove myself as an efficient, competent and calm new member of the team, what I am about to recount was clearly not a good start.

It was day three of my new job at Barton and I had to locate several files to begin reading them prior to contacting a family. I began my search for these files in much the same way as I have described to you above, but sadly without any of the caution born of experience (that came later!).

I think it would be fair to say that it was my enthusiastic desire to get to grips with my new caseload that was behind my undue haste in attacking the files which sat in seemingly undisturbed innocence on their appointed shelves. Perhaps they lived a very boring and abused life, in which they were constantly subjected to being torn out of their comfort zone, pushed into crowded briefcases, stacked any old how on floors and desks, ripped and damaged by thoughtless people. Perhaps, as a result, they occasionally livened things up by making malicious moves in retaliation, watching with enjoyment the discomfiture caused by their actions . . . Who knows?

Well, I had spotted the files I wanted quite quickly, delighted that a prolonged search was not necessary. I reached up to haul them out when it happened!

The rather fat file was crammed in beside two other similarly weighty tomes, so the mere movement of the first triggered a chain of collapse whereby first one and then another file launched themselves into the air, flapping their covers like poorly co-ordinated pigeons, as their contents floated down like a dense cloud of feathers. Everywhere! As if this was not enough, the next file followed, then the next . . . so precipitating the aforementioned avalanche. I leapt at the shelf and tried to staunch the flow with my arms, with limited success. There was the sound of one last remaining file sliding down in the unit but not falling out, and then . . . silence. Total silence.

There was no one else in the room at that point and I gazed horrified at the almost-empty shelf and sank down onto the floor to sit among the utter chaos I had created – papers from differing files all mixed up, torn covers, it was like a shot from Dante's *Inferno*.

This is the point at which a snap decision had to be taken: did I run from the building and apply for another job, sneak quietly out of the room and pretend I had been on a visit all morning or . . . I looked about me at the total mayhem, choked back the feelings of utter despair and panic and took a deep breath. I reached out to some papers nearest to me, looked at the name of the child they referred to and put them on one side. I quickly developed a system of piles: one for loose papers, one for named papers, one for . . . and so it went on. After about twenty-five minutes I began to see some hope, and it was at this point that another of the social work team came in to look for a file. She didn't even look mildly surprised to see me stacking piles of papers on the floor. So was this a common occurrence? Or perhaps the nature of the work made social workers almost bomb proof when it came to mundane fights with filing units? As far as I was concerned, until my 'system' was refined and in place, I developed a near phobia about the units, and felt that it was open war for some months.

Well, enough of my carefully honed system of file

control. I worked hard all morning on the review forms, struggling to find all the detailed information required and then typing it onto the online format. I finally finished the second form at about 11.30, and knew there was no time to complete the task, as I had to get off to see the foster carer, Rose.

16

Rose

I closed down my computer, gathered everything I needed for the meeting with Rose and signed out but, as I made off, Marie leaned out of her room, and said, 'Becky, I have a student here, on his first day – are you able to take him on this visit?'

I said this was fine, and Marie introduced me to a young man, Mark. Mark was tall, with dark intelligent eyes set in a thoughtful-looking face. He enthusiastically thanked me for taking him along and we set off for the car. Traffic was light for once and the foster carer was not too far out of the centre of town, so by five to twelve we were arriving at her home.

On the journey I had been able to fill Mark in on the situation of the children we were visiting, and talk generally about the work. He showered me with questions and it was refreshing to talk to someone who was so new to the field that none of his idealism and energy had been drained away by reality. Someone who was fresh from their books and could discuss approaches in an academic way. It was always great to have students. That was always a worry in this work – it was easy to become cynical and lose the drive to make a difference. No child's life was ever changed much by a social worker who just, 'went through the motions, and no longer believed in better outcomes'. It needed real drive and involvement in the work to trigger change.

Rose was a quiet, cheerful woman in her late forties. Her two children had long since left home and tragically her husband had died suddenly about five years ago, causing Rose to review her life completely. She once told me that after the first three years following her husband's death, she suddenly realised that she was at risk of wasting the rest of her life mourning for him. He had been a really positive person and she knew that he would have regretted her doing this very much, so she began to think very hard about what she would really like to do, and that was when she read about fostering in a magazine in the hairdressers.

She says that, as she read this article, she felt tears come into her eyes and felt emotionally alive for the first time since her husband had died. The stories had really got to her and she felt this overwhelming desire to become someone who makes a difference to others in this life. After another year had passed, during which she spent time talking to people who had fostered, and to her family, she took the plunge.

There was no doubt: she was shaping up into an extremely good carer. She was thoughtful, caring and grounded; you only had to walk through her doors to feel the warmth she radiated. She had only been a foster carer for about a year and these children were her second placement; the last child had returned home to his mother. The two children she had at present, Alfie and Amy, were about eighteen months and three years old respectively, gorgeous children, but with serious problems that we were only just beginning to get a handle on.

Mark and I talked also about foster carers in general. I told him to always remember two things. One, that they are probably one of our most precious resources and they need all the support and help we can give them. Indeed, without good foster carers we would never be able to change the lives of any child; they are gold dust. However, secondly, whilst most foster carers are amazing, self-sacrificing and caring people, one must never lose one's critical judgement and forget that there are just a few carers who fall seriously short of the standards children need. We always have to be aware of this, because it is all too easy to become on such good terms with carers that we can no longer pass judgement in an independent light. Children deserve our constant vigilance.

Rose flung open the door to her home and I introduced Mark to her and the children. Before long, he was down on the floor with the children, trying to play with them. His silly antics did in time elicit a slight response from the baby, but Amy continued to stare at him with a look of suspicious doubt, her dark eyes never leaving his face, as if she couldn't make sense of him, didn't trust him and so kept up her guard.

We chatted generally and Rose laughed cheerfully at the banter. As she was putting the kettle on, I asked her if she would mind telling Mark her side of the children's situation to date. She was more than happy to tell him about the children. She reached for the teapot, selected some mugs and began. 'Well, really they were a great shock to me; this was only my second placement you see. You remember what a state they were in when they arrived, don't you, Becky? Oh, my goodness, what a state.

Honestly, Mark, they were just bags of bones, absolutely filthy, and seemed like some poor little wild things. Well, particularly Amy, who wouldn't speak, look at you, wouldn't wash, wouldn't sit in a chair to eat – everything terrified her.'

By the end of this sentence, Rose had lost her smile and her face had settled into a more serious and sad expression as she recalled that day. She looked at us very openly and said, 'You know, when I came into fostering, I knew the children would be neglected, but I never could have imagined any child in their state. Poor little lambs.' She looked fondly at the children, who picked up on her tone and looked up at her, but there was no confident childish smile, just an anxious recognition of their names.

This had been a dreadfully sad story and goodness knows what the outcome would be. The mother of the children had had a very severe mental breakdown some while after Alfie was born, and had been admitted to hospital only when the family's plight was discovered. She was currently not showing much improvement and her partner had disappeared off the scene long before this all happened. We could not find any relatives prepared to take the children on, or indeed to show interest in the situation, so they were taken into care.

They were in a terrible state. No one had been aware that these children were being neglected – the mother had not gone out, had no friends and her family didn't come near. Anyway, most of them lived a very long way away, so she lived in a twilight world of mere existence and loneliness. It doesn't bear thinking about.

It was sheer chance that the council was proposing to renovate the council houses they lived in and two housing officials were asked to go in and discuss the situation. They spoke to me at the time, and I recall they told me that the mother refused to open the door at first. But after a long time of persuading they were allowed into the front room only, where they held a strange and somewhat disturbing conversation with a very sick woman. They were unaware of the presence of children until a sound in the kitchen attracted their attention. Because the mother refused to allow them to go anywhere in the house, when they left, they walked around the house and peered in at the kitchen window. What they saw sent a chill down their spines – a small, thin little face peered up from the floor, where the contents of a bin was scattered. The child was so thin that her eyes seemed like enormous saucers, surrounded by dark, dark shadows. As one of them said to me, it was like looking into dead eyes, there was no expression, nothing, she just sat there pushing scraps into her mouth and gazing blankly up at them.

Needless to say, this was the saving of these children, and indeed the mother, whose life to that point must have been a living hell. The mother was taken to hospital and the children to Rose.

Rose stopped periodically in her tea-making to interact with the children. She gave Amy a banana to hold, then peeled it for her; she rolled oranges to them, which Amy eventually touched, but that was it – she tentatively touched it then stuffed it in her mouth in an attempt to eat it. Rose then continued with her tale and Mark listened, gripped by the horrors these children had been through.

'When they first arrived I was on twenty-four-hour duty. They couldn't sleep; they rocked themselves constantly for comfort, yet hardly ever cried. I think they had given up – you don't keep crying if no one ever responds. I heard that on our training course but really found it hard to believe. I do now!'

I agreed with that point: so many of the children who have experienced severe neglect have given up on crying, and it could feel surreal at times – when any normal child would give way to tears, these children remained dry-eyed. Tears demand a response and if there is none, in time, you learn to bottle it and carry on – not a good sign in a child.

Rose continued. 'I found it hard to discover that they never smiled either. It was as if they were locked inside themselves. They've been with me for about four months isn't it, Becky? I have now got them into some sort of routine on the sleep front, but they don't play. I spend my days doing things with them. I take them to the shops every day, although at first they were so terrified of going into noisy, busy places that I had to stick with local shops. Amy didn't speak a word when she arrived; we can't yet be sure that she hasn't got serious learning difficulties, so I have been really trying to encourage her to make sounds and noises to develop her speech. I talk non-stop to them both. Everything I am doing is carried out with a running commentary on my part . . .'

Rose stopped and laughed. 'My daughter says that I have to be the ideal person to teach anyone to talk, because I never stop myself! It's quite funny. Wherever I go I keep stopping and discussing the birds, every passing dog, the flowers, the weather, the things on the shelves at the shops – it takes me ages to get anything done and Amy just watches me, silently observing my chat, and . . .' Rose went very quiet, looked down at Amy and seemed to be struggling with her emotions. She then looked at us and I noticed that her eyes were glinting with unspilt tears and she added, 'Amy said her first word last week. We saw a big red setter near the play area, in the park, bounding about, and she suddenly pointed and said, "Dog, Doggie!" You two must think I'm potty, but I cried, I couldn't stop myself. For four months I have done everything I could – danced, sung, played with instruments to music and nursery rhymes, talked myself silly, everything, and not a word and then suddenly "Dog". It was amazing – I felt like I had won the lottery! There I stood, crying and smiling, because my three-year-old had said dog!'

We all laughed, but I couldn't help sharing her feeling of overwhelming emotion at what was, for Amy, a gigantic step.

'Since then, I have had one or two words from Amy. I really feel I am getting somewhere, though I am unsure what to do about her eating.' I listened to Rose's account of how Amy would scavenge about in the cupboards, trying to open jars, bottles, even tins. She would try to open drinks bottles and even take food out of the bin. Sometimes she gave food or drinks to Alfie. Rose then continued. 'If I try to divert her she becomes hysterical, so I can't do that. And as soon as I leave her for one moment she will have taken the food and hidden it. I've found food in some very odd places. Down the sofa, hidden in cupboards in their room, in the garden shed. It's not that I mind at all, it's just that I don't know how to deal with this, and it is clearly causing her such distress.'

I suggested that we went through to the sitting room and set the children up with their toys, so that we could chat this over. We all traipsed through and Mark and Rose organised the children with some quiet musical toys to look at. Amy was not inclined to play when on her own, so while Rose was talking Mark sat with them and instigated some play, even if most of it was on his part. Still Amy watched him – seriously and intently. His broad easy smile seemed to fascinate her and whenever he smiled at her you could see she was puzzled yet fascinated.

'OK, Rose, we need to think this through, don't we. It is clear that these two survived, certainly in more recent times with their mother, by scavenging food and drink. Well, Amy scavenged and has clearly fed Alfie. I think what their mother provided was scant and irregular. Prior to their mother's illness – and we simply don't know how long ago she became ill – I suspect from all we have now discovered, that the care these two received was not good, so food has enormous significance to them. What we need to try to begin to do is make food assume its proper place for Amy, as something that she enjoys but doesn't worry about. After all these two have been through this will take a long time, but you can make a good start. She has to be helped to understand that it is always there now, and is not a constant anxiety.'

Rose and Mark were listening and clearly thinking deeply, and from their very serious expressions were, I suspect, visualising a small child, frightened and hungry, searching for food in her mother's kitchen, crawling from cupboard to bin in search of food and drink. And also feeding her baby brother. This had to be a gut-wrenching image. There was a long silence, then Mark said it all. 'Poor little mites . . .'

Rose just looked up at me and I could see in her eyes exactly what she was feeling. I continued. 'How about we aim to make food less important by helping Amy to see that it is always available. You could buy some little colour-fully lidded containers that she knows are hers. Better still, let her choose them if you can involve her. Fill them each morning with healthy snacks, as long as they are things she can safely give to Alfie, things that he won't choke on if by chance you are not looking, because that is what she is likely to do for a while. Encourage her to help herself from the fridge. Maybe cottage cheese, apple purée, yogurts, rusks that both she and Alfie will like. As Alfie gets older you can put other things in. Then you could make sure there is always fruit at her level, and allow her unlimited access. I had one child we did this with, and she insisted on taking food everywhere with her. Her carer took packets of Rice Krispies wherever they went. I think she used those little ones you can get, and also bread rolls – whatever works – but that child couldn't tolerate the stress of being without food, even for a short time.'

Rose jumped in here and said, 'Oh yes, that's a good idea. When we are out, Amy goes mad if she sees food in the shop displays or sees another child eating. And it's not a normal tantrum, it's as if she is absolutely distraught. I have felt at a loss at times. I wasn't really sure what approach to take.'

I continued. 'Well, with this other foster family it became

a joke. Everywhere they went a trail of krispies or bread-
crumbs followed, like Hansel and Gretel. But the main
thing was, it freed the child up from her awful fear of
going hungry, so she was able to invest her emotional
energy in more important learning, and in building
relationships with her carer and others.'

'Did it work?' asked Rose.

'Yes, in time, but the foster mother had to take on
board that she too had to become absolutely laid back
about the food, and the trails of krispies. It simply had
not got to be an issue for anyone. After about a year, or
maybe longer, the child would sometimes forget to take
the packets out with her and nothing was said, but the
child slowly lost her obsession with food.'

Rose listened to this and said she would start doing
this, and would set it all up later that day. She sounded
enthusiastic and relieved to be pointed to something that
could help and I was just so pleased that Amy and Alfie
had been placed with her.

'Make sure you tell Amy clearly what you are doing,
so she knows she can help herself, and remind her
frequently. Let her see you smile at her if she takes some
food. We don't know what happened in their home, but
it is common for a child to have to obtain food secretly
or to get into real trouble for taking it.'

We chatted about the lack of speech and agreed that
the singing, nursery rhymes and constant clear chatting
and repetition were the key. It was going to be hard work
but I felt confident that Rose would give it her best shot.

'You know, Rose, you are clearly achieving a great deal
already. You're doing a great job.'

Rose looked at me and said, 'I've had less sleep than I've had for a long time, been busier than I have been for years, but this has got to be the most satisfying work I have ever done.'

I looked at her and the children, and found myself thinking, 'If Rose can't help these two, I doubt if anyone can. They are very lucky children.'

We thanked Rose for the drink and got up to leave. Mark had heaved himself up from the carpet where he had stationed himself with the children and I suddenly noticed that Amy's face crumpled and tears silently rolled down her face as she watched Mark move away. Rose noticed at the same moment and scooped the little girl up into her arms, talking soothingly, stroking her hair and explaining to Amy that Mark was a visitor, but would visit her again. As Amy calmed down and the tears dried up, she clung to Rose like a little monkey, not taking her eyes off Mark.

Rose looked strangely and inexplicably elated, and I was a little puzzled. She then said to us, 'Those are the first tears I have seen Amy shed, the very first. That has to be good doesn't it?' Now I understood her response I smiled broadly at her. 'Yes, I rather think it's yet another step in the right direction. OK, we'll be off. Bye, Rose. Keep up the good work and give me a ring and let me know how you're getting on. You're seeing the speech therapist soon aren't you? She'll have some more ideas that will help you.'

Rose grinned at us. By now she had a child on each hip, hugged closely. Amy was clinging to Rose with one arm and sucking her thumb with the other. Alfie was just clinging, but both children were watching us with solemn, uncomprehending eyes.

I could see that Mark was confused and, I suspect, rather upset. We got back into the car and I didn't turn on the engine straight away. Mark was very quiet and after a while I asked him, 'How did you feel about that visit?' He thought, and replied, 'I think a bit shocked. It's one thing to read about things in a textbook, but when you see the real-life children, its heartbreaking.' He paused and was obviously wrestling with his thoughts, and then he asked, 'How on earth do you cope?'

He turned to me and waited for my reply. I wanted to be as honest as I could but this was a difficult issue for many, perhaps most, social workers. It wasn't always easy to cope, that was the honest answer. But how would it help a new student, on his first day, to tell him that there were times that I lay awake at night worrying about some cases? How could I explain how some nights, when a really difficult decision had to be made about children, I would wake at two and lie there, going over and over the situations, re-evaluating all my decisions and ensuring I was happy with the conclusion that I had made, finally falling asleep hours later? How could I tell him about one of the most vulnerable children on my caseload, supposedly at home with his parents, yet whom I strongly suspected was wandering the streets alone at night, but I couldn't prove it yet? It is hard not to think about that child, wondering whether something could happen to him before you had enough evidence to act. In reality there would always be risks, but as social workers we have a responsibility to reduce those risks to the very minimum that we possibly can, and our concern for the child fuelled our efforts to do that.

To say that there will always be children in danger is not a statement that social workers should throw out glibly, allowing themselves the comfort to sit back smugly and absolve themselves from responsibility to act. But the risks *will* always be there. On top of those, there are so many restraints upon our ability to carry out the job we were trained for – caseloads, bureaucracy, paper overload, the stress of the work, legal thresholds and, not least, society as a whole. Society appears not to understand its responsibility in all this; it appears not to recognise its own power to influence policy and trends. One year, an over-sentimental viewpoint, which denies the reality of the lives some children have to live, and the damage they suffer, leading society to castigate social workers for 'snatching children from the bosom of their loving families with no reference to the human rights of the parents'. Another year, usually following another tragic child death, society denigrates social workers for not having removed children sooner, from parents who were clearly struggling. There should only be one agenda – the one that brings the best outcome for the child. Not an overly sentimental view, held by those who actually do not see, or understand, the damage neglect and abuse can cause, and who believe that every child is better with his or her own parents, no matter what. But a view that recognises reality, and yes, fully supports families who have problems and are prepared to work hard to improve, whilst also acknowledging that this improvement is not always possible, and further, must come in a timescale that minimises the damage to the children, who cannot wait for ever for stability.

Social workers also have to be aware. For their part, there has to be recognition that following current trends, either under the influence of society or those of popularised and therefore influential thinkers, has taken its toll. They need to guard against following the latest thinking too blindly. Instead, their practice should be based on well-conducted research findings, always using common sense to evaluate the theories thrown out by the latest gurus. Finally, and most importantly, they have to remember that the best outcome is always one that furthers the stable future of a child. The child must come first, in everything we do.

So, how did I answer Mark's earnest question?

What I said in the end was: 'Well, it can be tough. However, this job is so worth the strain and lives can be transformed. If that means sometimes we have to cope with some stress, so be it.'

I knew that, as he reached the point when he was carrying his own caseload, he would have worked out his own strategies. By then he would have savoured the pleasure to be had from helping children, both within or removed from their families, and would find this sufficient satisfaction to justify all the stress and strain.

Mark nodded thoughtfully and it was a more reflective pair who travelled back to the office.

17

Liam

On our return, Marie intercepted us. She had 'that look' on her face, which I just knew meant she was going to ask me to do something extra! I was right; apparently there had been an emergency call from the police to say they had a runaway teenager, found wandering in the shopping mall by an alert police officer.

Liam, the boy concerned, had run away several times in the last few months but was only fourteen and the police felt that Social Services should be asked to investigate before any further action on their part was considered.

Marie was very apologetic as she handed over the thin file. Both duty officers were out on calls and wouldn't be back, which left me, because all the other workers were either in court, out on visits or away. I was pressed for time, but frankly we had to do something about this situation, so I agreed I would arrange to go up to Liam's home and meet the police there. Marie added that I could take Mark with me if I felt that was acceptable. I looked at Mark and I could see that his eyes had lit up at Marie's suggestion. He was clearly keen to come and I knew he had spent some time on placement in an adolescent assessment unit, so would not be phased by what might happen. I took the file from Marie and sat down to read it. Mark thoughtfully offered to make coffee for me and disappeared off to familiarise himself with our coffee cupboard.

There was very little information in the file – literally a couple of referral sheets which logged that the police had picked Liam up from the town, the bus station and various venues over the last year but had precious little other information. So, before we went anywhere, I needed to collect some background information.

First, I rang his school, and finally got to speak to his head of year, Mr Clarkson, whom I had met in the past. Fortunately, he had known Liam for his whole time at secondary school, as his class teacher, his football coach, and also as his current physics master. When Mr Clarkson answered the phone and realised what it was I wanted to discuss with him, there was relief in his voice and he said, 'I am so glad for a chance to talk to someone about this boy. I've noticed such a change in him. Tell me what has happened.'

I explained that Liam had been picked up in the town by police, who had suspected he was truanting so tried to talk to him. Mr Clarkson sighed. 'It's such a pity, I just don't get it. Liam was always such a high achiever, a really decent kid – played in the football team, did well at school, even played the flute in the school orchestra. Truanting would just not have been an issue.'

'So, when did you see a change in him?' I asked.

Mr Clarkson replied, 'Well, it's hard to say, because one doesn't always notice individual kids until problems are big, but he began to be absent rather a lot about nine months ago.' Mr Clarkson went quiet and then continued, 'I hesitate to say much because I don't know, and it sounds such a dreadful inference to be making, but just over a year ago, his mother, who was on her own, began to bring her new partner along to all the school events and I gathered from odd comments at football that he had moved in.'

'So,' I continued, 'what's he like, this new partner?'

There was silence at the other end of the phone and Mr Clarkson seemed to be unsure how to answer my question. After a brief pause, he said, 'Well, I don't know how to be fair to the man; I have only met him a couple of times and seen him in the distance with Liam if he picked him up from football.'

'Look,' I said, 'allowing for that, how does he strike you?'

'Well I'd rather not be quoted but, off the record, I found him quite brusque and I did think he was rather harsh with Liam.'

'In what way have you noticed that?' I asked.

Mr Clarkson replied, 'It was one day when he picked him up from football and Liam had actually just had quite a nasty collision with the goalie. He had blood all over his head and was limping off the field. I asked his mum's partner to get him checked out at A & E and to be honest was rather taken aback at his offhand attitude. It seemed that this was just a nuisance to the man, who tried to infer the wound was trivial and that Liam was making a fuss about nothing. Believe me, I know the difference between trivial and in need of attention – I've seen enough injuries over the years. Also, he just seemed disinterested and cool with Liam. I felt rather sorry for the boy. I suppose he wasn't a man whom it was easy to take a liking to, but these are purely subjective comments – though his handling of Liam is fact.'

'Is there anything else you have noticed?'

'Well, quite a lot. Obviously, as I said, there was the truanting.'

'When did that start exactly?' I asked.

There was a pause, during which I could hear papers rustling as he searched through his records, and then he replied, 'Oh, it was in April. He had been absent on at least ten separate occasions and we had concerns about his general behaviour; he had just not bothered to hand in work and if challenged would be offhand and distant, as if he no longer cared. You know, I've known this boy for some years and he was never like this, he was always keen and enthusiastic. I wondered if he had got mixed up with drugs, and we've been concerned enough to have his mother in on two occasions.'

'So how was she about all this?' I asked.

'Well, again, it all seemed a bit strange. She seemed very anxious about him, but had nothing to offer by way of explanation, though the two of us who saw her did feel something was not right, as if she was hiding something. I really don't know; it's so difficult to know what is going on in the lives of these children.' He stopped here, and I was just about to end the call when he continued, 'There's one thing perhaps I should add. Liam had a nasty accident at home about four months ago. I only noticed this because he happened to have his shirt virtually torn off his back by a ruffian from another school, during a football match. His shirt was in strips and I couldn't help noticing that he had some appalling bruising on his back. When I commented on this he looked a bit awkward. I think that was what worried me. He then said he had fallen from his bike. Well, I suppose, oh I don't know, I just felt a bit uncomfortable, if you know what I mean. No real reason to, but I just did.'

Oh, I knew that feeling. I also knew that substantiating such feelings involved a lot of hard work.

We agreed we would keep in touch, and that the school would contact me if they had any further concerns. I put the phone down. I then phoned the police, to check if they had any records of difficulties with the parents that might be relevant to this child. The police rang me back – as they needed to be sure that I was who I claimed to be – and we then had a discussion. It appeared that there had been a call-out to the family home some six months ago to a domestic violence incident. This call had been made by an anonymous, young-sounding male claiming to be a neighbour. When the police arrived, there was the couple and a boy, whom I took to be Liam. The mother was not looking happy at all, but denied any violence, though it was clear to the officer at the time, simply by the demeanour of the man and woman, that there had been quite a violent altercation. There was nothing the police could do without any proof. This had been logged as No Further Action (NFA) and filed.

So, Liam was having a tough time.

I filled Mark in on my enquiries and made a quick call to the GP surgery where Liam was a patient, to see if they had any records of significance there. There was no record of Liam's accident, which almost certainly meant he had not been taken to A & E – but I could check that. Nothing else came up.

It's about collecting the pieces of the puzzle and then

putting them together. In time, with enough questions, someone will know something and little bits begin to sit together and form a picture. That picture will tell the story of a family.

I talked through with Mark how I would hope to manage this interview, clarified his role, which was that of an observer, and we set off. Liam's home was in an unfamiliar part of town. Neat detached houses lined the roads, four by fours littered the drives, and lawns were neatly manicured. He lived in a pleasant, modern house in a cul-de-sac. We drew up, very aware of the eyes of a neighbour who was out cutting his hedge but surreptitiously watching us. Careful to say nothing audible to reveal our purpose there, we made our way up to the door.

The door was opened to us by a red-eyed, exhausted-looking woman, who introduced herself as Liam's mother and invited us in. She was slim and smartly dressed and her name was Carol. But her demeanour spoke volumes. Her movements were slow, as if she were in a dream, her eyes were almost completely lacking in any expression apart from defeat and I wondered how she had got into this state. Behind her was a tall, well-built man, who was introduced as her partner, Callum. He shook hands and made eye contact, but what I felt from those eyes was not an open message; instead his eyes were dark and assessing.

We went through into the living room and met the police officer, a young woman in her twenties. Next to her sat a sullen, slim-built teenager, slouched in a chair in one corner. He barely looked up at us but moved his body in an irritated fashion and sank further into his chair, eyes glued to the floor.

I sat down and suggested that maybe we should all sit down to have a talk about things. Carol sank down onto the sofa, next to the police officer and her son. Callum took a chair on the opposite side of the room. I then introduced myself to the group.

Although Liam was intently not looking at me, I addressed everyone, and explained that clearly Liam had worries, and that we needed to talk about these and get to the bottom of them. I passed onto Liam the very positive things that his teachers had said about him – that he was a bright boy, well liked and well regarded, but that they had seen a change in him over the past year. There was a slight movement as I said this and from the corner of my eye I noticed that his mother had glanced very briefly at Callum.

I had intended to get the whole family around the table and set up a family conference, however, with the new evidence that was starting to point a finger at rather more than poor relationships in the home and the slight but significant reaction I had noted just now, I was fairly confident that no one would speak their minds in the presence of the other family members. I therefore suggested that I spoke to each family member on their own, so that I had a chance to get to know them, and then we would all have a chat together. I noticed a slight change of expression in Callum's face as I suggested this. He looked somewhat uncomfortable and irritated and said he had to leave shortly to meet a colleague. Rather than let him slip away, I suggested that I talk first with Callum to allow him to leave, and suggested we go into the kitchen and have a chat there.

Callum was edgy but answered my questions. He worked as a manager in a local computer software company, had been married before and was now divorced with two children by that marriage. He told me that the marriage had failed because his wife had become involved with another man. No, he said, he didn't see his children very often; his wife had a new partner and made it hard for him. Also, she had moved away so it was a logistical nightmare. He had met Liam's mother about two years ago through work and they had moved in together about a year ago.

When I asked him about Liam, he said that he had no idea what the problem was. He said that he felt the boy needed a firm hand, because his mother had been alone with him for a long time. It was Callum's view that Liam had almost assumed the role of the man of the house and he felt this was wrong. He maintained that he was very fond of Liam, but there are ways of saying things and ways of saying things, and somehow his declaration did not ring true. I would, however, expect that in this scenario there would be a period of settling in for a newly reconstructed family and it would not be surprising if there were problems.

Liam's father, Robert, had died many years before and Callum seemed to feel that he could step into the gap left in Liam's life. When I gently suggested that it would take time for a teenage boy to accept him as a new part of his family, particularly after the tragic loss of his father, to whom he had been very attached, Callum sneered and looked straight at me. In a harsh and loud voice which was suffused with submerged anger, he said, 'You know,

I haven't got time for all that psychological nonsense. He's lucky to have a father. It's more than I had! Mine was a waste of space, usually drunk and couldn't give a damn about me and my brother, then he walked out. Left my mother on her own to cope. Liam is very lucky to have someone about for him.' Callum then looked at his watch and claimed that he had to go. I suspected that he was so angry at being questioned by a social worker that he was not able to contain his anger and wanted out. He left, and I watched as he walked out, the door slamming behind him; there went one very angry man. So what on earth was he like with Liam?

It was Liam's mother Carol who talked to me next. She was initially withdrawn and monosyllabic. I then asked her to tell me about Liam, right from the start. At first, she spoke haltingly and with seeming difficulty, then slowly it was as if she really wanted to talk and the words came faster, and then simply flowed out. She told me that Liam had been a much-wanted child and she described a very happy marriage with Robert, who had been a patient, caring husband. She described her husband's death as something she thought had brought an end to her life. In her words: 'There I was, standing in the hospital at my husband's bedside – a heart attack had killed him at thirty-three. Thirty-three! I just couldn't take it in. People don't die at that age. I was told later that he had had a genetic condition from birth. But now I was alone, with a young child. I was no good at being alone, never had been, but here I was and I had no choice. How I got through the next months I will never know; it was like walking round with a lump of lead in my chest and a sack of stone on my shoulders. I felt physically ill all the time. I didn't care about anyone or anything; if my mother and sister had not been there I don't know what I would have done. I couldn't think straight; I couldn't care for Liam. It took me a long time to become something like normal, and then my mother died and my sister's husband got a new job in Scotland and they had to move. I was devastated. It felt as if I was back to square one. I had tablets from the doctor for depression but they didn't really solve anything much. It was a year after this that I met Callum. He seemed so dependable, someone to lean on; he was happy to organise me and I was only too glad to be organised. It was amazing; I felt such a relief. I didn't need to be in control all the time because Callum seemed to naturally take that role. I felt happy for the first time in ages; he was calm and cheerful and it was great. When Callum suggested we move in together, I thought it was a really good idea.'

I looked at Carol. She had come to the end of her recollections, and was clearly unsure where to go from here. So I asked her, 'And has it worked out well?'

She looked up at me and quickly looked away, as if she thought I could read her mind. Then she said, 'Well, it hasn't been easy for Liam to accept a new man about the house, but I suppose that was to be expected.'

'And how have you found the adaptation to having someone in the house again?' I asked.

Carol continued to look at the floor; I was waiting to see how she would handle this question, as I was pretty certain she was covering up. She answered after a minute's thought, 'Well, I suppose it has been an adjustment for me too, but it's fine. Callum has had a hard time, you know. His ex-wife gives him a tough time, won't let him near the children. He even went to court.'

'That must be hard for him. Very tough. How does that make him feel?' I responded.

'Oh well, sometimes he gets very angry about it, but what can he do?' she replied.

What she had told me about Callum's appeal to court, together with his ex-wife's resistance to contact, was making me wonder. Were there reasons for his wife to avoid him? I would have to check this out. I thought it was time to push her a little, and asked her what she thought had changed Liam from a happy studious boy into the boy we were seeing now. She seemed a little thrown and replied in disjointed sentences, 'Well, I don't know . . . Maybe . . . Oh, I don't know, perhaps it's just all the changes. Maybe . . . well perhaps he will settle down soon.'

I left her final thought hanging in the air, and said nothing for a moment. Then I asked her what her relationship with Liam was like. She became very withdrawn in a trice, so I had to coax her by reminding her of her words. 'You told me that Liam was a very much-wanted and precious child to you and your husband. Do you still feel like that about him?'

Carol glanced quickly up and looked at me, then looked as quickly down as if to avoid my gaze. Her head sank onto her chest and she studied her hands, twisting her ring on her finger in a desperate endless movement. My question was met with total silence, a silence that spoke louder than words. All I could hear was the distant barking of a dog and the ticking of a clock. I don't think she heard anything; it was as if she had been drawn back into those early days with Liam and her husband and was remembering what it had been like. It was a long silence, but something told me to allow her this time; she needed to think, and I was fairly sure she was doing so.

So suddenly that I was momentarily shocked, Carol looked up and said, 'Oh God, what have I done, what have I done? I've made such a mess of my life. If Robert knew what I had done he'd . . .' She stopped. There was a long pause and asked, 'What would Robert do?'

She thought long and hard, and then she replied in a softer voice, 'He'd help me out of the mess. That was what he was like. He was sensitive and caring; Liam is just like him. And yes, Liam is still very precious to me, but I wonder if I've almost forgotten him in searching for a way to help myself. But . . .' Carol stopped again, and wearily pulled up her trouser leg to reveal huge bruises.

'Callum has a terrible temper and I pay the price. He never touched me in the early days; he was so attentive and so kind to me, I thought I had found another Robert. It wasn't until he moved in that slowly I began to see another side to him and it scared me, so much that I couldn't do anything. Then he began to lay into Liam; he said that Liam is short of discipline and that what he needs is a good thrashing. It's awful, and I feel such a coward not stopping him, but I'm frightened to interfere. I'm frightened to tell Callum that he has to go.'

She stopped there and looked at me, then said, 'He does, doesn't he? I mean, he has to go?'

I replied, 'Well, the choice is yours, but we will have to act. Liam is clearly at risk living with you and Callum and I imagine the police will be looking into Liam's situation with serious interest. If you don't tell Callum to leave, we will have to protect Liam.'

'No, no,' she said in a flat voice. 'I wasn't really asking you. I know that Callum has to go, for Liam's sake, and for mine. I've ruined Liam's life with all this. I've lived in fear of Callum for too long, and just not found the strength to get away from him. I simply cannot believe that I've been so weak.'

I suggested that we went into the other room and she talked to Liam and told him how she was feeling and what she was going to do. I spent some time with Liam, and his relief at his mother's decision was enormous. He described the last year as 'an endless terrifying roller-coaster of avoiding Callum's angry outbursts and watching my mother get beaten when he lost it.' But Carol was now in a place to take hold of the reins again if she chose to.

It was a good time later that I left the family home. The police had taken Callum in for interview and they were going to issue an injunction against him to stop him going anywhere near that home. There was a long way to go for Liam and his mother, a great deal of trust to rebuild, and a lot of growing needed of Carol. I was going to ensure she had the details of a support group to help her and a referral to counselling if she was prepared to take that help to move her to a stronger position. It had, sadly, like so much in life, needed a crisis to bring the whole awful situation to the boil, but it is often at crisis points that resolution can be found.

As Mark and I walked away, Mark turned to me and smiled broadly. 'Well, that's a brilliant outcome isn't it?

Now that kid stands a chance of getting some stability back in his life.' I didn't reply; I was deep in thought about the family. He looked at me and read my expression. 'It is, isn't it?'

'Oh yes,' I answered. Then continued, 'Oh yes, if she can manage to sort herself out without slipping back to needing Callum.' 'Oh, surely not, not after all this,' he said in a tone of utter incredulity. 'Well, I really hope not. Carol seems to have insight and I'll do all I can to set up some real support for her, but women who do not believe in their ability to survive on their own tend to slip back, even into abusive relationships. There's a very long way to go yet, Mark. She will need to take up and really use the offer of counselling and group help, some of which will need to include Liam. Liam will need help and support to cope with all that has happened; that is something I need to check out.'

I could see he just couldn't accept what I was saying, and it troubled him. It troubled me, but was a sad fact. All too often, even at the expense of their own children, some women will accept abuse as a better alternative to being alone. Today was simply the 'crossroads day' for Carol. All I had done was structure a situation within which she could think freely about her life. It would then be for her to realise she had a choice, she now had the chance to choose the road she would take. The future for Carol and for Liam would all hinge on whether she could then walk that road.

18

A Difficult Time for All

It was a Wednesday. I woke early and lay there, thinking about the day ahead. That alone was sufficient to bring me into fully awake mode. My thinking was, I'll get dressed and out early today so I can tackle some of my paperwork before the team meeting. There was a three-line whip for the team meeting – we were all expected to be there, or else!

I reached work early and walked briskly up to the office in the hope of finding it quiet so that I could get on uninterrupted. I was in luck; only Paula was there, and she was typing away at a rate of knots, catching up on some of her reports. I waved a brief silent greeting and carried on. My email was bursting, as usual, so I sorted through that to begin with. Then I went to my post box, where there was a note from my senior: 'There will be a surprise inspection of files today, and the inspectors have at random asked to see those of Rebecca Smith.'

My heart stopped; well, it felt like it had. Rebecca Smith. Rebecca was one of four children who were in the same foster home, at the same school and had all the same contacts. Much of the work was shared, so apart from visits or reports, that were solely relevant to this child, all the paperwork for this family was typed up, copied for the other three children and then filed. I had done the copying

– it was all in a folder ready to file when I had a spare moment, and I had managed to file away her siblings' papers only the day before, so they were all up to date. But it just so happened that I had not yet filed Rebecca's papers, so the last two weeks of work was outstanding. That would be a serious black mark. Because there had been several meetings and a flow of reports coming in to me from other professionals there was quite a lot of filing to do. I felt sick. I felt that there was no justice. I prided myself on keeping my files up to date, because I recognise the importance of this should someone, in an emergency, need to check out any detail of a child's life. But I simply hadn't managed to get Rebecca's done.

I looked at the clock. This file had to be on the inspector's desk by 9.30 a.m., the team meeting began at a quarter to nine, and I had wasted over half an hour answering emails. I rushed off to the filing system, to get Rebecca's file. The filing units were still locked; usually, a member of admin was responsible for unlocking them early for those who came in at eight, but there was no sign. I dashed back to the admin drawers where the keys were kept, but couldn't find them anywhere.

Paula looked up from her work at my desperate searching in Sandy's desk and when I asked about the keys, she suggested trying the senior's pen pot! Success, but I had lost five minutes already. I went over to unlock the units and inserted the key. For some reason, there was no response. I jiggled it, shook it (I even gave it a bit of a bang!) but nothing moved. I panicked a bit and tried to shake it again. Then I studied it and realised that whoever had locked up last night (probably the senior), had closed it slightly bent. These were not state-of-the-art filing units! I managed to free the workings, access the cabinet and then searched for Rebecca's files. After a search – and it was more of a desperate hunt – I finally found her files, so tightly packed in with those around that it needed the strength of Hercules to push them back and find one specific file, particularly on a morning when the units were full. I grasped the file as if my life depended on it and rushed back to my desk. I hunted out my file of copies and began to file everything away. This was not a case of sorting them into date order then slamming them in. No, they all had to go into separate sections, here, there and everywhere. I found two important reports were missing and had to get the originals from her brother's file to get them copied. I rushed over to the next bay where the photocopier was housed in a small side area, a dusty messy area with a couple of dead and dying plants. I punched in the code and waited while nothing happened. I tried again, and again. Nothing. What on earth was the problem?

Our helpful stand-in temp, Simone, was now in the office and appeared round the corner, clutching her bag, into which she was putting her nail file. I called out, 'Oh, Simone, why is the photocopier not working?' She turned and said, 'Oh I think they changed the codes yesterday.' And with that helpful comment she wandered slowly and vaguely off to her desk, no doubt to continue filing her nails, which must surely need no more attention. I took a deep breath and asked whether she had the new code.

'Well no, I haven't. I think someone gave it to me on

a piece of paper but I haven't been able to find it yet, so you'd better use the one in Children with Disabilities.' That was on the next floor down. If I had been a balloon I would have burst by now. If I had been a bomb, I would have exploded and been heard as far away as Sweden. But I was human, and I wondered how much more of this I could cope with before I was carried off screaming.

By the time I had finally got the wretched papers photocopied it was much later and the team meeting had been going on for some time. One of the seniors sent a message down to see where Paula and I were. I looked up from my filing to see that glum admin – otherwise known as Simone – had given up on her nails and was answering the phone. But actually, no, this was yet another private call to a friend she was meeting for lunch. If she would only give me a hand I could get to the team meeting . . .

Well, that didn't happen. I rolled up late, only to receive a rather stony look from the senior who was taking the meeting, but I had left the file on the inspector's desk and was just praying that most of the papers were filed OK. I so wish that my training had included speed filing. For the hours we social workers spent filing, I often worked out that the department could employ any number of sensible, organised school-leavers to free up the social workers to do the job they trained for. But no. Let's make social work into the ultimate multitasking profession, so they can do everything as well as social work. Or, more honestly, everything *but* social work. Then let's pillory them when they haven't time to pre-vent tragedies happening.

The team meeting was the usual mix of advanced

warnings about training we would all be too busy to attend, documents we would be too busy to read, new ideas that we would doubtless find yet another pressure to incorporate in our day – with little visible benefit – and requests for 'ideas' to improve the team.

'Well, some extra admin help would be my current number one, and two and three . . .' But who's listening?

To end the meeting there was a short presentation from a local support group for young mothers. That was good and well worth the time; she had our attention and provoked genuine interest. One of us had to write up the minutes from the meeting, and we took this in turn. None of us needed this job either; it was yet another piece of paperwork. We broke up and I was just about beginning to feel a little less stressed after the dreadful start to my day. As I was gathering my papers together after the meeting, I noticed Paula was still sitting on her chair, looking as if she was not going to move. The rest of the team had gone by now and the room was empty. I turned to her and said, 'Hey Paula, you look like you're there for the duration!' She sighed and replied, 'Oh, I'm tired, so tired. I was up until two, working on one of my court reports, and I have a review for five children coming up, with the mountains of paperwork that will involve. But I'm on duty all afternoon. I feel like I can't move.'

It wasn't her words that disturbed me, the paperwork *was* an enormous burden and sitting up late to work on important reports sometimes left one tired and drained for days. It was the flat voice and blank expression that went with it. Her posture was somehow different: her shoulders were rather slumped, she seemed unable to smile and, as I talked to her, an all-pervading feeling of depression and hopelessness filled me. I found that quite alarming and my mind wandered back to one hot summer's day when, sitting in lectures during my training, the words of our very able and knowledgeable tutor, Miss Fry, penetrated my admittedly rather heat-sleepy mind. Her dictum being, 'If you forget much of what we have learnt this afternoon, you must promise me never to forget that if someone you meet in your work leaves you unaccountably depressed – start thinking. Hard! Depression is infectious. This is a key diagnostic pointer, and don't you dare forget it!' She had made this statement so strongly that not only did her words stay with me, I even remember the clothes she was wearing that day: a strong pink swirly dress with matching earrings! She had gone on to say that undiagnosed depression was a contributory factor in many of the problems we would meet, and the rest of the lecture was around that issue.

I knew that Paula had been through a really tough time with one of her court cases and had real worries about the family concerned. She had also had a complaint made against her by one of her clients. This was common. Most of these were simply clients who had grudges because of the work social workers had to do. Still, it was an extra stress and Paula would have had to go through all the processes. Several of her cases, which had to date been stable and jogging along nicely, had recently exploded for a multiplicity of different reasons. Some were serious parental problems, which meant the children could no longer remain at home and had needed placing with carers, which would involve a lot more work. Some were teenagers who had become persistent runners. And so it went on. We all knew she was probably carrying the caseload of at least two social workers at present. Because she was experienced, and an incredibly good social worker, we all assumed she would cope and just dismissed her throw-away comments about not sleeping. Perhaps the truth is, we were all so very busy that we had little time to dwell on anything, just keeping our own heads above water was a full-time task!

We talked for a little while and I suggested she should go to Marie, have a chat and tell her she felt overloaded. Paula replied, 'Oh, I don't think it will make any differ-ence. I mentioned I felt my caseload was becoming unman-ageable in our last supervision, but somehow she didn't understand. You know I really like Marie, and she can be great to talk to, but I think she has been put under huge pressures herself to fulfil certain targets, and almost cer-tainly would not choose to take on board any additional problems.'

I thought about this, and had to agree. Marie had seemed more distant recently and she had repeatedly mentioned inspections and targets in meetings. The drive to have no unallocated cases was affecting us all, with Marie herself having to carry one or two cases in a very perfunctory way.

Paula continued, 'You know, in my last supervision session, I was even asked if I could just oversee one new case allocated to an inexperienced worker; it was a quite complex and potentially dangerous case! I said no, and I think Marie did get some sort of message from my tone, as she seemed to sit up and talk over my cases with more thought for the stresses.' Paula hesitated and then continued. 'Oh, I don't know. There's no answer. I'll get an early night and perhaps that will make a new woman out of me.'

She took a deep breath and stood up, giving me a smile which was as empty as her expression, and saying, 'Hey we'd better get on; the morning is running away with us.' And with that she walked briskly off, leaving me rather concerned and wondering.

I didn't have long to dwell on Paula, my phone was ringing and I had a list of tasks to do as long as my arm or, more probably, my leg.

I was working on a report for three children for whom the plan was adoption. There were two little girls and their younger brother, who had cerebral palsy, which sadly was going to make life very hard for him. But it was looking as if we had several couples who were very keen to take all three children together, which would be so much better for them in this case. As part of the work for this I had to put together a very detailed family history, and a health history if at all possible, which involved visiting grandparents or other relations. It was important to children, particularly as they grew older, that they should have both a social and genetic history if this could be done. When a doctor asks you if anyone in your family has had diabetes or high blood pressure, as simple examples, you take it for granted that you know the answer, or can find out. But if you are adopted, and no one has acquired this information prior to the adoption, by the time you realise the need, the people who might have known may be dead or have disappeared.

It was for these reasons that I had arranged to visit the Josephs, one set of the grandparents of these children. The children's parents had become seriously involved in the drug world, both as dealers and addicts, and the children had been removed in very sad circumstances over a year before. I set off on this visit feeling a distinct sense of curiosity.

The address was a multi-storey block of flats on the edge of town. The flats were set in a very run-down area, rows of terraced properties, which could have looked quite attractive if not for the fact that they had been almost completely neglected – as if the community no longer cared for their environment. I think that says a lot about the state of mind of any community. I just don't believe that there aren't people in such an area who wouldn't enjoy gardening, or making things look pleasanter, but it seems to need someone to take a lead and without it being a whole community effort it is unlikely to work. Somehow, everyone needs to be involved, otherwise vandalism will always be a problem. Everyone needs to have a stake in their own bit of land.

As it was, it seemed to be a barren land, with nothing to rest the eye on apart from stark, grey buildings and the rubbish blowing about this desolate wasteland. What had started as a very grey day had begun to improve, and now the sun had forced its way through the clouds to give out glorious bursts of warmth and light, only to disappear briefly behind a cloud, leaving the world momentarily bereft and waiting until the cloud drifted slowly on its way. But even these brief bursts of sun didn't seem to subtract much from the feeling of bleak despair this place gave me. I found it sad and dehumanising and it made me angry that anyone could accept that this was how it was and not want to try and change things.

Youngsters were hanging about in what had been designated as play areas for young children; almost certainly this would be one of the many meeting points for dealers to trade their wares. I'm not sure how many young mothers would feel safe if they were out on their own but, then again, where were the teenagers supposed to 'hang out'? Unfortunately, there was little for them to do but hang about and this made them easy prey for the local drug dealers, who would often give out samples – trial supplies of drugs to youngsters – hoping to get them hooked and become a part of their future market. Once hooked, the youngsters would be paying dearly for their habit, whilst someone in the dealing trade got rich, very rich. When the newly addicted young people found that the drugs they now craved had become more and more expensive, they had to find a way to get that money. Whatever the cost, legal or not, the craving now ruled their lives; it was now their new master.

And why was it so easy for the dealers to enlist these young people? Because the young people are hanging around with little to do – no activities, no aims, no sport. If they are older, there are no jobs or it's too easy not to take one. With nothing to aim for, something that offers temporary excitement – well, it isn't hard to see how this works is it? Further, if many of your friends are doing drugs, peer pressure is very powerful, particularly if there are no strong role models in the home. All these factors, not to mention the role of the media (which consistently manages to glamorize drug use) produce a society that seems blind to the dangers it has created for its young people, whilst constantly asking why!

The tragedy is, when dealers or even 'friends' hold out the promise of an interesting experience to a young person, they conveniently omit to describe the downside, the life-shattering, degrading descent that drugs can spiral a person into, leaving them with a life of addiction and unreality. Young people value their freedom above most things and yet, in experimenting with drugs, they can open the door to an addiction that can then make them a slave to it, sometimes for the rest of their lives, with all the implications for both their physical and mental health.

I drove down several wrong turns, asking myself, not for the first time, just how difficult can it be to construct an estate where it is easy to find one's way about as a visitor. It was the bane of my life – well, perhaps not the only one – spending precious time searching for roads, then still worse, numbers to houses, and that's in the daytime. At night, and many visits were at night, how often did I find myself carefully picking my way up random paths, torch in hand, to read a number, only to find it had, like its neighbours, fallen off, never existed, or the odd numbers were somewhere else altogether?

The blocks were all identical and the signs erected to label them had been defaced or were hanging off their hinges, so reading them was quite a task. Eventually, I found Lilac Block, a singularly inappropriate name for this pale-grey edifice of concrete and glass which rose steeply upward from the ground like an alien structure deposited by one who had no comprehension of the human psyche, the need we have to coexist with the ground and with other humans. Here, you were simply a being, conveniently and space-efficiently slotted into a living space. And there certainly weren't any lilac trees in sight; apart from some almost completely worn-away grass there was little in the way of greenery at all. Not a tree in sight, not even a wild flower. Indeed, not even so much as a dandelion. Sad. Whoever built these flats must have had some inspiration to provide beauty in the surroundings, or why choose the name? It is quite possible that when this was new, some time in the 1960s at a rough guess, there may even have been some lilacs planted. If so, they were long since victims of thoughtless uprooting.

I looked for somewhere to park that hadn't got broken glass on the ground, having recently had a number of punctures, probably as a result of parking on all the rubbish so often left lying around. Still, I parked my car, found my way to the entrance and rang the intercom. A voice answered, and let me in, telling me they were on the fifth floor. When the intercom buzzed I pushed on the door. It was a heavy sort of door and I threw my whole weight against it to open it.

As the door shut behind me it was as if a sudden silence had swallowed up the rest of the world, leaving me standing in a cold, strange, parallel universe. It was so quiet that it was unnatural. I walked down the corridor to find the lifts. There was a dank odour about the building and I doubt if it had been painted for twenty years. The paint that remained was peeling off in chunks and the floors were black and ingrained with dirt. I suppose someone was employed to mop these floors from time to time, but perhaps they too had been permeated by the sense of depressive neglect and had lost heart, their mopping having become a cursory flip that made no discernible difference at all.

I walked on, unable to find where the lifts were, so I back-tracked, found they were hidden in a recess and selected floor five. While I waited, I listened. I could hear nothing – no voices, no children, just a deep silence that said, 'You are alone.' I was beginning to find this rather disconcerting, then the main doors opened and a young man appeared and came to stand at the lifts with me. He didn't look at me, didn't speak, and I tried to find a way to observe him covertly to decide whether I felt I wanted to go in the lift with him. I wasn't normally particularly nervous, but somehow this building was making me feel unsafe. He seemed unable to stand still, his eyes looked strange and there was a smell of what I thought was alcohol about him. I decided that it might be extremely unwise to risk sharing a lift, so I pretended to search for my mobile to take a call. I wandered over to a window to do this and hoped the lift would come soon, and that the young man would move on. It didn't happen. After a time, in which he had pushed the lift button with increasing levels of irritation, he kicked the lift doors and walked off. I concluded that the lifts were broken.

Oh great! The fifth floor! I found the stairs through a door at the end of the corridor and began the ascent. I walked up somewhat slowly and rather nervously, wondering where the frustrated young man had gone. As I climbed

I met no one. Did anyone actually live here? On each floor I could see through to long dark corridors with only door-mats to indicate the existence of human life. What must it be like to live in this environment? Well, that was rapidly becoming the least of my concerns. Would I actually make it to the fifth floor?

Each floor had three flights of stairs and they seemed to get steeper as I climbed up and up. My legs ached, my bursting briefcase felt like lead and I was just beginning to think I would soon need oxygen, or treatment for alti-tude sickness, when I saw above me the sign for the fifth floor. I stopped at the top of the stairs and tried to get my breath back so that I could actually speak when I arrived at the flat. I didn't want to be so breathless that the couple would open the door to a pathetic specimen gasping for breath like a fish too long out of water!

After a few minutes, and a freshly formed intent to take up more exercise, I pushed my way through the heavy doors and looked for the Josephs' flat. Finally, I found it. A big mat said 'WELCOME' (it could have added 'AND WELL DONE!'). I pressed the bell, which rang with a cheerful tune. I had made these musical bells the victims of some very scathing and cynical comments over the years, but now I listened to it with enormous relief and pleasure. It said to me: 'At the other side of this door is someone who likes pleasant sounds, is cheerful and some-what light-hearted,' and I felt a sense of returning to a world which was pleasant and safe!

Very quickly the door opened and a friendly face appeared – it was Mr Joseph. He had a warm smile and eyes that radiated intelligence. He stepped forward, shook my hand and invited me in without any of the reluctance that many, if not most, of my clients displayed. He took me through into the living room, where his wife was sitting in a chair with her leg resting up on cushions. She also had a warm, smiling face and said, 'Hello dear, I can't get up. I've just come out of hospital and they said I have to keep my foot up as much as possible, so please do sit down.'

I sat down and looked about me. The room was clean, comfortable and really cosy. It was as if I had stepped into a different world, and the contrast was almost disconcerting.

'The lifts were broken,' I mentioned.

Mrs Joseph responded: 'Oh not again, that's the third time this week, and there's a poor girl down the corridor with a young child. She is hoping to be re-housed, but she has to walk all that way if they break. We just don't go out when they break. Well, honestly we can't, it's too far.'

Mr Joseph insisted on making some tea and we got chatting.

This was a thoroughly delightful couple. I just wondered how things had gone so wrong for them. Well, I was soon to learn. After the preliminaries, the Josephs asked about the grandchildren. I explained what in fact they knew already, that we were searching for the right couple to adopt them because of all the problems. I also told them that the children were doing well and had settled with their foster carer.

The couple listened and then Mr Joseph spoke. 'You know, we'll be glad for those little kiddies to have a good home. We're too old to take them, and we don't hardly ever see our son Wayne these days. Last I heard he had bummed off to Scotland. We think he's still there.' He paused at this, sighed, and then continued. 'We often wonder if we could have done something to prevent all this happening, and maybe we could. We didn't have much money. but we worked so hard to make a life for ourselves; I worked nights and Elsie worked days. I tried to look after the children in the day, and slept while they were at school. But it was hard. Our son was always a good kid. He went to school, was fairly bright, didn't cause too much hassle, and it was only when he reached about fourteen that the problems began. A boy moved into the road that we lived in and he was trouble, with a capital T. Before long, he had established a gang and he seemed to make a dead set for our Wayne – and our son seemed to be almost flattered to be the centre of this boy's attention. Nothing we said made any difference; he seemed to be obsessed with this boy. And what did this boy do for him? He led him and others into trouble, that's what he did, and Wayne went into it with the best of them. At one point there was some very nasty violence, then it was theft, cars and the like. I was never sure if Wayne was involved with all of this. I just hoped not; it made us feel quite ill and totally helpless.' Mr Joseph stopped, and struggled to gain control of himself. 'I can't tell you what it has done to us, that one of our children has become a drug dealer, and sunk to these levels. We feel so ashamed. Not only that, but we've lost our son. For years now the only time we've seen him was when he needed money, and we ended up not trusting him so we had to change our locks . . . from our own son!' This last thought obviously distressed Mr Joseph. He dropped his head into his hands, was now clearly overcome with the telling of this story and had to pause while he wiped his eyes.

He went on. 'We often think that if we hadn't worked so hard and had been there for him, perhaps things would have been different. When we weren't working we were both so tired that it was easier to let Wayne have his own way. I remember being exhausted and then trying to talk to Wayne about his lifestyle. Well, he stood his ground, we gave up – that time and many others – because it was so hard. Much easier to give in, I know that.'

Mr Joseph paused and looked out somewhere in the distance. 'Somehow, we didn't get it right with Wayne and I do feel responsible, but if the children can be saved I will feel that is a better outcome.'

Mrs Joseph interrupted here. 'Stop it, you know it does no good.' She looked at me and said, 'If we've been over this once, we've been over it a thousand times. We will never know. We did what we could at the time and, yes, I'm sure we could have done more, but it was hard then and we did try.' She paused and then said, 'You know – and you will know in your job – but the streets out there are flooded with drugs. It's as easy as buying sweets to get drugs, and once they start it is nigh impossible to stop them.' She hesitated, and her voice changed. There was bitterness and anger as she continued, 'Once those dealers have got their claws into the kids you've lost them; it's . . .' She looked down, her face contorted by her anger and frustration.

I tried to bring them into a more positive frame of mind. I always worried about visiting people, stirring up vast hidden emotional turmoil and then just walking out. What right had I to do that? I tried to bring them to some level of resolution, sufficient for them to be able to talk more calmly and positively about their lives. We talked about the adoption process, which they were interested in, and then came on to their history.

Mr Joseph had grown up in a Yorkshire mining village. When his mine had finally closed he moved to find work and then met his wife, who came originally from Ireland. They both had interesting stories to tell about their own backgrounds and were able to talk about family members and grandparents, even great-grandparents, so by the time they had finished talking I had more of a history for these children than most of us have. That was good; there were some very positive role models in the family, which seemed to be dominated by hard-working, sound people. Somehow this made the situation even more poignant. It felt as if it shouldn't have happened, but it had.

I too began to feel that, had their son seen more of this lovely couple, whose ideals and aspirations were sound, perhaps it would have been better for him. Had the couple not been quite so committed to working, perhaps they would have had a more attentive and energetic finger on the pulse. But this is a difficult issue for many families – balancing work and home is never an easy task – and this couple were trying to provide as well as they knew how.

I left the Josephs, who were very strongly in support of their grandchildren's adoption and future. They asked to send these sentiments to the family who adopted them; they knew they would probably never meet the children, although in rare cases this could happen. But the Josephs were not asking for this: they were happy to know that the children would be placed in a 'loving, caring home, and know some security'.

These last words are almost exactly what that grand-father said to me, and his wife had nodded in agreement. I couldn't help feeling that this was real caring, not self-interest, just concern for the children's wellbeing. What a refreshing change. I left them feeling encouraged and positive; meeting them had restored some of my faith in human nature. As I walked down the corridor, towards the stairs, it was also a great relief to know that it was all downhill for me!

Before long I was back in my car and heading for the office. I had a meeting in the afternoon, in which Paula was also taking part. We were discussing a family that we both knew, and had had dealings with recently. Marie, plus one or two other involved people were there, so it was a full house. We had to discuss quite a difficult issue around the future action needed for the children concerned.

We all crowded into one of the conference rooms; it was cool and a welcome break from the hurly-burly of the office. I was only part of this meeting because of an issue that I had become involved with during one of my duty sessions, so my role was more one of information provision. For Paula it was considerably more stressful, as this was her case and the children of this family appeared to be at considerable risk. I also knew, from what Paula had said to me and from my experience with the parents during a duty call, that this family were extremely uncooperative and rather aggressive individuals – and I think I am being very generous in my description there!

I recall Paula telling me about an incident when she had popped into the local shop on the estate where this family lived. It had been a quick stop to buy a Kit Kat to keep her going, but she had the misfortune to accidentally bump into them and was subjected to lengthy abuse in the middle of the shopping centre. Four members of the family had encircled her very threateningly. This, I would add, was further exacerbated by passers-by stopping to enjoy the spectacle and clearly expressing allegiance with the family against Paula. For Paula, one of the most regrettable side effects of this was that it tarnished her love of Kit Kats, and she used to say that just thinking about them conjured up all she had gone through that morning. Now that was a tragedy!

Marie introduced the situation and we began to discuss the events surrounding the family over the past nine months. I noticed that Paula was unusually quiet – silent in fact – but I assumed she was thinking through all the issues that were being raised. Many suggestions were being batted about, and then Marie put a question directly to Paula, asking her whether she had taken one particular piece of action. Paula didn't answer.

After a minute, Marie repeated her question, worded slightly differently, only to be met again with complete silence. We all now looked at Paula, who was seated at the end of the table and appeared to be intently reading her file with her head down. Her body was hunched over the file and she appeared to be almost frozen, in what I assumed was concentration.

Marie then said to Paula, 'Paula, are you alright? Did you hear me?' Silence greeted this comment and then suddenly Paula sat up, looked straight at Marie, and burst out, saying, 'All I get are suggestions to do more, and then more still. It's, have I thought of this and have I thought of that, have I done this and have I done that.' Her voice became raised, with an almost aggressive edge to it. I had never heard her even mildly raise her voice before and somehow it seemed quite shocking to hear this very challenging tone. I noticed Marie looking very shocked too, and a red flush had sprung up across her face as she listened to Paula.

Paula continued, 'Yes, in reply, I've done all those things and another hundred more. I've worked my socks off to sort this case. I can hardly cope with half my caseload at present, how am I supposed to do all this on top?'

The room fell into an embarrassed silence; everyone chose a point in the room to stare at, and did so. It was an ironic thought I had at that moment: here we were, a room full of social workers who spent our lives dealing with the outbursts of people's emotions, yet when one of our own exploded under the stress of it all, we seemed unable to cope. Perhaps we all jogged along, preferring to close our eyes to the reality of stress in ourselves. Perhaps this was the last unspoken taboo for us. Perhaps in being confronted with the extreme stress of another social worker, we were brought face to face with our own demons of fear that maybe, one day, we wouldn't be able to cope. Perhaps we all played a game in denying the burdens of the work, and the rule of the game was never to admit openly that you cannot cope. I wasn't sure, but I could read cringing embarrassment and confusion on every face and I also knew that, as a group, we had probably all experienced more emotional outbursts from other people than people in any other job I can think of!

Clearly Paula had to be answered. Marie said to her, 'You are obviously feeling overloaded Paula. Perhaps we need to talk about this.'

'Well we can talk all we want, but the work still needs to be done, and I can't see how, I simply can't,' Paula replied. Her voice rose towards the end of this statement and I could see that tears were welling up in her eyes. I felt that Paula was right on the edge and I wondered how much more she could take. The answer came all too quickly.

In the next moment she stood up and fled from the room. No one moved for a second, then Marie said she would give her a minute and would then go and talk to her. No one in that room really believed talking was going to help, but what other option was there?

I said to Marie that perhaps it would help if I went to talk to Paula first as I knew her well. Marie turned, and with a smile said, 'You know, I think that would be helpful. You don't represent the system so much. Ask her to chat to me afterwards. I'll be in my room.' An awkward and stilted agreement to reconvene on another day followed. Everyone gathered up their belongings and, in very subdued mood, left the room.

I gathered my things and returned to our office. There was no sign of Paula. I looked in the loos – no sign – and then asked reception if they had seen her. 'Oh yes,' said one, 'I think I saw her heading out to the Quiet Garden.'

The Quiet Garden had been introduced a few years

ago, ostensibly as a restful sanctuary for us all. Somewhere to take a break and relax! That was a joke; in fact it was used most by the smoking fraternity, who would congregate in a sociable group for their regular 'smoke breaks'. Oddly, I often looked on enviously, not because I wanted to smoke, not in the least, but because of the regular breaks they took in the fresh air, with an opportunity to chat or joke away some of their stress. Without that addiction to propel me into stopping, I and most of my colleagues just kept going, when actually a break would have been valuable. Ah well, maybe I should make more of having a caffeine addiction, but that could easily be satisfied at my desk so that was not a winner!

I beat a path to the garden at the side of the office in the hope of finding Paula there, and I did. She was sitting at the furthest extreme, clearly hiding herself away. I was unsure if she would want my intervention, but someone had to speak to her.

I wandered over and sat down next to her. 'Paula, I can see you are feeling really overloaded, that's clear.' There was a long silence and then Paula spoke. 'You know, Becky, I don't know how anyone is supposed to deal with their job, the amount of paperwork they constantly push onto us, the number of cases.' She shifted a bit and went on. 'I lie awake at night wondering which of my cases, that I have not had time to work on as I know I should, will blow up in my face, with something awful happening to the children. I can't sleep most nights for worrying. The doctor gave me some sleeping tablets for a very short time, but once they were over I was no better. I wake up in tears and panicking some nights.'

I turned to her and asked, 'Have you talked to anyone else about this?' Paula replied, 'Only the doctor, and my mother last time I went home.'

'What did they say?'

'Well, the GP suggested I talk to my senior about case-load management, but you know what a waste of time that is. Who's going to deal with the cases if we don't? I don't want to abandon my caseload. Anyhow, there is a chronic shortage of social workers; the last two who left have not been replaced yet. My mother said I should give up the job, take a break and find some less stressful work. I know she's worried.'

'And what do you think?' I asked. I looked at Paula, sitting rigidly, shoulders hunched, arms tightly gripping the bench, and watched as tears slowly ran down her face, at first in a trickle, and then like a torrent unleashed. Between the tears, she tried to speak, and eventually managed to say, 'I don't know. I can't do this.'

There was a long pause, and then she continued. 'You know, for the first time in my life I feel so exhausted I almost don't care anymore. That scares me because that is so unlike me.' She stopped speaking and, after a while, she said, 'I can't walk away from some of my cases that are in a critical stage. I've got two going through court in the next two weeks and two more that I am preparing reports for court. I would need to have done all my closing summaries and updated my recordings. How can I leave those? Then there's . . .'

I stopped her. 'Look, Paula, you've been under pressure for too long. What do you feel is the right step to take?' There was silence. Paula didn't speak; she looked exhausted and seemed to be almost beyond thinking. But I knew she was. It was from her inner self that the next words came. 'Becky, I want to go on, but I can't, I simply can't. I've been dragging myself out of bed for the last few months, often thinking I couldn't cope, but carrying on. I can't concentrate, I keep forgetting things and I've even had funny dizzy spells. I even burst into tears at the supermarket yesterday when a cashier was rather sharp with me. I just feel I've reached the end, I just feel it is all too much. I want to run away and hide, where no one can get me. I want to forget it all and sleep for months . . .'

Silence followed this outburst of truth, and then I said, 'OK, look, you need to explain this to Marie and decide what you want to do.' Paula nodded, and I said that I was going to get her a drink first, to give her time to calm down and think through what she felt was best for her.

We sat in the garden for some time, while we both sipped our drinks. Beside us was a little water feature, installed, I assumed, to calm the workers, but which somehow seemed almost irrelevant in the face of such distress. There would be no easy solutions, but if Paula could get through the next few hours and sort out a way forward, that would be a start.

I went along with Paula to see Marie, and then left them to talk. After about fifteen minutes Paula emerged, tears running down her face again, and tore off to her desk where I saw her stuff a multiplicity of belongings into her bag from her desk: brushes, pens, notebooks, periodicals, her special mug. Without a word to anyone, she almost blindly tore out of the office, not stopping to respond to the words of a colleague who had just returned to the office and was passing her. I looked out of the window and saw her go to her car, get in, pause, then drive. I took out my mobile and sent her a text: 'I'll ring you tonight, take care.'

Marie came out of her office and called me in. She looked tired and extremely serious and, as I came into her office, she closed the door and said to me, 'Look, Becky, could we keep this confidential for the moment. Paula doesn't want anyone knowing what has happened, and I think we have to respect that. She has decided to take extended leave and see her doctor. If she feels able, she will return in three months. How we will manage I do not know; I need to ring the agencies to get some emergency cover. But, I repeat, please don't tell anyone what has happened – she wants it to be known that she has been taken ill with something.'

I replied that I certainly wouldn't, and cynically wondered if this request had a dual purpose. Firstly for Paula, who quite understandably wanted to keep her private struggles private, which she was very much entitled to, but secondly, such an event seriously undermined the morale in a team, which was already low. I understood that part of a senior's role was to maintain good morale and wondered if the secrecy also served this purpose.

Paula was off for much longer than the three months and I met up with her regularly over the time she was on sick leave. I vividly recall her words after about three months: 'I feel like a burden, so heavy that I could hardly breathe, has been lifted from my shoulders and sometimes now I occasionally feel pleasure in little things again.'

*

Paula never did return to the job. After her period of sick leave she decided to take a social work post with Care of the Elderly, a job not without stress, but not of the order of Child Protection. I know she settled well in this new field and enjoyed working with a different age group. But there were times when I was chatting about work and about the children that I sometimes saw a look in her face, one of longing and of regret, and once I asked her whether she missed Child Protection work. She looked at me and replied, 'You know, I really did love the work, it gets under your skin. I enjoyed the challenges and, yes, even now I still sometimes miss the work dreadfully – the children and the enormous buzz – but I came too close to being unable to cope anymore and I dare not step back.'

There was a pause, and I could almost see her mind ranging over the last year at work, and many of its critical moments. She took a deep breath of relief and freedom, rather as someone takes when they arrive at a pleasant destination after a long car journey, looked up at me with a real sparkle in her eyes and, in a less serious, even light tone, added with a grin I was so glad to see, 'Not many of my elderly clients do runners, and that makes for a much easier life!'

19

Mena

The months had rolled on. I recall one particularly wet morning, when the sky was so grey that it seemed the rain would never stop, it was coming down in sheets that no umbrella seemed to be designed to handle with any degree of proficiency. My car windscreen wipers struggled to handle the sheer volumes of water the sky was producing and everywhere on the journey to work people scuttled along, bowed under umbrellas or desperately trying to pull collars up to protect themselves from a total soaking.

I arrived in the office, shook myself rather ineffectually free of raindrops, hung up my sodden raincoat over the radiator and started to walk over to my desk. Before I managed to even achieve that short distance, Marie called me into her office.

I was intrigued, because not only did she suggest that we grab a coffee each first, which we did (well, actually I made the coffee), but then she handed me 'the' biscuit tin! Nothing wrong with that – it was a very nice biscuit tin. Well, it had been – a long time ago. It was covered in heather and men in kilts, and had clearly been brought back – probably by Marie – from a Scottish sojourn, doubtless acting as a happy reminder of the home country. No longer full of shortbread, it was now home to Marie's very special selection. We all knew that this only came out on certain very specific occasions, those being 'coating the pill' or entertaining important visitors. Well, clearly I was not in the latter category, so . . . I waited.

There was a brief pregnant pause. Never a one to waste valuable time on meaningless small talk, she launched in. 'Look, Becky, I need to run something past you. Norbeck Junior School rang this morning and are expressing extreme concern about one of their families, the MacDonalds. This case was allocated to Tom, who left last month, but I know that he hadn't had time to do more than a very preliminary visit, and I doubt if he had scraped the surface. It's a complex situation, extremely worrying and needs experience. But we need to get onto this situation pronto.'

Marie paused and seemed to gaze very deliberately, if briefly, out of the window, as if she might find inspiration out there. She then continued. 'I know you're up to your eyes in work at present but I need to give this to a worker who has the appropriate experience and there simply is no one else.' Here she paused, and looked straight at me. Unusually, I noticed that she was fiddling with the paper clip in her hand in a way that suggested she was rather concerned about all this. She then reached for a pad and pen from her desk and said, 'There must be work you could offload to a newer worker, or some way we could free you up to take this case on. How would you feel about brainstorming your caseload to see what we could do?'

I was very aware of just how much work I had on, but could equally see her dilemma, and understood this request. However, where on earth was I to find the time? My mind scanned all the court work I was involved in and the families that I was working with – with whom, indeed, I had after long hard months built up a rapport and trust. Then there was all the paperwork – review forms and assessment work – awaiting my attention. I could see no easy answer.

I listened to her description of the case: a very young single mother, Mena, with five young children, three girls and two boys. The mother was simply not coping and the eldest three rarely reached school. Goodness only knows what was happening at home. The school reported grubby, often-hungry children, who not infrequently fell asleep at their desks. The mother was chaotic and seemed unable to handle any requests to go into school and have a chat, and if cornered by a member of staff became either aggressive or walked off in a huff.

In spite of everything, I felt challenged by this case. I actually felt that this was something I would enjoy getting to grips with, so my brain began churning. I would need time – a lot of it. I would need to do a great deal of talking: to school, health visitors, doctors and the family.

'Marie,' I began, 'I would actually like to look at this family, but I can only manage this if I can offload as you say. So, yes, let's have a go with your brainstorm, and see what is possible.'

We sat for a good hour, discussing options and listing tasks to be done. One of my long-term, very stable, foster placements had several meetings coming up and reams of forms and paperwork, which I needed to circulate to all and sundry for the meetings. I had no concerns, and knew that if I spent an hour talking it through with someone who could stand in for a couple of months that would give me a window to concentrate time on the MacDonald family. I could also ask someone to begin work on some of my chronologies that were not required for court but needed doing. It was a real no-no to have chronologies not updated, and for good reason. If a social worker should be off sick or, heaven forbid, on holiday, a good chronology at the front of a file will have all the significant happenings listed in date order, allowing any duty worker to quickly pick up on all the significant events of that family. As I thumbed through my diary, we agreed to have a social work assistant take on several appointments in non-critical cases, and tackle much of the routine paperwork. We both knew that in turn this worker would need to leave on hold many things they had lined up, such as contact meetings, and in some instances we would need to get agency workers to fill in.

Marie and I talked at length about the family, and finally I scooped up the file and began to walk out. As I made for the door at my usual speedy pace, Marie said, 'Just a moment, Becky.'

She gave a rather cynical half laugh, and then said, 'Given all I was told by the school, this should have been on our radar long ago. We've failed these children so far, and now is when that ends. But there are so many issues; it's a lot to cope with, so just a warning – take great care, this could be the one that gets you into the Sunday papers! Please keep me fully informed at all times, and for this case don't be afraid to ring me any time.' She paused as if she was weighing up what she was about to say, and

then added, 'Becky, you need to be very aware of something else in this case. I've checked this out with the
police, who suspect that the local drug barons may have
got their claws into this girl. We think they may be using
her. She may be a victim or she may be a willing con-
spirator. Hopefully, you will find out. But remember, you
will not be a welcome presence to them; don't be taking
any risks. Use the police if needed.'

I took a breath, perhaps a little deeper than usual,
thanked her for this, and laughed. What else could I do?
But I knew that was her 'flashing red lights' warning.
It was a rather serious, somewhat fixed smile that was
held on my face as I walked out of her office, clutching
several bursting, rather ageing files.

Returning to the main office, I made myself a coffee
and struggled to clear a space on my desk. I spent over
an hour reading the files, which was all the time I could
spare for the moment. I'd have to sacrifice an evening's
TV to read the rest in peace and quiet. Now for some
information gathering! For two hours I sat on the phone.
I sought to contact as many as possible of the outside
agencies that had had any dealings with the family. I
spoke to past and present schools, playgroup leaders, health
visitors, housing, the GP, to name but a few. As time went
on, I became more and more concerned and a clearer
picture began to emerge.

If the comment, 'I'm amazed nothing has been done
about this family before,' was said to me once, it was
repeated six, maybe seven, times and those who did not
use those words expressed great concern. Some were fairly
disdainful about the lack of action from Social Services.

I had long since stopped allowing these hints to unsettle me. I was not personally responsible for the failures of the whole system, or indeed for the whole of society's problems, and it was a frequent feeling to wish different actions had been taken in the past. But the wisdom and self-righteousness of hindsight are wasted emotions. What I did feel in such cases was a strong desire to right any failings by making sure that I missed nothing at the time. That I could do, and hope that where I failed today, another would do the same for me one day.

I began to get a feel for this family. I had discovered that class A drugs had been found in the home on many occasions; there had been several incidents of the police being called to fights, always between visiting individuals, with the children sometimes lurking tentatively in the background. I had also learnt from one of the local police officers that when certain groups of local low life were missing, this mother's home was always considered a good point to start the search.

I rang the mother, Mena, explained that I would like to meet up to have a chat, and organised to visit that afternoon. She wasn't keen, to say the least, so I had to be fairly determined because I knew I would never find a time she was happy with. I needed to make a start, and this situation could not be left any longer. I had made some space in my diary, but I still had to hurry through rather a lot of paperwork to make time to visit Mena that afternoon.

On my way out I signed in the red book, and flagged up Sandy to monitor my visit. Sandy double-signed the entry in the book and, with her usual kindly grin, wished me luck. This was standard procedure if we did a slightly higher-risk visit. Any new client came into this category, along with known threats. This woman had no history of violence, but I rather wished that James was not away!

I passed Marie in the corridor. When I told her where I was off to, she wished me luck and reminded me to ensure someone was checking on me; I continued on my way. As I was halfway down the corridor, she shouted after me, 'Oh Becky, on a slightly lighter note, have you got a hair-band? The GP, health visitor, one teacher and two teaching assistants have all managed to catch the children's head lice. Don't say I didn't warn you!' 'Oh great,' I thought, and was glad that I had an Alice band and some elastics lurking in my car from visits to another rather 'alive' family!

In what seemed a very short space of time I found myself driving down Alton Crescent, a 1950s council estate, where the care given to the little gardens at the front varied considerably. I had visited a few homes in this road and nearby. I had sat in some that were beautifully cared for, with gardens tended in a way that would earn them a slot on any gardening programme. Others were so filthy that you chose your chair carefully, with a view to avoiding the insect life which probably dwelt abundantly in the soft furnishings, where it could multiply undisturbed by man, beast or hoover.

Mena's home was at the end of the road. I pulled up, trying to park were there was no broken glass, gathered my things, pulled my hair back in a band and headed for her home. Any pretence to a garden had long since been abandoned. The ground was mud, with a line of broken paving stones. A generous covering of rubbish coated the mud – nappy sacks, pizza boxes, broken bottles, squashed cans – all jostled for space, and many more had been partially buried long ago. The fence that had once so proudly defined the square had long since given in to the vagaries of life and assault from passers-by, visitors or family members. It hung split and rotten in various grotesque positions, with huge rusting nails projecting meaninglessly from the posts.

I picked my way up the path and knocked on the door. There was a tremendous racket going on in the house, with a woman's voice raised in exasperation, and I wondered, as I often did, what the family I was about to meet would be like, and where this would all end.

Mena's head poked around the door, while she pushed back two small grubby faces. 'You the Social?' she said in a clearly unwelcoming voice. And then, with a shrug of her shoulders, in a resigned voice she said, 'You'd better come in.'

Reluctantly, she opened the door, giving me a very clear and antagonistic scrutiny. As I was wondering about Mena and family, she jolly certainly was trying to assess what on earth I was going to bring upon her. From her expression, I could see clearly that she was in no way pleased to see me, nor did she want my intervention or help.

Mena had very pale, almost translucent skin, shiny dark brown hair, which she dragged back into an apology for a pony tail and very expressive, dazzlingly blue eyes. She was a pretty young woman, in spite of the well-worn and grubby tracksuit that she must have been wearing for a while. She spoke with a fairly strong Glaswegian accent, reflecting the city of her birth. She was only in her very early twenties, but looked even younger. At moments she looked vulnerable, and appeared more like a child; at others she struck one as a tough streetwise kid.

We walked through to the kitchen area, where the other children were playing on the floor. The kitchen was filthy; there was stuff everywhere – bits of discarded food lying in corners of the room, the bin overflowing, with more rubbish stacked by it, washing-up piled high in the sink and surrounding it. The cooker would need sandblasting to get off the deposits of – at a rough guess – many, many years of grease and spills. Her table was piled high with papers, packets, old take-away wrappings, nappy bags complete with contents and more plates covered in congealed leavings. The floor looked as if the last time the pattern on it had been visible was when it was initially laid, it was so ingrained with grease and stains that any generalised dirt was less visible. Clearly there was an animal in the home that had had an accident a while back and this remained another undealt-with problem, now desiccated and a part of the general mess lying about.

We sat down and chatted. I told her very clearly about the concerns that were being expressed all round, and that we really did need to look at what was going on. She listened to me, surprisingly quietly, and said little. As we talked, I was able to watch her with her children. They looked as if nothing they had on had seen soap and water for a long time, and they were pale and rather listless. The eldest was at home with a 'cold' – probably yet another day that Mena had not made it to school. From time to time, the older one wandered over and wanted her mother's attention, leaning into her side and looking up at her. Mena would pause and look down at her daughter, stroke her hair, deal with the request and then come back to our conversation. The younger ones came and sat on her knee in turns, or together, but she was patient, physically affectionate and loving with her children. A small ray of hope switched on in my mind as I watched and we talked, but the enormity of the task was enough to extinguish the least flicker of light.

What did I hope to achieve in this first visit? Well, I needed to make sure that Mena understood clearly the gravity of the situation, that things had to change, but that I was there to support her if she wanted to accept help – that was her choice. I talked, and at first I wasn't really sure if I was reaching Mena.

As the time went by, I began to notice that Mena was actually starting to look straight at me; she was listening, almost as if she was beginning to believe me. She went very silent when I fairly bluntly spelt out to her the enormous risks that her lifestyle was exposing the children to, and because of the serious nature of these risks, she was going to have to decide where her priorities lay. I felt certain also that she was trying to assess just how far I meant to go, and how determined I was and, moreover, whether she could pull the wool over my eyes. I had seen that look so often before, from so many clients.

I hoped she got the message when I said, 'Look, Mena, I'm not going to mess you about or deceive you. I'll be straight and fair, but things will have to change here, and radically. No child is safe from violence, abuse or being pulled into other rackets as long as your door is open to the people that at present you allow through. On top of these appalling risks, you also need to consider what you are doing to the children by failing to get them to school.' The state of the home, I felt, had to wait for another day.

Mena watched me as I spoke; her eyes filled with fear and her arms tightened involuntarily around two of her daughters. Then in a low voice she said, 'Are they going to take my kids away?'

I paused. This was the nub of the issue for her and, without dramatic changes, these children were far from safe with Mena. She was doing nothing to protect them and, yes, this was a likely outcome. Unless I was totally honest I was no help to the children or to her, so, after a moment to consider what I was going to say, I replied.

'Look, Mena, my priority is to ensure the safety of your children. As things are, they are not safe and this cannot continue. But I promise you that I will move heaven and earth to help you if you are prepared to work with me and change things. However, if you don't or won't, then I know that we will have to act. I will be forced to report that you are not co-operating and something will have to be done. I need to get to know you, and you me, and we need to work out a plan to help you. But I cannot help you unless you want desperately to be helped. You would have to work hard, very hard; it would be the hardest work you have ever undertaken, but I will be here with you. If you want to change you can, I'll make sure of that, but the choice must be yours and yours alone.'

Mena had listened very intently to my words; she had sat very quietly as I spoke and it seemed as if all the bravado and fight had drained away. When I finished speaking she continued to sit still and quiet, her hands fiddling with the torn edges of her tablecloth, her posture bent, weary and defeated. There were a few long minutes of utter excruciating silence, when it felt as if she was undergoing an enormous internal struggle. Then she looked up at me. Her eyes were changed – they held a bleakness that was almost chilling, and her words have remained engraved on my mind from that day to this because of the terrifying emotion behind every drawn-out breath.

'I can't do it, I'm so tired, I'm drowning, and I'm too scared to stop all this, I just can't . . .'

She paused, and after another minute added, 'You don't understand. They'll kill me.' A silence hit the room, it was tangible.

Then it was my turn to draw a deep breath, and I leaned forward to look very squarely at her. 'Mena, you've got to trust me. I will help you, but you need to tell me what is going on here that puts you and your children at such risk, and yet you can't stop it.'

Mena was silent for a time, looking down and wringing her hands in a relentless battle with her emotions. Mena had possibly never been able to trust. How could she now? I felt almost breathless in her long pause. Was she going to trust me and allow me in, or would she recoil and shut me out? Desperation was writ large in her eyes when she finally looked up; there was no light in those deep-blue eyes, no expression but despair in that face. She then spoke up, very quietly, as though she hadn't the energy to speak any louder, and summed up her situation, saying,

'If I do tell on them I'm at risk of my life. If I don't I will lose my kids, won't I? I can't lose them, but I'm no good to them dead. What can I do?' With this final effort a tear began to trickle very slowly down her cheek. She rubbed at it ineffectually, simply leaving a dirty streak across her weary face. In a low, at times scarcely audible, voice, Mena began to talk. She talked without stopping; it was almost as if someone had taken the top off a bottle that had remained closed for years. Out streamed stories of horror and fear. She talked for nearly two hours about her childhood, her few short years when she had been taken into foster care and seen a brief time of love and affection, and her life when she returned to her family and ever since.

In spite of everything, Mena was clearly a fairly intelligent young woman, but came from a really tough background. Her mother had died when she was very young, and her father drank himself to death two years later. There were no family members who actually wanted Mena, but she went to an aunt, where she was treated as less than a servant. Raised in that home, she developed a tough exterior, learnt to expect not to be valued, loved or considered and, worse, became easy prey to anyone who appeared to want her. Her brief period in care came when her aunt was ill for a while, and she recalled her foster carer with considerable warmth. However, she had never mentioned her life at home and so when the aunt recovered she was reclaimed from her foster home. Clearly there were the welfare benefits for the aunt in reclaiming her and, further, Mena was turning into an attractive young girl and her aunt could spot a business opportunity when she saw one!

Mena's teenage years rolled out dancing to her aunt's tune, making money on the streets and finally becoming pregnant. Relationship followed relationship; each time she was looking for someone to fulfil her need to be loved, but along with the relationships came five vulnerable children, whom she struggled to care for. It was clear from what she said, and perhaps more so from how she said it, that she knew she was failing her children badly but she was at a loss to know how to escape all this. And she wasn't really sure if she wanted to or whether she could. She said that she could not accept losing her children; this was the bottom line for her – she could not allow it. But then they all said that and I had become cynical over the years. Actions speak louder than words; indeed, actions are the only things that change children's lives, not words!

During the last two years Mena had fallen victim to a local gang of drug dealers, who saw her as a ready source of cover, a place to use as a dealing centre and a young woman to make use of in whatever way it suited them. She told me that in the early days she had fallen for one of the main leaders of the gang and been in what she had thought was a committed relationship. So she was reasonably happy with the arrangement, believing he would bring security to her chaotic life and also believing he really cared for her. However, in the last year he had added two other young women to his entourage. She had become old hat, no longer needed, redundant and she felt depressed and desperate. By now she was in it all so deeply that even the realisation that he was simply using her had to be pushed to the background so that she could survive. She wanted to avoid becoming another in the line of casualties that she had heard of over the years – left beaten, assaulted or dead in a gutter or nearby woodland. She also knew they had guns and knives aplenty and were not afraid to use them.

I listened with the growing realisation that this woman was risking everything in telling me all this. Both of us knew that the word would be out that I was there and it was only a matter of time. It was a casual glance through the window that caused Mena to stiffen. She dropped her voice and told me that the youth who was so casually hanging about on the corner was one of the gang informers, who would be watching and noting exactly how long I was there.

I sat back, and did some fast thinking. As Mena had talked, I had become increasingly convinced that she really did want to get away from all this. Her concern for the children had spilled out everywhere and she had admitted to finding their care quite overwhelming, but she wanted to change things. In spite of my tendency to cynicism, I felt she meant it and I believed she deserved a chance to prove this. I was thinking hard about how I could progress things and was beginning to introduce ideas with Mena. But what happened next superseded any actions I was planning.

As I sat there with Mena, there was a sudden crashing sound in the kitchen. Mena and I rushed out to see what had happened and were confronted by a young man freaking out in the kitchen, hurling things about in a rage and seemingly completely out of control. He had clearly been there for some time, because his first words to Mena were, 'You bitch! You traitor!' He continued to pull out

drawers and throw the contents everywhere, quickly followed by the drawers themselves. He smashed all the
china sitting in the sink, then kicked the unit doors until
they split under his assault. Chairs were turned into mis-
siles and the children screamed hysterically. He then
grabbed Mena and, in a voice half-crazed with rage and
half-crazed with whatever drugs he was taking, he threatened Mena with what he was going to do to her. The
eldest two children were shouting out in fearful voices
and wanting their mother; two of the younger ones were
crying uncontrollably and one of the small boys had hidden
himself in a corner, hiding his head in his arms and rocking
and moaning. In this home I wondered how often they
had seen addicts freaking out.

Mena tried to speak some words of comfort to them
but this provoked an even worse reaction from the young
man. He snarled at her and taunted her, repeating her
words from our conversation and making it very clear
that he had been eavesdropping for some time and had
heard much of it. Looking at the young man's face, I was
fairly sure he was well out of his mind, which meant
there was no way to predict what he might do. Further,
from my earlier conversation with Mena, I found myself
wondering whether he was carrying any weapons.

Mena collapsed onto the floor in sheer horror and the
young man pushed her aside. Just at that moment my
mobile went. It was my set-up security call from admin
because I had not returned as expected and was on a
'high-risk' visit. The young man snapped at me to ignore
it, but I said that if I did it would bring several workers
immediately to investigate, so he told me to get rid of

the caller and say nothing or we would all suffer.

I found it hard to handle my phone, because I was shaking, but the familiar sound of Sandy's voice steadied me momentarily. Sandy asked me if I was OK and reminded me of the case conference at four. I said I wouldn't be making it and asked her to pass that message onto Bill Thomas. There was a silence at the other end: firstly, she knew that I had to be at this meeting, as I had set it up and, secondly, Bill was our police liaison officer, totally unrelated to the meeting.

'OK,' she replied. 'I take it you'll need Betty to assist then?'

'Yes,' I replied, 'I do.' My relief in having conveyed the seriousness of my situation in the code-word 'Betty' was so great that I had to fight to hide any sign of relief, because the boy was getting irritable. I pretended to turn off my phone, but left it on, enabling Sandy to eavesdrop; fortunately the racket of the first child's crying was distracting the youth.

We were forced to sit on the kitchen floor and soon had three more crying children to add to the tension. By dint of the conversation that followed I hoped I had conveyed to any listener that we were under threat.

As time progressed the boy became more excitable and erratic and I feared that he was becoming *very* unpredictable. He was trying to contact the other members of the gang on his mobile, and with every failed attempt he became even angrier. We couldn't placate the children; their crying was winding him up dangerously. I have never felt so helpless in my life. Talking was not an option; he merely became more upset and angry, screaming at me to 'shut up'. Believe me, I did – discretion is definitely the better part of valour.

It was a long fifteen minutes later that I spotted a movement outside the window behind our captor. I felt a fresh burst of fear coursing through my body. Had the gang arrived in response to his calls? What followed happened so fast that I hardly know quite what did happen, but the back door burst open and three figures dressed in stab jackets rushed in, screaming, 'Police! Get down!' They had the youth grabbed before any of us knew what was going on. Within seconds they had the young man safely restrained; he had been too taken by surprise to act but as soon as the immediate shock wore off (a minute or two perhaps), he began to swear vehemently and abuse the police officers, at the same time struggling to get free. Fortunately, it was clear that he would be going nowhere; they had him firmly in their grasp, thank goodness.

Mena, her children and I stood in the midst of organised chaos, with police everywhere. I wanted to sit down and cry, as a release from the appalling tension, but knew this was a luxury that would have to wait. A very kindly police officer made us both a cup of tea, which we drank in a state of total shock, struggling to actually hold the mugs in our shaking hands. I found that I was shivering and barely able to string words together. Once the initial shock had passed, I began to gather my thoughts and I told Mena to pack some things for herself and the children. I rang a refuge I knew would take Mena and then went to help her with the packing.

One of the police officers escorted us to the refuge, which was well out of the area and a good distance away from any possible contacts. There was no other option for Mena and she didn't even suggest that she should stay. She knew that she was now a marked woman and wouldn't live long if she was found. Effectively, Mena disappeared. Just like that.

This has to count as one of the most terrifying incidents in my career. We later learnt that the youth who had held us captive had a serious mental illness, caused or exacerbated by a cocktail of hard drugs. He also had a long record of violence. He would not have thought long about attacking any of us, if indeed he had thought at all.

I will always remember Mena as one of my most rewarding cases. Sadly, her story is not an uncommon one, but the outcome shows what can be done when a parent really decides to change their way of life, and has the ability to do so.

She lived in the hostel for some months and then was re-housed a long way away from her old home, on the absolute fringe of the area we could cover. So, for some time I continued to work with her. Re-housing was the easy bit; Mena hadn't got a clue about how to cook or how to care for children or a home, and routines were a complete unknown to her.

We helped Mena to furnish her new home, and I organised for her to have help in the form of an older, very sensible, motherly home help, called Linda, who went in daily at first and helped Mena to organise routines for school, cleaning, shopping, cooking and general homemaking. She took Mena shopping, taught her to budget and, without a shadow of exaggeration, transformed that girl. She worked with Mena to show her how to play with the girls, and we sent her to a family centre to reinforce all these activities, to learn more and to make friends. The children blossomed and even Mena began to look very different. Mena worked so hard, and fought to learn everything that Linda suggested.

The one huge blessing, which probably made all this possible, was that Mena, almost beyond all probabilities and in spite of being surrounded by drugs, had never become involved with taking them. I still don't know how she managed to avoid them, but when asked she just said, 'I didn't want to.' Had we had to get her off an addiction I really doubt that she would have coped with any of this, or she would always have been vulnerable. Instead, Mena was able to learn, and very slowly we could withdraw the daily support to become every other day, then less frequent. Mena went from strength to strength and the children got to school.

On the day, well over a year later, that I told Mena that I would be closing her case and passing her over to her more local office so she had support if needed, she turned to me and said, 'I am so proud of everything I have achieved, so proud, and this is just the beginning. But I couldn't have done it without you and Linda, you've saved my life.' The smile in her eyes and the tears that accompanied those words will remain with me. Thanks of that sort are not common. I thought back to our first meeting, and the dramatic events that followed. Yes, things could have ended so differently. Yes, without our help she could probably never have climbed out of the total mess her life was in, but without her determination we could not have helped her. Sadly, that was more often the case. So what did Mena have that others didn't? I'm not sure, but there was something in her that grew with increasing strength over the years.

Some eight years later, when I was working in another area, I met her by chance when I was taking a client to visit a Family Support Centre that had been recommended to me. We walked into the centre together and were greeted by the manager, a smartly dressed, well-groomed young woman. It was Mena! She was now running this support centre on one of the rather difficult estates in a town some thirty miles from where she had originated. She was clearly loved by the mothers seeking support there, and was obviously a very different woman from the victim I had met all those years ago.

She turned from the conversation she was having and looked at me. We both stared at one another in amazed surprise for one brief moment. But it was the bear-hug I received from her that was very nearly my undoing. Tears threatened, because I knew how very nearly she had lost everything, how far she had come and just how tough it had been . . . and so did she. Brilliant. It doesn't come any better.

20

Tap, Tap, Tap

I sat listening to the tap, tap, tap of Tina's biro on the desk opposite me as she chatted gaily to someone on the phone, completely oblivious to the effect her repetitive tapping was having on me. I struggled to drag my mind back to the review papers that were staring at me from the computer, and tried to blank out the noise. I had been typing for over two hours already, but needed to keep going; I'd never finish this report if I didn't focus. I tried a quick mind game to bring back my concentration, and typed on for another five minutes at least. Slowly, I found my concentration slipping back onto the persistent tapping. She was still talking . . . and tapping . . . this was a very unfortunate habit she had, but any moment now I felt as though I was going to explode, so I closed down the file on my computer and decided to take a short break. This reaction was unlike me but I could self-diagnose stress at 100 metres.

I had a mountain of paperwork stacked up on my desk – no longer in neat piles; that level of organisational order had stopped after the first two inches. The piles had now assumed a life of their own, leaning at crazy angles, spreading across the desk and threatening to envelop me. If, with one wrong move, I nudged them whilst leaning to reach for the phone or a pen, they would be sent cascading across the floor and it would take ages to retrieve and sort them, at which point I knew I would be at risk of losing the plot.

Some of the review papers I was working on had to be completed today, so that they could be mailed out to all and sundry. I had a whole family of five children, all having a review shortly, so that was five forms to start with. I had several foster carer review forms which were needed for the regular reviews of carers, and on top of this I had to make applications to various centres for two of my clients, along with some feedback forms. Feedback! The likelihood of returning any feedback forms any time soon was not high.

At the rate I was going I'd be lucky to complete one form all morning. Every time I thought I was getting somewhere, I would need to find yet another elusive fact or date which entailed shuffling through the files. On top of this, at 12 o'clock the computer specialists were holding a special training meeting, 'to introduce us to the latest format for our recording of caseloads'. This, we were told, was going to save us time. So, great – I could do with that – except that I didn't hold out much hope. Computer buffs seem to believe, with evangelical fervour, that all the problems of the world would be solved if only another, better, more specifically designed program could be loaded onto our computers. That would be great if it worked, but firstly it usually entailed even *more* work and, secondly, I have never met a client yet who has benefited from my spending more and more time at my computer. But we had been told in no uncertain terms that we were all required to attend!

I decided to go over to the next office to check out some details on childcare facilities for one of my young mothers, and at the same time hoped that the walk and change of scene would calm me down. I was halfway there before the truth dawned; the only answer was to get my wretched paperwork sorted! There was no escape! I shortened my break and returned to my desk, stuck in my earplugs, which I kept in my briefcase for moments such as these, and in the muzzy silence that this created, slogged through the review forms, hoping that I would be able to find all the information I needed.

It must have been a good hour and a half later that I became aware of a gentle nudge and then a voice somewhere in the distance saying, 'Becky, are you coming to the meeting?' I realised that it was nearly 12 o'clock and our training session beckoned. I removed my earplugs, surfaced to the din of the office, closed down my report and stood up, re-orientating myself to the world around me.

It had been Ginny who had gently brought me back to earth, and she was waiting for me to join the clearly very unenthusiastic group of social workers who were making their way to the computer room. Had it not been for the three-line whip put out by our seniors, none of us would have been there! I am sure we could all think of at least a hundred tasks which were genuinely more urgent.

Shortly, we all found ourselves seated in front of individual screens, waiting for the trainer to arrive. Spot on time, she whisked through the door, carrying a neat file with a few handouts in it. She was a petite, neatly dressed, perfectly made-up young woman with an American-style smile that said, 'I'm here now, don't worry, your problems are over!' Hmmm!

We sat and listened whilst she explained the problems she was going to overcome with this new system. Confidently, she extolled the virtues of the 'new system', and then explained to us how it worked. There was an almost embarrassing atmosphere in the room, which spoke of the scepticism and weariness of the course participants, who, with the exception of one new starter, did not seem to share her enthusiasm. It was explained that, for every case, we would have to enter in our visits, legal status, review dates and medicals, plus a multiplicity of other pieces of information. In addition, there was a chart for the many codes that we had to enter alongside these facts, which would indicate certain aspects of any particular case. These codes, she emphasised strongly – and her expression assumed the look of a fearsome headmistress – were an essential part of the whole process and must be completed at all times. This statement caused a surge of fruitless adrenaline in my body, as I recollected the amount of time I already spent in my week searching for the 'correct' codes for all the other forms we had to complete (and the near panic that ensued if they were wrong or, even worse, missing!). I found myself wondering vaguely where I could keep this reference sheet of codes, alongside those I held for many and varied other reasons; I foresaw losing the form within days. Maybe I could photocopy it and keep a copy in my briefcase, but I already had so many other photocopied 'important reference forms' there that I would never find it in the bundles.

Whilst my mind had diverted off briefly on this train

of anxious thought, the trainer had hurried on with her detailed explanation of the 'new system'. Oh bother, I was now lost – completely. I sat there feeling hot, now knowing that losing the code sheet was the least of my worries. Now I had lost track of the increasingly complex instructions and stood about as much chance of achieving the completion of this form as breaking into the Bank of England! When she asked whether there were any questions, how could I say I needed her to start right back at the beginning, and maintain any level of credibility?

I then heard her saying to us that this work was to be entered onto the computer daily, so that it was always up to date, and that this was how it would lead to greater efficiencies. My mind then moved on. What if I'm out of the office, or too busy one day? I often struggle to find time to read all my emails and sometimes I cannot get round to opening half my post. I just carry out a brief skimming of it for any seemingly important letters, the rest sit and wait. I sat there feeling a mounting sense of panic, thinking, 'They must be insane. Don't they realise how pressurised we are already? Surely they don't really mean us to do this?' Alongside these fairly tame thoughts of personal stress were a few less commendable ones involving the perpetrators of these ideas. In order to keep my dignity I will leave those to your vivid imaginings.

Somehow I did not have the energy to express these thoughts. The morning's desperate attempts to catch up on this week's ongoing paperwork had left me drained. I began to feel depressed and trapped by yet another bureaucratic nonsense that was to be imposed upon us.

It was into that feeling of near desperation that I suddenly realised someone was talking, assertively and definitively. It was Hilary. A breath of fresh air – indeed a much-needed mountain breeze.

Hilary was a relatively new social worker in my team, but very experienced, and she was a great addition. She was committed, caring and passionate about the rights of both clients and her co-workers. I wouldn't call her militant because that conveys a sense of putting one's own wishes or ideals before others', whatever the situation. She was flexible enough to appreciate that this was not an ideal working environment – indeed, where do you find that? – but Hilary did not suffer fools gladly; she spoke her mind and didn't hold back.

I heard her saying, 'I'm sorry, but I need to say this.' (I doubt she was very sorry, and nor were the rest of us.) Anyway, she continued: 'This is yet another attempt at the bureaucratic burial of social workers. You cannot honestly expect us to take this on. We're all already seriously over-burdened with paperwork and bureaucracy. This is just too time-consuming a routine to be consistent with our daily tasks. Also . . .' Hilary paused here to think. 'Also, this information is mostly held on the sheets at the front of our files, the info sheets which were introduced only last year; we don't need a repetition, those forms work.'

There was a slight, almost undetectable, pause whilst, I suspected, the trainer regained her composure after this unexpected attack on her project.

'Ah, but they are not on your PC,' the trainer interjected in a somewhat artificially calm and slightly patronising tone, as if she were talking to a young child. 'It is so vital for you to have this level of organisation. Supposing you are away and this information needs to be accessed.' This final comment was accompanied by a broad, triumphant flourish of a smile which seemed to say, there you are, it's self-evident, problem solved!

She had reckoned without Carla, another social worker in the team. Carla had both Latin American and Yorkshire blood in her veins – an interesting mix. She was warm, passionately outspoken and blunt. Many ascribed the latter to her Yorkshire father and upbringing. Whatever, we all loved her, but she *was* blunt!

She passed judgement on the trainer's last comment, with a single dry sentence. '*If* we are away, and *if* someone wants to access this information, they can bloody well open the file and read it. Or have the literacy levels in the UK sunk to even new lows recently?'

A now more subdued and quietly desperate voice, recognising the determination in Carla's tone, returned by saying, 'Well, I do think you will find this a great help, and a timesaver.'

Hilary broke in at this point, and the contempt was clearly visible on her face before she even opened her mouth to reply. 'There is *no* way I can undertake to adopt this piece of imaginative form creation. Who invented this rubbish? Someone whose remit is clearly to persecute social workers and ensure that what little bit of time they have to escape their desks and visit clients is eaten up with even more bureaucracy!'

There was a generalised, quite passionate, nodding and murmur of agreement with this. The young woman was clearly losing her grip on the situation and although I felt immense pity for her personal situation – being on the receiving end of Hilary and Carla's 'telling it like it is' – I so wholeheartedly agreed with them that I could not but be glad that they were able to say what the rest of us were thinking, but were too chicken-livered to actually say. The trainer began to shuffle her papers because the time allocated to this session had expired, and the next group waited at the door. In a somewhat deflated voice she suggested that we talk to our seniors about this.

'We certainly will,' said Hilary. 'Someone around here needs to learn to say No!'

It was a somewhat negative group of social workers who left the training room. I suppose it had been a change of scene, but my morale had not been improved by this interlude. The feeling I had was of being transported back to school, where, as teenagers, we had to accept rules and procedures that we had had no part in setting up. But the feeling here was that we were expected to carry out a very difficult and stressful job, but have no say in the organisational set-up that dictated our use of time. None of this should have happened. We should have been able to express our frustrations with this 'brilliant scheme' long before that poor young woman had been sent to sell her scheme.

On the way back to our desks we shared our frustrations at the elephantine bureaucracy which too often weighed us down. But by the time we were back in the office, the phones were ringing and our return was greeted with long lists of calls to be returned. Before we had even reached our desks our minds had already been re-deployed to the job in hand. Social work! It simply wasn't possible to spend time grumbling – there was too much to do. Of course, this had the negative effect of us being unable to find time to invest in improving our lot. Survival was the name of the game.

I sat down and stared at my computer screen for a moment, took a deep breath, rebooted the monster and returned to my review forms. I had a great many to do. Lunch was my usual banquet at my desk.

I had a visit to do in the afternoon to a new referral. This new case was not going to get me a place in any popularity ratings. The referral had come from the police, who had been called to a domestic dispute and because of the presence of children in the home there were concerns. On Monday mornings we often found these cases in the referral pile. We each took them in turn. They were usually one-off warning visits, pointing out the dangers for the children and offering advice and sources of counselling. I typed on.

By 3 o'clock I had to head out to my visits. I reached my second appointment – with a Mr and Mrs Cokes – some time after 4.30 p.m. and knocked on the door.

It was opened by a smartly dressed woman in her mid-thirties, who looked very suspiciously at me and wanted to see my ID. I introduced myself; we had already spoken on the phone. She hurriedly took me inside, with a furtive glance around. I imagine she was anxious that I might be seen by her neighbours.

She asked me to sit down and nervously sat down opposite me. She told me that the children would be in later and that her husband was walking the dogs. Then she began to explain the row that had led to the police involvement.

'You see, Marty, my husband, is under a lot of strain. He's just lost his job and he hasn't been very well and, to be honest, he had had too much to drink on Saturday. If he doesn't get work soon, we'll lose the house.' She paused and then added, 'I wish he would try to get work instead of drinking. This was a one-off; he just lost it with me.'

It was as she paused after her last comment that a shattering barking erupted in the house, swiftly followed by the appearance in the room of two huge black lurcher dogs. They say that real fear can be a paralysing experience. Well, at that moment, I felt unable to move out of the sheer terror that one of these dogs would finish me off if I did. I sat frozen in my chair. Mr Cokes followed them into the room, looked aggressively at me and snapped at his wife, 'Kathy, is this that social worker?' She nodded, and he turned to me. Already nervous at the proximity of the dogs, which were so far just leaping about the room, his speech did nothing to reduce my discomfiture. 'What the blazes is it to do with you what goes on in this house? This is my house, and it's none of your blasted business!'

The dogs picked up on his none-too-friendly attitude to me and clearly decided that I was an undesirable – someone that it was their responsibility to dispose of. I had little doubt that their idea of disposal was not going to be humane either! They came right up to me and there was a low rumbling in their throats. The couple seemed to feel this was quite harmless behaviour on the dogs' part! As I was still seated (feeling that to rise might be perceived by the animals as a threat, and lead to an attack on me), I was now face to face with the dogs and could even feel their rather hot breath on my face.

Mr Cokes continued his tirade and began to get increasingly worked up into a state. I explained to the couple that, when the police are called to arguments (the police actually described it as 'a very unpleasant fight') and there are children present, we are asked to visit the family to see if we can help, because children who are exposed to violence do suffer considerably. I maintained a low calm voice at this point, though it took every thread of self-restraint to do so; I continued to try to get Mr Cokes to understand my presence. I told him that the police had said that he was having a really tough time, what with having been unwell and that, with the closure of his company, he had lost his job. There was a slightly responsive pause from him as I said this, and I continued to say that he must feel under enormous pressure, and all this must be very hard to cope with, particularly because he had never been out of work before. Silence followed my words and I wondered what was going to happen next.

My verbal acknowledgement of his clearly extremely difficult and worrying situation seemed to touch his mood. Perhaps no one had been able to recognise his stress before. Let's face it, his wife was also under tremendous strain. I don't know why, but suddenly he sat down. I turned to him and for the first time he looked me in the eyes. What I saw was a beaten man – tired, weary and unable to see a way out. It was after this look that he sharply called to the dogs, 'Ben! Boris! Get out! Go to the kitchen!' Both dogs jerked around to look at Mr Cokes and, on a swift repetition of his commands, they raced off into the kitchen.

I quietly breathed a deep sigh of relief, and felt the adrenaline surge I had been experiencing slowly subside, though I still felt pretty awful. However, Mr Cokes suddenly seemed almost glad to talk. It was like a river flooding out; he seemed almost unaware of anything at times, and he just talked and talked and talked.

His wife sat rigidly on the edge of her chair, her eyes glued to his face as he spoke, and periodically she interjected in quite a sharp tone with comments such as:

'You never told me that.'

'I didn't know you felt like that.'

'Why didn't you tell me that?'

As the time passed her voice gradually softened and I could see mounting compassion in her face for this man who, for the first time in his life, had no work, couldn't find any yet, and had lost all his pride. He talked about his role always having been to provide for his family, and when he said that, his wife said, 'But you always have. This isn't your fault, Marty.' With this last comment, he turned to her and said, 'But I should be able to provide for my family. I don't want to be like my father. He was hopeless, drank himself into his grave and left us all destitute. If my mum hadn't worked her fingers to the bone, we'd have been homeless and hungry.' He paused and went very quiet, almost as if he couldn't decide whether to continue. This was a private burden he had kept hidden. Could he say more? I think he felt he was at his wits' end, and nothing mattered now.

'You know, Kathy, I remember as if it were yesterday. I

must have been about eleven, coming home to find my father dead drunk again, my mother crying and distraught because he had drunk all the money, again. I went up to my room and sat, so angry that my father could do this to her and, I suppose, to us all. I remember punching my pillow and crying. I can still see all that as if it was yesterday. I hated him so much. He died a few months later and the guilt was terrible, but I was glad. I had wanted him to die. Then I feared that my wish had been granted and that I had caused his death. I know now he died of liver failure from the drinking, but it took me a long time to accept that.'

Mr Cokes had been looking at the floor all through these revelations, and now suddenly he looked up, turned to his wife and continued, 'You know what I swore on that day, Kathy? I swore that whatever else I did in life, I would never, ever, be like my father: a drunken, nasty, lazy, waste of space, never . . .' He sighed. 'Look at me now. That's exactly what I have become – like father like son. It would be better for you and the children if I was dead.' At this, he broke down, and Kathy rose immediately and sat with him, putting her arm around him.

There was a lot going for this family, but up to this point there had been little understanding. Before I left that day, I set up a series of appointments with Kathy and Marty, to go on for a limited time. I left a very sober couple, who had much thinking and talking to do in order to process all that had come out in this very dramatic meeting.

As I left the house, I hoped the dogs were in the garden,

but no. Marty stopped them in mid flight to beat me to the front door. He made them sit, and insisted that they offered me a paw to shake. I appreciated that this was Marty's way of lightening a very emotional moment, and of putting his precious dogs in a better light, so I took the proffered paws in turn. I didn't linger in my paw shaking; I felt that discretion was very much the wiser side of common sense! The look (which I can only describe as somewhat malevolent) in the dogs' eyes as they allowed their paws to be shaken was not consistent with Marty's intentions, and it said to me, 'I am obeying my master, because I have to. I wouldn't choose this but I don't forget people like you. Don't forget – don't step over the line, or else.'

I left their home with a mix of feelings. I was so glad to leave the intense emotional atmosphere, but I felt an enormous satisfaction from having helped this couple to open up, share their feelings and begin to move on. There is no question that the more intense interviews with clients leave one drained and very tired. Add fear to that intensity, and you will understand why my journey home was so welcome and, even more welcome, putting the key in the lock of my little house and closing the door between me and the world.

That day turned out to be a pivotal moment for Kathy and Marty. They began to talk to one another, and then I was able to agree with them some steps they could take which would enable them to get their lives back on track. I met up with them regularly over the following months and each time we set targets and they would work on these; and things really did move on.

Marty was great: he accepted that he needed help with his drinking and his temper, and determinedly took up the help on offer. As a couple, they worked on communication, and as the weeks went on I could really see them growing closer. I saw the children regularly and checked that there were no problems at school. Any hiccups had clearly been related to the problems at home and the worrying change in their father – who had in the past always been involved, caring and responsive. As things improved at home, so the boys had fewer problems.

I finally closed the case after about five months. Marty and Kathy were coping well without anyone's help, and that is the perfect outcome. Marty had really taken his problems seriously, worked hard on them, accepted that he needed help from various sources including Alcoholics Anonymous, and he had become a much stronger man as a result. He also started up his own business, taking on odd jobs and decorating – something he was good at – and he was doing quite well.

It had been time well spent and I was pleased to be able to close the case knowing that Marty and Kathy had now taken charge of their lives and no longer needed me to keep them focused. I love being made redundant in these circumstances – it makes the job worthwhile!

21

A Home for Sarah

I can hardly recall the months that finally led up to Sarah's court proceedings. I was so busy, day after day, that the weeks raced by. I did have one week's leave booked but on day two managed to go down with flu and spent the next three days in bed, aching and moaning about my state. For the following three days I slowly tottered about the house, feeling as if I was at least 100 years old. I took the view that at least my brain was having an enforced rest and by day five I was able to cope with some of the light reading I had stored up for my leave.

The adoption team, thank goodness, were not languishing in their beds but were hard at work sorting through possible families for Sarah. It is the rule that in these cases plans are made for both outcomes. So there has to be planning to support a reunited family, alongside finding a possible home for a child should this not prove possible.

The court hearings went ahead; I wrote endless court reports, often in the early hours of the morning. Because there was neither time at work, nor peace, I often had to stagger to my car carrying all the files home, where my tiny dining room became my newly appointed study. I defy anyone to be able to write a clear, logical report in the noisy open-plan offices in which we spend our days, and which management planners many years back must have decided were the way forward. The noise levels were truly unbelievable at times.

In spite of there being about eight huge bursting files on Sarah and her family, it was good that in the silence of the evening, or sometimes the early morning, I could read through every detail of her sad life until I felt I really had a true picture of the family. In the silence I felt able to think and write down a clear case for what had become, with every passing week, increasingly obviously the right recommendation for the local authority. And that was that Sarah should be freed for adoption. Her mother simply wasn't managing the changes in her lifestyle that were needed to improve things.

There were many meetings and telephone calls with the guardian – the court-appointed social worker. There were regular reviews with the foster carer, the mother and her partner. And there was ongoing contact with the mother's drug and alcohol counsellor, overseeing contact arrangements, statutory meetings of all kinds and medical follow-ups. There were many reports, some very lengthy, associated with Sarah's future as well as discussions with the long-term fostering/adoption team, who were trying to make a preliminary adoptive match for Sarah. I could go on. It was non-stop work to bring this whole situation to a critical point – the final hearing at which the judge would decide whether Sarah was to return home, if further work had to be done to enable the mother to try to parent the child again, or an order should be made to free Sarah for adoption. As part of this work it is a statutory rule that we *must* check through the extended family to see if there is a relative willing and able to parent the child. This alone was quite a task, and I mention this because people often think we whizz children out of their homes, away from the bosom of their families, and never look back. I spent weeks endeavouring to contact every possible relative. We knew that the maternal grandparents were known drug dealers and the paternal grandfather was dead. The paternal grandmother had severe arthritis and was adamant that she wanted no part of this. Sarah's mother had only one brother and he was in prison. I also had to track down Sarah's father, long ago off the scene. This was like a piece of serious detective work.

Eventually he was traced to a remote seaside town, where he was living in a small, rather cramped terraced cottage with a girlfriend and her four children; and another child, his, was on the way. He was happy to meet me, in spite of having had no contact in any way with Sarah since her birth. He told me that his relationship with Sarah's mother had been brief and stormy, that he had been very young and stupid to, in his words, 'get mixed up with that lot', but their short time together had resulted in Sarah's birth. His house-bound mother was still living on the estate where Sarah's mother lived. She kept him informed about things on the estate, so he had no illusions about the life Sarah probably lived. To my surprise, he was pleased to know that Sarah had been taken away from Julie and her family, and his view was that she should never return home! He seemed a reasonable, fairly sensible sort of guy and his girlfriend came across as sound. He was working regularly now and was trying to make a life for himself and his family. He was very clear that there was no way he wanted to be any part of Sarah's life, but he was happy to sign the necessary documents should adoption be the decision. He had wanted to see a picture of Sarah, and he did say that if ever she wanted contact he would write. He had no other family apart from his rather elderly and infirm mother.

When I finally received a letter from Julie's uncle in prison, it was interesting that he said that he believed that Sarah would have the best chance in life if she was taken away from the family! I have a great deal of respect for this level of honesty and concern. Sadly, that particular relative had had many years of thinking time inside to view his family life more objectively, but many in his position never gain this level of clarity about their lives.

All this work went on and we all had an objective: to be ready by the final court date to take the right steps and minimise any delay for Sarah. The adoption team had identified several possible families who were seeking an older child to adopt and who matched Sarah's needs. We wanted a family that would have energy and time to invest in her development, because she was so far behind in every way. It was also, we all felt, very important that Sarah was the youngest by quite a good number of years, so that the carers would have more emotional space for her and she would not be competing with another child or even children at a similar stage of development. She would need a great deal of time to help to heal some of the damage resulting from her early experiences, so a very emotionally warm and stable couple with a great deal of spare capacity was what we were hoping for. I spent a great deal of time with the adoption team, talking over

Sarah's needs and looking at the possible families. I felt I really knew Sarah and had a fairly clear idea of what sort of family might be right for her.

It was a few weeks before the final hearing that I travelled to meet a couple who had been picked out as one of two strong favourites, should adoption become the path. Jenny, who was the social worker from the adoption team working with me on the selection of a family, decided to travel up with me so that we could use the time to talk over any issues. It was a horrible wet day; the rain fell in a constant heavy drizzle, covering the countryside in a shroud of grey mist and dampening the spirits as only non-stop rain can. As we finally approached the junction turn-off on the motorway I began to feel slightly anxious. I couldn't help it; I felt I had been through so much with Sarah, directly and indirectly, and I wanted the couple to be right. We navigated our way through the confusing signs to the town where the couple lived and soon found ourselves walking up the path of a lovely old Victorian terrace with neat rows of colourful plants lining the path. The door was flung open and a bouncy, slim, red-haired woman greeted us with a welcoming smile. Sue was quickly joined by her husband, Tony, a tall, somewhat more retiring person than his wife. They ushered us into the sitting room and very soon we were sitting with coffee, chatting to the couple.

We talked for a long while, exploring the situation. Sue was working as an IT specialist in a large company and intended to stop work if they had a child placed with them. Their own two children were now grown up and off their hands. They had always talked about adoption, rather than having their own third child, so now seemed the right time, and they felt ready. Sue was lovely, lively company and Tony a very sincere, much quieter and reserved person.

We were shown around the house and then returned to sit down. I took a back seat in the discussions, letting Jenny take the lead, which gave me the opportunity to observe the couple and try to get a feel for them. Something was not quite what I felt I wanted. I tried to get my mind around this. I needed to see Sarah here; I needed to feel that Sarah would be at home here. I went over all we had talked through. I was trying to get a feel for the family; they were a really pleasant couple but I just couldn't see Sarah here. I struggled with guilt. They were a nice couple, really nice – what was wrong with me? They had a very strong commitment to adoption, and all the right attitudes to the issues we covered, so what was my problem? Was it something about the couple that resonated with a personal issue of mine? If so, what? Did they remind me of someone from the past? Was it something they had said? Sitting there, as Jenny was chatting to them, I continued to fight with myself.

The meeting went well; issues that needed to be discussed were discussed, though I left much of the talking to Jenny and just listened for most of the time. After an hour or so, it came to a close and the two of us left, saying we would be in contact with them through their link worker.

As we walked to the car, I was quiet. We sank back into the car seats; there was a silence and then Jenny said to me, 'Becky, would you just drive around the corner and stop the car? I don't want to chat outside their home.'

I did as she asked, managed to manoeuvre my car into a very tight parking space and stopped. I turned off the ignition and a deep silence fell over the car, a silence that was bursting with unspoken words. It was Jenny who broke it. She spoke more slowly than normal, as if she was considering every word. 'Becky, this is a decision about Sarah's whole future. It's so important. Come on, I know you well enough to see when you have concerns. What did you feel?'

I was glad this was Jenny, for whom I had much respect and with whom I had worked several times. I took a deep breath and said, 'Jenny, I'm really struggling with this one. I usually get a feeling about people and I didn't. Is it me? Am I being unfair?'

Jenny went quiet for a moment and then said, 'OK, let's think. What does Sarah need – really need – most?' There was another silence as I mentally conjured up Sarah as I had met her that day at school, Sarah as she clung to me in the hospital, Sarah as she leant into Patty when she told us her fears. I knew. 'Nurturing, Jenny. Nurturing, nurturing and more nurturing. She is timid, wounded and vulnerable – she needs copious amounts of Mother-Earth-style nurturing.' I paused briefly then said, 'That's it, Jenny. They were lovely but they were not naturally warm, nurturing people. They will make really good parents for another child, but not, I feel, this one.'

Jenny turned to me, and smiled. 'I'm really glad you've put it so clearly. I didn't feel convinced either but I couldn't put my finger on it. Also, I don't know Sarah as well as you do, but you're right. So, OK, we'll visit no 2 or 3 on the list. We will do the very best we can to match this child up with the right family.'

On our return to the office the following day, I could see that Marie was disappointed that the visit had not proved positive; I could see it all too clearly. It was all precious time out of the office, and didn't I know it! I hardly dared to think about the mountain of paperwork piling up in my absence, but Marie respected our decision.

Jenny and I went back to the drawing board and took out the F Forms of the other families who were in the final choice selection. We pored over the forms of the other two on the short list and spoke to their link workers. It was a very hard choice but we finally agreed on one, organised a date to visit and, before the week was out, found ourselves waiting at the door of a modern, brightly painted house, being observed by a rather scruffy black cat who removed his gaze occasionally to re-wash a part of his paw that he had clearly missed. His face said, 'And who do you think you are; this is my step,' and, as the door opened, he streaked in like a flash of light.

We were greeted by Zoë, a woman in her late thirties. Dark brown curls framed her face, in which was set a pair of large brown eyes which looked straight at you and reflected her smile. A friendly but rather large fluffy dog rushed up with a brief woof, but the accompanying tail-wagging and almost-smiling face led us to conclude that he was no threat to anyone. A brief word from Zoë and, true to our supposition, the dog turned and almost sheepishly crept into the kitchen, where, as we saw later, he took up what was clearly his favourite spot on a nice warm mat by the radiator. He had done his job, had welcomed his guests and would now retreat to comfort.

Zoë's husband, Michael, appeared behind her and ushered us into the house, offering us coffee. The couple had two sons who were now aged fifteen and sixteen, and they had thought of adopting ever since the boys had reached their teens, feeling that they still had lots of energy and space in their lives to help a less fortunate child. Zoë was not working; she had given up her job about a year ago when they had first applied to adopt. They had a child placed at that time, but at the last moment the court had allowed the birth parents to have their child returned to them as they appeared to have made great strides and turned themselves around. Zoë and Michael told us all about this – and the appalling hurt they had experienced on losing the child, who had been with them for some time. They had coped with this blow, not without a lot of heartache, and felt they must try again, but were clearly and quite naturally anxious about Sarah's situation.

Before we could sit down, Zoë scooped up two more cats that seemed to have hogged the best seats. 'Oz and Coz', she smiled. 'We took them from the RSPCA centre a couple of months ago; they had been dumped in a bin as kittens by their owner, and we couldn't resist them.' With a gentle nuzzle on the cats' heads and a word of explanation to the clearly much-loved animals, Zoë put them out in the kitchen, returned with an apologetic smile and sat down.

We chatted through Sarah's situation at length. Zoë and Michael asked lots of questions and sometimes they would go quiet while they digested things we had said. Zoë's questioning became more and more detailed. She looked with fascination at the pictures of Sarah and I could see in her eyes that she felt drawn to the child. In the time we were there, I began to feel increasingly that this was a family that could parent Sarah and that, if they took this step, they would give it their all. As a couple they made you feel not just welcome but something more – they had a real warmth that made you feel as if you had known them for a long while.

We toured the house and garden, during which time we were able to chat generally with the couple. After about an hour with them their two sons arrived home from school. There was a sound of crashing bags in the hall and all the usual laughter and hustle associated with teenage boys, and then the couple's sons appeared in the doorway. They were friendly, full of life and hungry, so, after a brief introduction they disappeared in the direction of the kitchen with a few suggestions from Zoë about the contents of the fridge!

Later, we had a chance to chat to the boys and it was clear that they were supportive of the idea; they were both very involved in their own lives, out a great deal and had a large circle of friends, but were excited by the prospect of a new sister. The boys were clearly very outgoing and spent much of their spare time at the gym or playing in the various sports teams they belonged to, so they had a healthy number of outside activities to keep them from being over-dependent on the family alone. They had also been raised as very much part of an extended family, with cousins, aunts, uncles and grandparents playing a regular part in their lives. Children like that had a greater experience of multiple relationships, had a bigger emotional support network themselves, and more people to talk to and share any difficulties with. Generally, such children had less of a shock when someone new – and often someone very needy – came into their family and demanded time and attention from their parents. The boys also had many younger cousins, and were quite used to having a younger child tagging along at times, with all the irritations that could cause. They had been quite sad at the loss of the last child, as it had all been going well and they had become quite attached, but they were realistic boys.

When we felt that we had given the couple as much information as they needed to come to a decision, we left, saying that we would talk things through with their link worker and give them a chance to think about things from their side. They waved us goodbye and I could imagine how they were feeling; it is a very difficult process for couples in their position. I felt for all these couples, but I knew that our ability to choose what was best for Sarah was no reflection on them personally. Just as we all choose different friends or partners, what is right for one child is not right for another.

22

The Court Day

It was a very thoughtful journey back to our hotel. Jenny and I chatted in fits and starts during the drive: we talked and then fell quiet while we thought, talked some more then fell silent again, and so it went on. I struggled to keep my attention on the road as I wrestled with all the issues that were preoccupying our minds.

I had felt very positive about this last couple. Zoë had a very warm and nurturing personality, while Michael was warm and calm, which would give Zoë much-needed support when times got tough. The family as a whole felt welcoming, judging from the way they talked about the aunts, uncles and grandparents. Further, this family had space emotionally to accept and meet the needs of a very vulnerable, attention-deprived child. Their link worker had spoken highly of them and felt that although they had been very upset at losing their last placement, they had had time to grieve and had now accepted that they needed, and were ready, to move on.

When we arrived back at the hotel, we had a quick coffee to unwind after what had been quite an intensive time with the family and then we spoke to the couple's link worker. It was now some two hours since we had seen the couple and it appeared that they had been on the phone to their link about an hour ago. Their link worker told us that the couple had talked it through within the family and then with her and they were very keen to be considered for Sarah.

After a long discussion, we agreed that, given the distance, we would make another visit before we left in the morning and give the couple a chance to see some video runs showing Sarah in her foster home. I also had a long chat with my senior, Marie, and Jenny spoke to hers, and we all felt that this couple appeared to tick all the boxes. We needed to be certain, before we took any further steps, that the family felt a basic ability to bond with Sarah, and a real commitment. It would also enable them to begin to prepare themselves for her possible arrival, should the court decide in favour of adoption.

Jenny and I had a restful evening – we needed it. The whole interview process had been emotionally very draining and, as far as I was concerned, detachment was not easy to maintain at all times. It was essential to remain objective in one's judgement and analysis of a family and of the personalities within that family. But as time moved on and you began to see that there could be a really good outcome for a child if they were to become a part of that family, it was hard not to feel that little creeping hope and excitement. Yes, I would find myself having little daydreams about the future for Sarah, but the structure of the whole process pulls you back from any risk of over-involvement. Much hinged on my remaining detached and so maintaining my judgement, unclouded by wishful thinking.

The next day dawned bright and fresh. It was one of those beautiful, clear, sunny mornings after a night of heavy rain – the world looked washed clean and even the trees seemed greener and fresher; all around gardens were full of colour and life. It felt as if the whole world was soaking up the sunshine and glorying in its warmth. I think I noticed all this more because it echoed my mood. I felt optimistic and bursting with hope. Then, alternating with these feelings, there would be moments when I would sink back to earth, with the recollection that however watertight I felt the court case was, it was always possible that the judge who sat on the day of the hearing would take a completely contrary view and request more time for the mother to turn herself around. It had happened before, even in seemingly clear-cut cases.

Most judges displayed immense wisdom, were extremely knowledgeable and invested enormous time, energy and training in trying to grasp and deal with immensely complex family situations. However, there is no doubt that there are some judges who lack a sense of reality in abuse cases – not seeming to understand the long-term consequences of their decisions – and I fear that in many cases they do not receive feedback, unless they happen to sit at any subsequent hearings. There were times when the wisdom of Solomon was required. Child Protection is probably one of the toughest fields they could have chosen to practise in, professionally and intellectually, and the additional requirement for an immense fund of emotional intelligence places even greater demands upon them.

But . . . Because it had been me who had stood by Sarah on that day the previous year in the hospital A & E . . . Because it had been me who had seen her pathetic little damaged body . . . Because it had been me who sensed her lean into me for some form of protection . . . Because it had been me who watched her bloom with her foster carer . . . Because it had been me who had spent hours and hours with the mother, talking about her life, working out where her problems lay . . . Because it had been me looking at ways to support the mother, taking her to support groups, trying so hard . . . Because it had been me offering her help to change her life in ways that would help her to parent Sarah better . . . Because it had been me who had monitored her efforts and seen that she simply would not, or indeed could not, even begin to accept help to change . . . Because it had been me whose heart had jumped with frustration when the mother's drug counsellor once again reported her non-attendance or that her blood tests had come up positive for certain substances . . . Because of all this going on for long months, and having listened to the horrors that Sarah had been exposed to throughout her whole life . . . Because of all these things, I saw no reason to feel that Sarah could ever be safe with her mother. And because of all this I was convinced that Sarah needed a chance to live a normal life in which she received proper care, and unconditional love and protection. A life that would equip her to one day parent her own children and prepare them to walk into the world loved, confident and cared for, able to break the generations of abuse that had dogged this family.

Over breakfast we had talked through once more what we needed to achieve in this morning's meeting with the couple, and which of us would lead different parts of the meeting.

Before long we were driving to Zoë and Michael's home. The meeting that followed was good – very good. We were able to provide Zoë and Michael with a much more detailed account of Sarah, now that they had been selected as the first choice. We again went over Sarah's behavioural issues and talked through helpful contributions about Sarah from the foster carer. We spent more time talking about Sarah's life experiences to date and what the likely consequences could be for any potential adoptive family, and they also looked at information provided by her school. They then watched the video. This showed Sarah, with her favourite blue ribbon tying up her now-glossy brown hair, in her foster home. It showed her having her lunch, chatting to her carer, on a swing, chasing about with the 'therapy dog', painting a picture and listening to a story. It was magic – and very well filmed. Not by me, I hasten to add!

Zoë tried to cope with her tears in as controlled a way as she was able; she just kept on pulling out more and more tissues from the box on her coffee table. Michael just sat riveted to the screen. It was one of those moments in social work that will remain with me. They are worth all the work, worry and stress, and while I will never be rich on my salary, at moments like this I felt rich beyond measure – better than any win of millions could ever make me feel.

It was some weeks later when we finally all found ourselves in court. I had slept very badly the night before, having read and re-read my court reports, thought through any possible difficult questions I might be asked, and then endeavoured, with complete failure, to distract my mind into sleep.

Well, today was the start: the court now had to decide on the facts of the case, as presented in the multiplicity of reports submitted by everyone involved. This included reports from the Family Centre, the guardian, the paediatrician and the child and adult psychiatrists, in addition to the local authority report, which I had prepared. It was the clear view of the local authority that Sarah should be freed up for adoption, and that this should be actioned as speedily as possible for the sake of the child, to prevent further damage.

Sarah's mother had simply not been able to turn herself around; we had given her endless support, groups to help with parenting, and drug and alcohol support and she had been seen by numerous experts in various fields. Sadly for her, and to our utter frustration, no matter what help she was offered she found herself unable to use any of it. This was the tragic consequence of her own childhood experiences and the added problems caused by her longstanding addiction to drugs and alcohol. Sarah needed to be in a permanent home as quickly as possible so she had a chance to begin to build up new relationships which would provide the opportunity to enable some of her damage to heal.

The guardian was in agreement with us but Sarah's mother was appealing for another period of drug and alcohol rehabilitation. Matthew had been investigated by the police but it had not yet proved possible to put together sufficient evidence to conclusively prove his alleged violence; it seemed he might get off free. Further, Matthew was claiming that he now lived with his mother! We all knew what had been going on, but without evidence that was it.

I felt that I knew the family situation inside out by now. There had been never been any commitment to this child; she had been placed at a very high risk of danger. Sarah's mother, Julie, was too damaged – barely able to cope with herself, let alone a child. Her life consisted of her need to feed her own relationships, no matter the cost, and drugs were likely to always be her number one priority. It was tragic, and if you were to ask me how I felt about Sarah's mother, I would have to say that I was very sad for her. In her life to date she had never experienced unconditional love, she had been used and abused, and this was all she had ever known of 'love and care'. Julie kept her many partners by being a slave to their whims; she would do anything to keep them, irrespective of any damage that reflected onto her child.

The court case dragged on for several days. I was in the witness box for quite a long time, as were others involved, and that is never an easy situation. Endless questions were fired from the opposing barrister. He was there to challenge us at every count. I had to think very hard before every word I spoke, so as not to mislead or appear unhelpful. The barrister did his best to try to prove that we had neglected some issues, or that there was other help we had not provided. I had no doubt at all that we had given Julie vast amounts of help, but what the judge would decide was another matter. It seemed as if the case would go on for ever, then suddenly it all came to an end and the judge went away to consider his verdict. We all filed out of the court – subdued, preoccupied and very anxious. The outcome would have vast consequences whatever the decision. But I was very involved; I felt deeply for Sarah and however sorry I might feel for the parents, I really believed, along with my department, that this child needed a chance.

Returning for the verdict was quite a day. My mind was buzzing; I had hardly slept, again! Would I be heading up another rehabilitation period for Sarah's mother, and summoning all my resources to give this yet another try, or would I be organising an adoption? I kept coming back to Sarah – how would she cope with all this? I have to say, my mind was in serious overdrive. This decision could be the making or breaking of Sarah.

I really did not feel that Sarah should continue to be left in a temporary foster home, however good (and it was very good), while even more assessments were made of her mother. I believed that this child needed to move now. No messing about; give her a chance. Children need certainty and commitment and the longer they are living without that, the more damaged they become. There is sometimes a risk of the child's needs being overridden by a sentimental or legalistic tendency to consider the human rights of the parent as being paramount in these situations. This is in spite of legislation clearly requiring that the child is always to be put first. I hardly dared to believe that the judge would *not* free Sarah in this case, but I had heard and seen too much. Nothing was set until the judge ruled.

On the whole, I am all for families staying together.

However, I also believe that if parents consistently abuse the privilege of parenthood – and having a child *is* a privilege – then they should lose their rights. And this should happen before such great damage is done to a child that they would be forever struggling. When the family cannot fulfil their responsibilities, then adoption works – very well indeed in most cases – but the younger the child the better. Sarah would already carry many issues with her.

Inside the court, it looked like another world. The sun was shining through the ancient stained-glass windows; coloured patterns moved across the old tiled floors. This was one of the older courts – cool, with high vaulted ceilings and soaked in history. Perhaps the sun was a little like the justice the court stood to give, struggling through the glass of circumstances to shine truth on the issue. How many lives had this court seen made and broken here? How much emotion had these walls and floors absorbed?

We all rose as the judge appeared in court to give his verdict. I could see Sarah's mother sitting on the other side, nervously fiddling with her cardigan, with Matthew at her side.

When the judge began to read out his verdict and his reasoning, we all listened intently. And when he spoke the words, 'and it is my considered opinion that this child, Sarah Peters, be freed for adoption and that placement should take place without any delay,' I think my heart stopped briefly, and at the same moment Sarah's mother began to mumble across the court.

It was in everyone's mind, apart from Julie's, that this was the right decision, and a bit of me feels that even the mother's declared wish to be allowed to care for Sarah was based more on a territorial feeling than on any commitment to the child. She would now have one less burden in her life.

How did I feel? I felt almost overwhelmed and indescribably happy to be able to give Sarah a new life. There was so much to do, but first I knew I had a phone call to make to two very anxious and uncertain people. Zoë and Michael had begged me to let them know the outcome of the case as quickly as I could. They wanted to know if their tremendous hope that Sarah might become their daughter was now a reality, or a dashed dream from which they must wake, shake themselves, mourn and force themselves, yet again, to move on. Well, that was a call I was very happy to make. When I broke the news, Zoë burst into tears and it was Michael, who had taken the day off work to be at home, with whom I then made the plans to begin the introductions.

I had one even more important call to make, and that was to Sarah. First, I called Patty to break the news. She was very pleased, as she had become very fond of Sarah and wanted to know all was going to go well for her. It was only three o'clock, so I set off to her home. When I arrived, Sarah was expecting me, although she didn't know the purpose of my call. I was greeted by the usual doggie welcome, added to which Sarah was leaping about with excitement at my visit. She was dressed in her pink ballerina outfit and insisted that I watch her dancing. She called out to me, 'Watch me, Becky. I'm a swan!'

If I dared to switch my attention for a second to my tea and cake, it was a constant stream of, 'Watch me,

Becky! I'm a swallow now! Look at me, look at me, I'm a seagull! Becky you're not watching!' (I had bent to pick up a stray crumb!)

'Watch me now – look, see how I can swoop!'

Patty gently persuaded Sarah to calm down and settle on the sofa and I began to explain what had happened that day. Sarah knew that something had been 'going on'; she had been anxious, and had actually asked Patty on several occasions whether she would have to return to her mother. It is hard to explain to a child that this was a decision yet to be made; living in limbo must be horrendous for children in this situation. One had to be honest and not build up any false hopes, yet prepare a child for change.

I explained to Sarah that it wasn't that her mother did not want to look after her, but she had so many problems that it was just too difficult for her. I then went on to tell Sarah that we had found a family who very much wanted a little girl just like her to look after, and would like to meet her. Sarah's immediate response was, 'What about Patty?' She had been told many times that Patty only cared for children for short times, so I repeated this now. But I was able to say that Patty would come with her to meet the new family and would be with her until she got to know them well.

Sarah became quiet, thinking about all of this. I waited to see what came next.

'So . . . would I be able to take my dancing dress?' she asked.

'Of course,' I responded. 'And, in fact, I told them you loved to dance and they wondered if you might like to go to dancing classes.' Sarah looked up at me with a look of stunned excitement on her face. You would have thought I had offered her the world.

'Honest? Are you sure? I've always wanted to go to dancing classes, and have those little pink shoes.' She then went quiet again and added, 'Laura, at school, and all her friends go to dancing classes and they play dancing in the playground but they won't let me join in. They say I'm useless.' Here she paused and, carried away by the glamour and excitement of dancing classes, she seemed to have forgotten what we were discussing as she came out with a defiant comment, 'I'll be better than them, then they'll let me play.'

I decided to ask Sarah if she would like to see some pictures of the family, to which she gave an excited response of, 'Oh yes!'

Patty, Sarah and I went through the little home book with Sarah, which showed the couple, their sons, their home and the animals. Sarah was riveted, studying Zoë's face in fine detail for some time. She finally thrust the picture away and looked at me rather stubbornly before saying to me, 'Becky, I won't go there if she drinks. Patty doesn't drink so I'll stay here!'

We were taken aback at this turn of thinking, but clearly Sarah was bright enough to have worked out where many of her problems came from. We were able to re-assure her on this point, and she accepted this, picking up the picture and again studying Zoë in detail. Oddly, no one else was mentioned at that point.

We left matters there; she needed time to absorb things at her own pace. I must say that I made a mental note to talk to Zoë about Sarah's concern and make sure she was not seen drinking so much as a glass of lemonade for a little while until Sarah felt secure!

That evening I drove home tired – very tired – my mind in a whirl, but happy, so happy. The world seemed a better place. Everything I had worked for since my first meeting with Sarah had been fulfilled. I could do no more. In another case it might have been that the mother or parents of a child had seriously turned their lives around and learnt to parent their child. Well, that would also have been a huge success. The outcome I wanted was the one that gave a child the best future, as quickly as possible before the damage became too deeply ingrained.

As a footnote, I want to tell you about Sarah's mother. She left the court quickly at the end, with Matthew beside her, and I felt very sad for her. Her future was to continue much as it had always been, with a succession of part-ners who were also heavily into drugs and alcohol. She would not seek help for herself. I so wished she had. In truth, it was unlikely that she even wanted to change her life; her many partners and friends, however abusive and callous, were all she had.

I believe, from information that came into the office, that she was badly beaten by Matthew and hospitalised, but refused to press charges. It was only some years later, when he was imprisoned for grievous bodily harm against a dealer, that she had the opportunity to escape Matthew's clutches. Sadly, her next partner was equally violent and only his death from an overdose saved her. She is only in her thirties, but looks old and wizened.

There is nothing positive one can say or feel. Her life has been wasted through addiction and need. Sarah has at least been saved from this and I hope that in her mother's saner moments Julie may come to see that, and gain some comfort.

The following weeks were hectic. The work needed to move Sarah had to a large extent been completed; I had made sure of that to avoid any unnecessary delay. The introductions were swift and organised and, within months, Sarah had moved to live with Zoë and Michael. She had exchanged many visits, they had stayed with her at her foster home, had learnt about her routines, likes and dislikes, and this process had continued until both Sarah and the couple felt ready and prepared to make the move.

The day finally came when Sarah was moved to become the much-longed-for newest member of her new family. During the early months after Sarah had moved into her adoptive placement, and before the adoption took place, I did the welfare visits. These were to ensure that the family and child had all the necessary support in this difficult stage and that the child was settling well into the new home. It is one of the unforgettable highlights of one's career – to be privileged to watch a child who has been seriously abused blossom when permanently placed, and blossom Sarah certainly did. She was very behind in all areas of development but, with support, began to taste 'normality', success even, in some small fields. However, the most important thing was the pleasure in her eyes when she told me the latest episode in the lives of 'her family'.

The teenage sons had become her 'slaves'; they indulged her totally and she lapped it up. For many reasons this was a placement that threw up fewer problems than the average, though there would be lots of issues. Sarah was dangerously trusting of strangers, and this had caused a few worrying incidents. She was also clingy, in quite an exhausting way. The family was able to absorb Sarah's understandable need to cling, and understood that she was making up for lost time – the hours left screaming in her cot, roaming the streets alone or scared for hours into the night. They just let her cling, in the knowledge that when one day she had learnt to trust them she would begin to feel safe enough to dare to let go and trust they would still be there.

It was some time later that the adoption was finalised. Sarah came to court with her new parents, their solicitor and myself. I looked at her standing there, proudly wearing the new dress that she had chosen for the occasion, blue with little flowers scattered all over, and the inevitable blue ribbons. She sat in court, between her new parents, happily leaning into Zoë, with her 'big brothers' on the other side smiling delightedly down at her. Sarah had a huge smile, which seemed to encompass the whole courtroom; she was so proud to be the centre of this big occasion.

My mind wandered back briefly to the little waif in A & E all that time ago. Could this really be the same girl? Well, it was and it wasn't. She was very different. This was a child with hope; this was a child with the knowledge, growing more firmly entrenched in her understanding with every passing week that she was loved, valued and safe.

ACKNOWLEDGEMENTS

I would like to thank the Hodder team, in particular Fenella Bates for her endlessly good humoured and patient support during the editing of this book, also Ciara Foley and Lucy Zilberkweit for all their help. A more professional team one couldn't ask for.

There must be many more whose names I do not know, who have worked long and hard reading the scripts, designing the art work, setting the type . . . thank you.

Thank you also to Luigi Bonomi, my agent, for his sound advice and huge encouragement for which I am very grateful.

Finally my thanks also must go to my husband and family who have encouraged me throughout in the writing of this book.

Somewhere, as you are reading this book, Sarah is close to becoming an adult. Perhaps, one day soon, she will be rearing her own children. It is my hope that this is something she will now be able to do. And that, with the help of her adoptive parents, she will bring stable happy children into the next generation.